Interactions 2

Reading

Interactions 2

Reading

4th Edition

Elaine Kirn
West Los Angeles College

Pamela Hartmann
Los Angeles Unified School District

McGraw-Hill/Contemporary

*A Division of The **McGraw-Hill** Companies*

Interactions 2 Reading, 4th Edition

Published by McGraw-Hill/Contemporary, a business unit of The McGraw-Hill Companies, Inc., 1221 Avenue of the Americas, New York, NY 10020. Copyright © 2002, 1996, 1990, 1985 by The McGraw-Hill Companies, Inc. All rights reserved. No part of this publication may be reproduced or distributed in any form or by any means, or stored in a database or retrieval system, without the prior written consent of The McGraw-Hill Companies, Inc., including, but not limited to, in any network or other electronic storage or transmission, or broadcast for distance learning.

Some ancillaries, including electronic and print components, may not be available to customers outside the United States.

 This book is printed on recycled, acid-free paper containing 10% postconsumer waste.

6 7 8 9 0 QPD/QPD 0 9 8 7 6 5 4

ISBN 0-07-233105-4
ISBN 0-07-118016-8 (ISE)

Editorial director: *Tina B. Carver*
Series editor: *Annie Sullivan*
Developmental editor: *Louis Carrillo*
Director of marketing and sales: *Thomas P. Dare*
Project manager: *Sheila M Frank*
Production supervisor: *Laura Fuller*
Coordinator of freelance design: *David W. Hash*
Interior designer: *Michael Warrell, Design Solutions*
Photo research coordinator: *John C. Leland*
Photo researcher: *Amelia Ames Hill Associates/Amy Bethea*
Supplement coordinator: *Genevieve Kelley*
Compositor: *David Corona Design*
Typeface: *10.5/12 Times Roman*
Printer: *Quebecor World Dubuque, IA*

The credits section for this book begins on page 279 and is considered an extension of the copyright page.

www.mhcontemporary.com/interactionsmosaic

Interactions 2

Reading

Interactions 2 **Reading**

Boost your students' academic success!

Interactions Mosaic, 4th edition is the newly revised five-level, four-skill comprehensive ESL/EFL series designed to prepare students for academic content. The themes are integrated across proficiency levels and the levels are articulated across skill strands. The series combines communicative activities with skill-building exercises to boost students' academic success.

Interactions Mosaic, 4th edition features

▪ updated content

▪ five videos of authentic news broadcasts

▪ expansion opportunities through the Website

▪ new audio programs for the listening/speaking and reading books

▪ an appealing fresh design

▪ user-friendly instructor's manuals with placement tests and chapter quizzes

Photos and illustrations activate prior knowledge of the topic.

Vocabulary Preview allows students to anticipate unknown vocabulary.

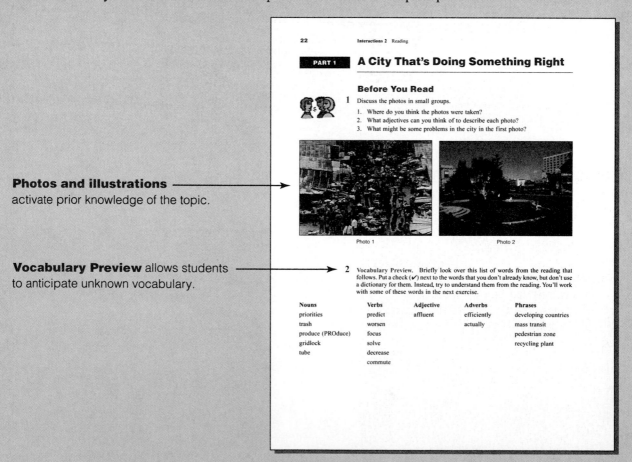

22   Interactions 2   Reading

PART 1 **A City That's Doing Something Right**

Before You Read

1 Discuss the photos in small groups.

1. Where do you think the photos were taken?
2. What adjectives can you think of to describe each photo?
3. What might be some problems in the city in the first photo?

Photo 1   Photo 2

2 Vocabulary Preview. Briefly look over this list of words from the reading that follows. Put a check (✔) next to the words that you don't already know, but don't use a dictionary for them. Instead, try to understand them from the reading. You'll work with some of these words in the next exercise.

Nouns	Verbs	Adjective	Adverbs	Phrases
priorities	predict	affluent	efficiently	developing countries
trash	worsen		actually	mass transit
produce (PROduce)	focus			pedestrian zone
gridlock	solve			recycling plant
tube	decrease			
	commute			

Prereading questions help students do *active* reading,

The first reading selection is in the style of a magazine article or essay.

Skill development prepares students for standardized tests through reading skills, print conventions, and critical-thinking activities.

---

4. Under his leadership, city planners established <u>priorities</u>—in other words, a list of what was most important.

_____

5. In neighborhoods that garbage trucks can't reach, people bring bags of <u>trash</u> to special centers.

_____

6. They exchange the trash for fresh <u>produce</u>—such as potatoes or oranges—or for bus tickets.

_____

7. At a <u>recycling plant</u>, workers separate bottles, plastic, and cans from other trash.

_____

8. Curitiba needed a <u>mass-transit</u> system but couldn't afford an expensive subway. City planners began, instead, with an unusual system of buses.

_____

Read

4   As you read the following selection, think about the answer to this question: what is Curitiba doing right?
Read the selection quickly. Do not use a dictionary. Then do the exercises that follow the reading.

A City That's Doing Something Right

[A]   There's good news and bad news about life in modern cities—first, the bad. People who study population growth predict a nightmare by the y... global population will be more than 8 billion, and almost 4 billion of will be living in cities in developing countries such as India and N... lation growth is already causing unbelievable overcrowding. Na... has basic services for 200,000 people but has a population of 5 m... City is home to almost 25 million people. By the year 2025, popu... predict, 660 *million* people will be living in cities in India. Due to... these cities have problems with air pollution, disease, and crime.... hours in gridlock—that is, traffic so horrible that it simply doesn't... they commute daily from their homes to their work and back. Ther... water, transportation, or housing. Many people don't have acc... services or jobs. Now the good news: in *some* cities, instead ... urban life is actually getting much better.

A City and Its Mayor
[D]   It might not be a surprise to find that life in affluent cities is improv... about cities that *aren't* rich? The city of Curitiba, Brazil, proves tha...

---

6   **Understanding Italics.**   Writers use *italics* (slanted letters) for several reasons, among them for emphasis. The italics indicate that the word is important. Find the words in italics in the reading selection "A City That's Doing Something Right." Read these sentences aloud. Place emphasis on the words in italics.

7   **Understanding Contrast.**   Sometimes writers use contrast to express an idea. In other words, they begin with the opposite of the point that they want to make. The reading selection "A City That's Doing Something Right" can be divided into two parts. What is the first part? What is the second part? How do these parts show contrast?

8   **Making Inferences.**   Writers usually state information clearly. However, they also often imply information. In other words, they just suggest an idea without actually stating it. It is important for students to be able to make inferences—that is, to "read between the lines" and understand information that is not clearly stated.
Here is information about Jaime Lerner. Which information is stated in the reading? Put *S* on those lines. Which information is implied but not clearly stated? Put *I* on those lines. Look back at Paragraphs B and E to decide.

1. _____ Jaime Lerner was the mayor of Curitiba.
2. _____ Under his leadership, the city established a new mass-transit system.
3. _____ Jaime Lerner was mayor for a long time.
4. _____ Under his leadership, city planners established priorities.
5. _____ Jaime Lerner was an architect.
6. _____ He was practical.
7. _____ He was a creative thinker.
8. _____ He talked with owners of factories and stores about street children.
9. _____ He was a persuasive person.
10. _____ He was a good leader of the city.

9   **Summarizing.**   A reading may express several important ideas, but there is one main idea that sums up (summarizes) all of the important ideas.
Circle the number of the main idea of the selection "A City That's Doing Something Right."

1. Population experts predict a nightmare by the year 2025, especially in urban areas in developing countries.
2. Curitiba has a creative method of garbage collection that not only gets trash off the streets but also provides food and jobs for poor people.
3. Curitiba's mass-transit system consists of buses, not a subway, but offers an efficient new way for people to get on and off.
4. Curitiba has laws to protect the environment and to make the city more beautiful.
5. Curitiba is an example of how careful planning and creative thinking can lead to solutions to urban problems.

Talk It Over

Genes for Crime It is highly possible that there is a genetic link or contribution to violence or criminality. In other words, our genes may contribute to the possibility that we will become a thief, murderer, or other type of criminal.

Psychologist David Lykken believes that people who want to become parents should be tested and given a license. If both the man and the woman have genes for violence or criminality, they should not be allowed to have a baby. He says that this will reduce crime in society. What do you think?

Beyond the Text

New discoveries in genetics—many due to twin studies—appear very frequently these days. Search the Internet for the most recent discovery. Share the information with the class. Discuss the information and any new vocabulary.

PART 3   Building Vocabulary and Study Skills

1   Words with Similar Meanings The words in each of the following groups have similar meanings, but they are not exactly the same. Match the words with their definitions by writing the letters on the lines. If necessary, check your answers in a dictionary.

1. _____ brain   a. a way of thinking or feeling
2. _____ mind   b. the ability to remember
3. _____ memory   c. an organ of the body that controls thought and feeling

4. _____ equipment   a. an instrument
5. _____ machine   b. the things that are needed for an activity
6. _____ device   c. a manufactured instrument that needs power in order to work

7. _____ insight   a. a way of thinking with formal methods
8. _____ knowledge   b. understanding that comes from experience
9. _____ logic   c. the power of using one's mind (especially to understand something suddenly

10. _____ colleague   a. a person of equal status or age
11. _____ peer   b. a person who works in the same place as an
12. _____ co-worker   c. a person who works in the same profession

Talk It Over and **Beyond the Text** encourage students to evaluate arguments and to do independent research related to the topic of the chapter.

Vocabulary and language-learning strategies for synonyms, antonyms, context clues, and word families give students comprehension and self-assessment tools.

PART 4   Reading in the Real World

Focus on Testing

Timed Tests

On any test, some questions will seem easier to you than others. If you are taking a timed test, it will help you to answer the easy questions first and then to come back to the harder ones later. In this way, you will be able to finish more—or all—of the test without wasting time.

The following two articles are about an unusual punishment for a crime. Read the first article and answer the questions about it. Work as quickly as possible, as you would on a test. (Your teacher might decide to give you a time limit.) Remember to answer the easy questions first. If you finish before the time limit, don't begin the second article. Instead, check your answers. Your teacher will tell you when to begin reading the second article.

Tribal court may banish teens to Alaskan islands

• **Admitted robbery:** Indians making restitution to Washington victim.

KLAWOCK, Alaska (AP)—A panel of Tlingit elders began a hearing Thursday to decide whether two Indian teenagers should be banished to uninhabited islands for severely beating and robbing a pizza deliveryman in Washington state last year.

5   Cousins Adrian Guthrie and Simon Roberts, both 17, pleaded guilty to robbery in May for attacking Tim Whittlesey of Everett, Wash., with a baseball bat. Whittlesey's hearing and eyesight were permanently damaged.

Rather than sending the teens to prison, a Washington state judge agreed to send them north to face the Kuye'di Kuiu Kwaan Tribal Court. The youths could still get prison time later.

Rudy James, a tribal elder who proposed the alternative at the behest of the youths' parents, says the punishment probably will be banishment for up to two years to separate, isolated islands in Alaska's vast Alexander Archipelago. The hearing in this southeast Alaska fishing village may last through today.

The tribal elders held court in the Alaska Native Brotherhood-Alaska Native Sisterhood hall, a single-story building used for weddings, funerals, town meetings and bingo games. It was the first time the Klawock court was convened to determine a sentencing referred from a state court.

20   About 75 people attended Thursday's hearing, which lasted two and a half hours and was scheduled to resume this morning. No one was allowed into the hall until it had been ritually cleansed with branches of devil's club, a thorny plant native to the region.

(continued on page 275)

Focus on Testing prepares students for standardized tests by analyzing question types, practicing timed readings, making analogies, and understanding figurative language.

Real-life materials connect the classroom to real life through ads, dictionary entries, newspaper stories, and other realia.

Video Activities: An Online English Class

Before You Watch.   Discuss the following questions with your class or in a small group.

1. Do you ever use the Internet? What kinds of sites do you visit?
2. Do you ever do research for a paper online?
3. Did you ever take an online course?
4. Do you know the expression "virtual reality"?

Watch.   Check the following things students can do in Dr. Wesley's virtual English class.

1. _____ get announcements
2. _____ listen to a lecture
3. _____ link to Websites for research
4. _____ construct a personal web page
5. _____ take tests
6. _____ talk to classmates
7. _____ send an e-mail to the teacher

Watch Again.   Virtual courses have both advantages and disadvantages. Compete the chart below. Afterwards, share answers with your classmates.

	Advantage(s)	Disadvantage(s)
For students		
For parents		
For teachers		

After You Watch.   A "compound" word is one word that is made up of two connected words. There are several compound words in the video clip. The first one is listed below. Watch the video and try to find the others.

a. black + board = blackboard
b. _____
c. _____
d. _____

Video news broadcasts
immerse students in authentic language, complete with scaffolding and follow-up activities to reinforce reading skills.

Don't forget to check out the new *Interactions Mosaic* Website at www.mhcontemporary.com/interactionsmosaic.

- Traditional practice and interactive activities
- Links to student and teacher resources
- Cultural activities
- Focus on Testing
- Activities from the Website are also provided on CD-ROM

Interactions 2 Reading

Chapter	Reading Type	Vocabulary Development	Reading Skills/Strategies
1 Education and Student Life **Page 1**	■ Description (education)	■ Using context clues ■ Suffix -wide	■ Previewing vocabulary ■ Predicting reading content ■ Identifying main ideas ■ Skimming for main ideas ■ Scanning for information
2 City Life **Page 21**	■ Exposition (city planning)	■ Using context clues	■ Previewing vocabulary ■ Predicting reading content ■ Making inferences ■ Skimming for main ideas ■ Scanning for information
3 Business and Money **Page 43**	■ Exposition (finance)	■ Using context clues ■ Words with same or similar meaning ■ Noun and adjective suffixes	■ Previewing vocabulary ■ Predicting reading content ■ Identifying main ideas ■ Understanding conclusions ■ Making inferences ■ Skimming for main ideas ■ Scanning for information
4 Jobs and Professions **Page 63**	■ Exposition (career trends) ■ Proverbs and quotations	■ Using context clues ■ Adjective phrases and noun phrases ■ Compound words	■ Previewing vocabulary ■ Predicting reading content ■ Identifying main ideas ■ Understanding details ■ Skimming for main ideas ■ Scanning for information
5 Lifestyles Around the World **Page 83**	■ Exposition (popular culture)	■ Using context clues ■ Dictionary entries	■ Previewing vocabulary ■ Predicting reading content ■ Identifying main ideas ■ Skimming
6 Global Connections **Page 105**	■ Exposition (world trade)	■ Using context clues ■ Understanding idioms	■ Previewing vocabulary ■ Predicting reading content ■ Identifying main ideas ■ Understanding outlines ■ Skimming for main ideas ■ Making inferences ■ Scanning for information ■ Increasing reading speed

(continued on next page)

Chapter 1

Education and Student Life

IN THIS CHAPTER

The first reading selection discusses the educational system in four countries. Next, you'll read about college life in the United States today and how it is different from college life in the past. Finally, you'll read a passage from a sociology textbook that explains similarities and differences among elementary school curricula in several countries.

PART 1   # Education: A Reflection of Society

Before You Read

1   Discuss the pictures in small groups.

1.   Where is each scene taking place? What is happening?
2.   What might be similar about education in these countries? Make guesses.
3.   What might be different about education in these countries? Make guesses.
4.   In your opinion, what are important cultural values in each of these countries?

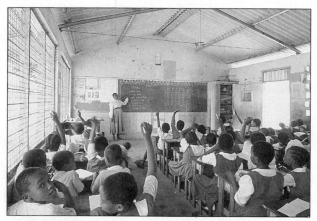

Primary school students in Kenya

Members of the Maasai tribe, Kenya

University student in England

High school in Japan

High school in the
United States

2 **Vocabulary Preview.** Briefly look over this list of words from the reading that follows. Put a check( ) next to the words that you *don't* already know, but don't use a dictionary for them. Instead, try to understand them from the reading. You'll work with some of these words in the next exercise.

Nouns		**Verbs**	**Adjectives**
a primary school	agriculture	reflect	identical
tuition	status	afford	rural
discipline	a vocational school	determine	egalitarian
relevance	a statistic	startled	

3 **Getting Meaning From Context.** When you read, you do not need to look up the meanings of all new words in a dictionary. You can often guess the meanings of many new words from the context—the other words in the sentence and the other sentences in the paragraph. Here are three types of clues that will help you guess new words.

■ Sometimes a sentence gives a definition of a new vocabulary item or information about it. This information may be in parentheses ( ), after a dash (—), or after a comma (,).

Example

There is a <u>drawback,</u> a disadvantage.

What does <u>drawback</u> mean? It means "disadvantage."

■ Sometimes a clue to the meaning of a new vocabulary item is in another sentence or sentence part.

Example

A school system in one country is not <u>identical</u> to the system in any other country. It cannot be exactly the same because each culture is different.

What does <u>identical</u> mean? You see the meaning in the second sentence— "exactly the same."

■ Sometimes simple logic helps you to guess a new word.

Example

The educational system is a mirror that <u>reflects</u> the culture.

You probably know the word *mirror,* so you can guess that <u>reflects</u> means "shows."

This exercise will help you with vocabulary that you will find in the first reading selection. Figure out the meanings of the underlined words and write them on the lines.

1. The economy is based on <u>agriculture</u> (especially the sale of tea leaves and coffee beans).

   _____

2. Visitors from another country might be <u>startled</u> by one <u>statistic</u> about education in Kenya. They might be surprised to learn that about 90 percent (%) of all students who finish <u>primary school</u> (elementary school) don't continue on to secondary school.

   startled = _____

   statistic = _____

   primary school = _____

3. Education in Kenya is free only through primary school; students must pay <u>tuition</u> in secondary schools, and many people can't <u>afford</u> this.

   tuition = _____

   afford = _____

4. Also, far from cities, in <u>rural</u> areas, children need to quit school to work on their families' farms.

   _____

5. They don't see school's <u>relevance</u>—its connection to real life.

   _____

6. Public schools are all both free and <u>egalitarian</u>; all students are considered equal and learn the same material.

   _____

7. Japanese students need great <u>discipline</u>; in order to make time for their studies, they need the self-control to give up hobbies, sports, and social life.

   _____

8. Results on these exams affect the <u>entire</u> family because there is high <u>status</u>, or social position, for a whole family in which children have high test scores.

   entire = _____

   status = _____

9. They attend one of three possible secondary schools: college-preparatory, <u>vocational</u> (for job training), or comprehensive.

   _____

10. Students themselves decide if they want college-preparatory or vocational classes in high school; no national exam determines this for them.

    _____

Read

4   As you read the following selection, think about the answer to this question: what can we learn about a culture from its educational system?

Read the selection quickly. Do not use a dictionary. Then do the exercises that follow the reading.

Education: A Reflection of Society

[A]   Visit schools anywhere in the world, and you will probably notice a number of similarities. There are students, teachers, books, blackboards, and exams everywhere. However, a school system in one country is not identical to the system in any other country. It *cannot* be exactly the same because each culture is different. The educational system is a mirror that reflects the culture. Look at the school system, and you will see the social structure and the values of its culture.

Kenya

[B]   Kenya, a developing country on the east coast of Africa, has a rapidly growing population. The economy is based on agriculture (especially the sale of tea leaves and coffee beans) and tourism. Visitors from another country might be startled by one statistic about education in Kenya. They might be surprised to learn that about 90 percent (%) of all students who finish primary school—elementary school—don't continue on to secondary school. One reason is economic. Education in Kenya is free only through primary school; students must pay tuition in secondary school, and many people can't afford this. Also, far from cities, in rural areas, children need to quit school to work on their families' farms. The other reason is social. Some rural tribes (such as the Maasai) don't *want* their children to have a formal education because they don't see its relevance—its connection to real life.

Japan

[C]   In contrast, the Japanese value education highly. They place such importance on it that 88 percent of all students complete not only primary school but also high school. Public schools are all both free and egalitarian; all students are considered equal and learn the same material. For social reasons, it's important for a student to receive a university degree—and a degree from "the right university." To reach this goal, students have to go through "examination hell." There are difficult exams for entrance to all universities, to many of the better primary and secondary schools, and even to some *kindergartens*! Japanese students need great discipline; in order to make time for their studies, they need the self-control to give up hobbies, sports, and social life. Results of these exams affect the entire family because there is high status, or social position, for the whole family when the children have high test scores.

Britain

[D]   In the United Kingdom (Britain), the educational system reflects the class system. All state schools—primary, secondary, and university—are free, and the first nine years are egalitarian; all students learn the same material. At age eleven, students take an important national exam. After this, they attend one of three possible secondary schools: college preparatory, vocational (for job training), or comprehensive (with both groups of students). However, 6 percent of

British students attend expensive private schools. These are students from upper-class families. Half of the students at Oxford and Cambridge universities come from such expensive secondary schools. Although all universities are free, only 1 percent of the lower class goes to university. Because graduates from good universities get the best jobs, it is clear that success is largely a result of one's social class.

The United States

[E]   Education in the United States is more democratic than in many countries, but it also has serious problems. Public primary and secondary schools are free, and almost 80 percent of all Americans are high school graduates. Students themselves decide if they want college-preparatory or vocational classes in high school; no national exam determines this. Higher education is not free, but it is available to almost anyone, and about 60 percent of all high school graduates attend college or university. Older people have the opportunity to attend college, too, because Americans believe that "you're never too old to learn." However, there are also problems in U.S. schools. In many secondary schools, there are problems with lack of discipline and with drugs and crime. In addition, public schools receive their money from local taxes, so schools in poor areas don't have enough good teachers or laboratory equipment, and the buildings are often not in good condition. Clearly, U.S. education reflects both the best and the worst of the society.

Conclusion

[F]   It is clear that each educational system is a reflection of the larger culture: its economy, values, social structure, and problems. Look at a country's schools, and you will learn about the society in which they exist.

After You Read

5   **Understanding the Main Idea.**   Write T on the lines before the statements that are true, according to the reading. Write F on the lines before the statements that are false. Don't look back at the reading.

1. _____   In Kenya, many students don't go to secondary school because they need to work or because their society doesn't see the need for it.

2. _____   In Japan, it's necessary to be rich to go to good schools.

3. _____   In Britain, social class seems to be very important.

4. _____   In the United States, it's important for students to pass a big national exam for entrance to college.

6   **Understanding Reading Structure.**   Paragraphs divide reading material into topics, or subjects. In the selection "Education: A Reflection of Society," there are letters next to the six paragraphs. One paragraph is usually about one topic. Match the paragraphs with their topics and write the letters of the paragraphs on the lines as in the example.

1.   __F__   Conclusion: Education as a reflection of society

2.   _____   A country that places a lot of importance on education and makes students take difficult examinations

3.   _____   A country that offers education to everyone but also has problems in its schools

4.   _____   A country where most people can't—or don't want to—attend college or university

5.   _____   A country where social class is very important

6.   _____   Introduction: Education as a mirror of a culture

7   **Recognizing the Main Idea.**   A reading passage may include many ideas, but there is one *main* idea. This is the most important idea of the reading. It is an "umbrella" that includes all of the more specific ideas. This main idea is usually stated in the introduction. Often, it is repeated in the conclusion.

   Circle the number of the main idea. All of these statements are *true,* but only one is the main idea. If necessary, look back at the introduction and the conclusion.

1.   Public education in primary school is free for students in Kenya, Japan, and the United States.

2.   There are important national exams in Japan and the United Kingdom.

3.   The educational system of each country can show us a lot about the culture of that country.

4.   Advantages of education in the United States are the students' amount of choice and the availability of a college education, but disadvantages are problems with drugs, lack of discipline, and also the poor condition of many school buildings.

5.   There is a relation between education and status in both Britain and Japan.

8   Turn back to page 5 and answer the question immediately before the reading selection. Then check your answers to Exercise 5 on page 6. Correct the false statements.

Cross-Cultural Note: Education in North America and Asia

In a Western society, such as the United States or Canada, which has many national, religious, and cultural differences, people highly value individualism—the differences among people—and independent thinking. Students do not often memorize information. Instead, they find answers themselves, and they express their ideas in class discussion. At an early age, students learn to form their own ideas and opinions.

In most Asian societies, by contrast, the people have the same language, history, and culture. Perhaps for this reason, the educational system in much of Asia reflects society's belief in group goals and traditions rather than individualism. Children in China, Japan, and Korea often work together and help one another on assignments. In the classroom, the teaching methods are often very formal. The teacher lectures, and the students listen. There is not much discussion. Instead, the students recite rules or information that they have memorized.

There are advantages and disadvantages to both systems. In North America, students learn to take the initiative—to make decisions and take action without someone telling them what to do. This prepares them for a society that values creative ideas. The system in Asia prepares students well for a society that values discipline. However, one drawback of the North American system is that students don't learn as many basic rules and facts as students in other countries do. And a drawback of the system in Asia is that it involves a lot of exams and memorization, but students often forget the information after an exam.

Discussing the Reading

9   In small groups, talk about your answers to these questions *about your country*.

1.   Are there both private schools and public schools? Is public education free, or do students need to pay tuition?
2.   Do most students go to secondary school? Do most students complete high school? Do many students go to college or university?
3.   Are there any important national exams? If so, tell about them.
4.   Are there different types of high schools (for example, college-preparatory or vocational)?
5.   What are some advantages of the educational system?
6.   What are some problems with the educational system?

PART 2   # Campus Life in the United States Today

Before You Read

1   **Skimming for Main Ideas.**   A paragraph usually tells about one topic (subject). Often one sentence is the topic sentence. It tells the topic and the main idea of the paragraph. The other sentences give details about the main idea. For example:

Life on U.S. college campuses is always changing. One change these days is that there are more foreign students than ever before, especially in certain majors and in graduate schools. There are almost half a million foreign students in colleges and universities in the United States. Over 100,000 international students attend graduate school—more than 25 percent of the total graduate enrollment. Most of these students are studying business and management. Almost as many are majoring in engineering. Other practical courses—mathematics, computer science, and some life sciences (such as biology)—are also popular majors. Not many foreign students are majoring in the humanities (literature, art, drama, philosophy, etc.) or the social sciences (anthropology, psychology, and so on) probably because they don't believe these fields offer the best job opportunities.

Topic: _foreign students in the United States_

Topic Sentence: _One change these days is that there are more foreign_
students than ever before, especially in certain majors and in graduate schools.

Read

2 Read the following paragraphs quickly. Do not use a dictionary, and don't worry about the details. When you finish, write the topic and topic sentence of each paragraph. (*Hints:* The topic is just a word or noun phrase—a few words. It is not a sentence. The topic sentence can be found in different places in the paragraph: beginning, middle, or end.)

Campus Life in the United States Today

[A]   For many years in the United States, most undergraduate students (in their first four years of college) were eighteen to twenty-two years old. They attended college full-time, lived in a dormitory on campus, and expected many "extras" from their colleges, not just classes. But things began to change in the 1970s and are very different now. Today, these "traditional" students are less than one-quarter (1/4) of all college students. These days the nontraditional students are the majority; they are different from traditional undergraduates in several ways. They are older. Many attend college part-time because they have families and jobs. Most live off campus, not in dorms. These nontraditional students don't want the extras that colleges usually offer. They aren't interested in the sports, entertainment, religious groups, and museums that are part of most U.S. colleges. They want mainly good-quality classes, day or night, at a low cost. They also hope for easy parking, short registration lines, and polite service. Both time and money are important to them.

Topic: _____

Topic sentence: _____

[B]   Psychological tests reflect different learning styles in this new student population, too. Each person has a certain learning style, and about 60 percent of the new students these days prefer the *sensing* style. This means that they are very practical. They prefer a practice-to-theory method of learning—experience first and ideas after that. They often have difficulty with reading and writing and are unsure of themselves. Most of these students are attending college because they want to have a good job and make a lot of money.

Topic: _____

Topic sentence: _____

_____

[C]   In contrast, other students (but not as many) prefer the *intuitive* learning style. These students love ideas. They prefer a theory-to-practice method of learning and enjoy independent, creative thinking. These "intuitives" are not very practical. They are attending college because they want to create unique works of art or study philosophy or someday help in the field of science.

Topic: _____

Topic sentence: _____

_____

[D]   There is a drawback for the students who prefer the sensing style of learning. A majority of college professors prefer the intuitive learning style. These teachers value independent thinking and creative ideas. Students in the sensing group are at a disadvantage because their way of thinking doesn't match their teachers'.

Topic: _____

Topic sentence: _____

_____

[E]   Politically, too, students these days are different from students in the past. In the 1960s and 1970s, many students demonstrated against the government and hoped to make big changes in society. In the 1980s, most students were interested only in their studies and future jobs. Today, students seem to be a combination of the two: they want to make good money when they graduate, but they're also interested in helping society. Many students today are volunteering in the community. They are working to help people, without payment. For example, they tutor (teach privately) children in trouble, or they work with organizations for homeless people. In these ways, they hope to make changes in society.

Topic: _____

Topic sentence: _____

_____

[F]   On all college campuses, student life is very different from what it used to be, due to technology—specifically, the Internet. At most colleges, all entering first year students receive an e-mail address. Dormitory rooms offer high-speed Internet access. Computer systems are available to everyone in computer labs, the library, and student centers. Application for classes and registration are usually now possible online. Some schools offer entire courses online. Many professors still have "office hours," when students can come to talk with them about class work or ask for help. But increasingly, students can contact professors twenty-four hours a day, thanks to e-mail. Perhaps most important for both students and professors, research is now easier and faster because of the new technology.

Topic: _____

Topic sentence: _____

_____

After You Read

3   **Understanding Pronoun Reference.**   As you know, pronouns take the place of nouns. When you read, it's important to understand the meaning of pronouns, to know which noun a pronoun refers to. To find the noun that a pronoun refers to, look back in the sentence or in the sentences that come before it.

Example

Over 100,000 international students attend graduate school. Most of <u>them</u> are studying business and management.

What does *them* refer to? <u>international students</u>

Look back at the reading selection "Campus Life in the United States Today" to find the meaning of the following pronouns. What does each pronoun refer to?

1. they (Paragraph A, line 2)   _____

2. they (Paragraph A, line 7)   _____

3. them (Paragraph A, line 14)   _____

4. their (Paragraph D, line 4)   _____

5. their (Paragraph E, line 4)   _____

6. them (Paragraph F, line 7)   _____

Discussing the Reading

4   This reading was about campus life (and students) in the United States. In small groups, talk about your answers to these questions about *your* country.

1. In your country, are there foreign students in colleges and universities? If so, where do they come from? Are there many?

2. In your country, are students today different from students in the past? If so, how are they different?

3. What are the main reasons that students in your country go to college?

4. Do students in your country do volunteer work? If so, what kind?

5. How has technology—especially the Internet—changed campus life in your country?

Talk It Over

Politically Correct Usage

Part of college life in North America these days is an understanding of being P.C.—politically correct. It's important for students to be sensitive to differences among various groups of people, to respect each group, and to be more careful about their use of language. Most students and teachers try to be politically correct, but many think that "things have gone too far." What do *you* think?

Here are some words and phrases that people used in the past and the more careful, politically correct words that many people use now instead. Can you think of reasons why people who use the politically correct words don't like the less politically correct words? Which P.C. words seem good to you? Why? Do any seem strange? If so, why?

Less Politically Correct	Politically Correct
blind	visually challenged
disabled, handicapped	differently abled
fat people	people of size
mankind	humanity
Orientals	Asians
pets	animal companions
policeman	police officer
remedial classes	basic classes
Third World countries	developing countries

PART 3   Building Vocabulary and Study Skills

1 **Recognizing Word Meanings.**   Match the words with their meanings. Write the letters on the lines, as in the example.

1. __g__ agriculture
2. _____ afford
3. _____ reflect
4. _____ memorize
5. _____ drawback
6. _____ recite
7. _____ discipline
8. _____ majority
9. _____ tuition
10. _____ startled

a. learn and remember
b. disadvantage
c. most; larger number
d. say aloud
e. control
f. surprised
g. farming
h. have enough money for
i. show
j. fees (money) for school

2   **Words in Context.**   Write the missing words in the blanks. Choose from these words.

statistic	rural	status
primary	relevance	egalitarian
determine	value	vocational
available	demonstrate	access
due to	major	

1. Children often have art lessons in _____ school.

2. He couldn't get a good job _____ his lack of education.

3. At first, I didn't see the _____ of a typing class, but my parents pointed out the importance of knowing how to type on a computer.

4. Some people _____ against the government to express their political opinions.

5. She went to a _____ school for job training.

6. Some societies _____ individualism and original ideas.

7. She plans to _____ in engineering.

8. This exam will _____ if I can go to the university or not.

9. It's necessary for college students to have _____ to the Internet.

10. Here's an interesting _____: only 29 percent of high school graduates in Germany go on to a university.

Focus on Testing

Answering Questions

On reading exams, there are different types of questions. Three of these are literal, opinion, and application. Students need to read each question carefully and determine what type it is.

Literal questions simply ask students to find answers in the reading and copy them. These are the easiest questions to answer.

Opinion questions ask for the student's opinion. These answers cannot be found in the reading.

Application questions ask students to apply information in the reading to a fresh situation from outside the reading.

Identify each of these exam questions. They are based on the reading on pages 5–6. Write *lit, op,* or *app* in each blank. Then discuss your answers to these questions with a small group.

1. _____ What do you think about the system of examinations in Japan?

2. _____ What percentage of Kenyan students don't continue on to high school?

3. _____ What are three problems in many U.S. high schools?

4. _____ How is the system of education in your country similar to (or different from) the system in Britain?

5. _____ In which of the four systems of education described in "Education: A Reflection of Society" do students have to pay tuition in secondary school?

6. _____ Some rural Kenyan tribes don't see the relevance of a formal education. What might be relevant to them instead?

7. _____ What are other countries in which students face "examination hell," as in Japan?

8. _____ Why do you think only 1 percent of the lower class in Britain goes to a university?

PART 4 # Reading in the Real World

1   **Scanning for Information.**   Often, as a student, you'll need to read material that seems too difficult—usually due to the number of new words but also because there might be grammatical structures that you don't understand. What can you do in these situations?

- Focus (concentrate) on what you understand, not on what you don't understand.
- Whenever possible, guess the meaning of new words from the context.
- To find information quickly, have a question in your mind. Then **scan** the reading—look quickly for the important words. Run your finger down the page until the answer "jumps out" at you. Don't read any more than necessary in order to answer your question.

Look over these questions *before* you read the following selection from a college textbook, *The Global Society: An Introduction to Sociology,* by William C. Cockerham. When you finish reading, write your answers.

1.   Look at the first sentence and the last sentence. What is the main idea of this passage?

_____

_____

2.   How many countries did the group of sociologists study?

_____

3.   Did the group find more similarities or differences in elementary education in these countries?

_____

4.   In what ways is instruction similar in these countries?

_____

_____

5.   In what ways is instruction different in these countries?

_____

_____

Knowledge for the Masses

An international group of sociologists from Israel, Japan, South Korea, and the United States has determined that children in elementary school around the globe are taught essentially the same subjects. Utilizing data from the United Nations and their own international survey, Aaron Benavot and his colleagues (Benavot, Cha, Kamens, Meyer, and Wong, 1991) analyzed information on education in 125 countries. They found considerable similarity in primary school curricula throughout the world. These researchers suggest that in an effort to achieve progress and equality, the world's educators have developed strikingly similar national educational systems and school curricula.

On a worldwide basis, instruction in foreign languages is increasing in primary schools, and a set of core subjects—reading, writing, grammar, mathematics, natural science, and social sciences—is taught everywhere. The percentage of time allocated to these subjects is also similar.

Some differences were found. Developed nations provide more instruction in physical education and the arts, while developing countries teach more vocational education. In predominantly agricultural nations, where most people do not attend school past the elementary grades, practical knowledge like farming and household work is emphasized. These differences, however, were not great when school curricula were considered on a global basis. Similarities clearly outweighed differences. Benavot and his colleagues (1991: 98) therefore conclude that "we may speak with some confidence about a relatively standard world curriculum."

[Source: "Knowledge for the Masses," from William C. Cockerham, *The Global Society: An Introduction to Sociology*, p. 406. Copyright 1995 by McGraw-Hill, Inc.]

2 **Getting Meaning from Context.**   Scan the reading passage to find a word for each definition. (Note: Look for these words in the same order as the definitions.)

1. world _globe_____

2. basically _____

3. using _____

4. information _____

5. material that people study _____

6. basic, most important _____

7. were more important than _____

3   **Expanding Vocabulary.** The reading passage included this sentence: "On a <u>world-wide</u> basis, instruction in foreign language is increasing in primary schools . . ."

    Worldwide means "everywhere in the world." What might be words for these definitions? Use logic (not your dictionary) to give a word for each.

1. everywhere in the nation   _____

2. everywhere in the country   _____

3. everywhere in the state   _____

4. everywhere in the city   _____

5. everywhere in the school   _____

6. everywhere on the campus   _____

Beyond the Text

Find *one* of the following and bring it to class. Share it with your classmates. Discuss the information and vocabulary.

■ a catalog (from any college) that includes a list of the courses

■ information (from the library or the Internet) about a college in another country

■ orientation information from a local college or university

Video Activities: An Online English Class

Before You Watch.   Discuss the following questions with your class or in a small group.

1. Do you ever use the Internet? What kinds of sites do you visit?
2. Do you ever do research for a paper online?
3. Have you ever taken an online course?
4. Do you know the expression "virtual reality"?

Watch.   Check the following things students can do in Dr. Weshkey's virtual English class.

1. _____   get announcements
2. _____   listen to a lecture
3. _____   link to Websites for research
4. _____   construct a personal web page
5. _____   take tests
6. _____   talk to classmates
7. _____   send an e-mail to the teacher

Watch Again.   Virtual courses have both advantages and disadvantages. Compete the chart below. Afterwards, share answers with your classmates.

	Advantage(s)	Disadvantage(s)
For students		
For parents		
For teachers		

After You Watch.   A "compound" word is one word that is made up of two connected words. There are several compound words in the video clip. The first one is listed below. Watch the video and try to find the others.

a. black + board = blackboard

b. _____

c. _____

d. _____

Chapter 2

City Life

IN THIS CHAPTER

The first reading selection discusses the problems of overcrowding in big cities and explores one city that has found some creative solutions to these problems. Next, you'll read about indoor air pollution—just one example of a problem that occurs in modern cities.

PART 1   # A City That's Doing Something Right

Before You Read

1 Discuss the photos in small groups.

1. Where do you think the photos were taken?
2. What adjectives can you think of to describe each photo?
3. What might be some problems in the city in the first photo?

Photo 1

Photo 2

2 **Vocabulary Preview.**   Briefly look over this list of words from the reading that follows. Put a check (✔) next to the words that you don't already know, but don't use a dictionary for them. Instead, try to understand them from the reading. You'll work with some of these words in the next exercise.

Nouns	Verbs	Adjective	Adverbs	Phrases
priorities	predict	affluent	efficiently	developing countries
trash	worsen		actually	mass transit
produce (PROduce)	focus			pedestrian zone
gridlock	solve			recycling plant
tube	decrease			
	commute			

3 **Guessing Meaning from Context.** You do not need to look up the meaning of new words if you can guess them from the context. Here are three types of clues that will help you guess new words.

■ The words *for example, for instance, such as*, and *among them* introduce examples that may help you. (Sometimes examples appear without these words, in parentheses, or between dashes.)

Example

Almost four billion people will be living in cities in developing countries such as India and Nigeria.

You can guess that developing countries are not rich.

■ Sometimes another word or words in another sentence or sentence part has the opposite meaning from a new vocabulary item.

Example

In some cities, instead of worsening, urban life is actually getting much better.

You see that worsening is the opposite of "getting better."

■ A definition or explanation follows the connecting words *that is* or *in other words*.

Example

The downtown shopping area is now a pedestrian zone—in other words, an area for walkers only, no cars.

A pedestrian zone is an area for walkers only.

Guess the meanings of the underlined words and write them on the lines. Use punctuation, logic, examples, opposites, and connecting words to help you guess.

1. People who study population growth <u>predict</u> a nightmare by the year 2025: the global population will be more than 8 billion, and almost 4 billion of these people will be living in cities in developing countries.

   _____

2. People spend hours in <u>gridlock</u>—that is, traffic so horrible that it simply doesn't move—when they <u>commute</u> daily from their homes to their work and back.

   gridlock = _____

   commute = _____

3. It might not be a surprise to find that life in <u>affluent</u> cities is improving, but what about cities that aren't rich?

   _____

4. Under his leadership, city planners established <u>priorities</u>—in other words, a list of what was most important.

_____

5. In neighborhoods that garbage trucks can't reach, people bring bags of <u>trash</u> to special centers.

_____

6. They exchange the trash for fresh <u>produce</u>—such as potatoes or oranges—or for bus tickets.

_____

7. At a <u>recycling plant</u>, workers separate bottles, plastic, and cans from other trash.

_____

8. Curitiba needed a <u>mass-transit</u> system but couldn't afford an expensive subway. City planners began, instead, with an unusual system of buses.

_____

Read

4 As you read the following selection, think about the answer to this question: what is Curitiba doing right?

Read the selection quickly. Do not use a dictionary. Then do the exercises that follow the reading.

A City That's Doing Something Right

[A] There's good news and bad news about life in modern cities—first, the bad. People who study population growth predict a nightmare by the year 2025: the global population will be more than 8 billion, and almost 4 billion of these people will be living in cities in developing countries such as India and Nigeria. Population growth is already causing unbelievable overcrowding. Nairobi, Kenya, has basic services for 200,000 people but has a population of 5 million. Mexico City is home to almost 25 million people. By the year 2025, population experts predict, 660 *million* people will be living in cities in India. Due to overcrowding, these cities have problems with air pollution, disease, and crime. People spend hours in gridlock—that is, traffic so horrible that it simply doesn't move—when they commute daily from their homes to their work and back. There isn't enough water, transportation, or housing. Many people don't have access to health services or jobs. Now the good news: in *some* cities, instead of worsening, urban life is actually getting much better.

A City and Its Mayor

[B] It might not be a surprise to find that life in affluent cities is improving. But what about cities that *aren't* rich? The city of Curitiba, Brazil, proves that it's possible for even a city in a developing country to offer a good life to its residents. The mayor of Curitiba for twenty-five years, Jaime Lerner, was an architect and a very practical person. Under his leadership, the city planners established a list of priorities—in other words, a list of what was most important to work on. They decided to focus on the environment and on the quality of life. With an average income of only about $2000 per person per year, Curitiba has the same problems as many cities. However, it also has some creative solutions.

Garbage Collection

[C]   One creative solution is the method of garbage collection. In neighborhoods that garbage trucks can't reach, poor people bring bags of trash to special centers. At these centers, they exchange the trash for fresh produce—such as potatoes and oranges—or for bus tickets. At a recycling plant, workers separate bottles, plastic, and cans from other trash. *Two-thirds* of Curitiba's garbage is recycled, which is good for the environment. And the plant gives jobs to the poorest people, which improves their lives.

Transportation

[D]   Due to careful planning, Curitiba does not have the same traffic problems that most cities have. The statistics are surprising. The population has grown—now *twice* the size it was in 1974—but traffic has actually *decreased* 30 percent. Curitiba needed a mass-transit system but couldn't afford an expensive subway. City planners began, instead, with an unusual system of buses in the center lanes of five wide major streets. At each bus stop, there is a forty-foot-long glass tube. Passengers pay *before* they enter the tube. Then they get on the bus "subway style"—through wide doors. This allows people to get on and off the bus quickly and efficiently. People don't crowd onto the bus; loading and unloading takes only thirty seconds. This makes commuting more pleasant and also helps to solve the problem of air pollution.

Street Children

[E]   Then there is the problem of street children. To help solve this problem, Jaime Lerner talked seriously with owners of factories and stores. Each factory and store owner agreed to take care of a few street children—to give them a meal every day and a small amount of money. In exchange, the children do small, simple jobs in the garden or office. In addition, the city hired teenagers to keep the public parks clean.

The Environment

[F] To make the environment both cleaner and more beautiful, Curitiba has strict laws against polluters. But it also has low taxes for companies that have green areas, so several hundred major industries such as Pepsi and Volvo have offices in the city. Bringing natural beauty into the city is a priority. For this reason, Curitiba gave 1.5 million young trees to neighborhoods to plant and take care of. And the downtown shopping area is now a pedestrian zone—in other words, for walkers only, no cars—and is lined with gardens.

A Symbol of the Possible

[G] Clearly, overcrowding in big cities worldwide is the cause of serious problems. However, the example of Curitiba provides hope that careful planning and creative thinking can lead to solutions to many of them. Curitiba is truly, as Lewis Mumford once said of cities in general, a "symbol of the possible."

After You Read

5 **Understanding the Main Idea.** Which of the following statements are true about Curitiba, according to the reading? Write T on those lines. Which statements are false? Write F on those lines.

1. _____ Curitiba is a rich city.

2. _____ Curitiba has some creative ways to collect garbage.

3. _____ Because the population is growing, traffic has increased 30 percent.

4. _____ Curitiba is doing something to help street children.

5. _____ Curitiba has taken action to create a clean and beautiful environment.

Cross-Cultural Note: Language

Some words in English might sound similar to words in your language. Usually, this helps your English vocabulary. However, sometimes the meaning is completely different. This can cause you problems! Words in two languages with a similar sound but a different meaning are called false cognates. *(You saw two examples of one of these in the reading.) As a student of English, you need to remember that false cognates exist. Do not try to translate them. Here are some examples.*

■ Actualmente *(in Spanish) means "presently, now," so Spanish-speaking students think that* actually *(in English) means the same. But it doesn't. In English,* actually *means "really, truly" or "although this seems strange."*

Context: The population has grown, but traffic has <u>actually</u> *decreased 30 percent.*

■ Manshon *(in Korean and Japanese) means "an expensive apartment building." However, in English,* mansion *means "a large expensive single-family house."*

Context: If I win the lottery, I'll buy a <u>mansion</u> *in Beverly Hills.*

■ Magazi *(in Greek) means "store, shop." However, in English, a* magazine *is something to read.*

Context: I read an interesting article yesterday in a news <u>magazine</u>.

■ Lunatik *(in Russian) means "a sleepwalker—a person who walks in his or her sleep." However, in English,* lunatic *means "a crazy person."*

Context: Everyone thought he was a <u>lunatic</u> *when he decided to quit school.*

Are there any false cognates that give trouble to people who speak your language? If so, share them with the class.

6 **Understanding Italics.** Writers use *italics* (slanted letters) for several reasons, among them for emphasis. The italics indicate that the word is important. Find the words in italics in the reading selection "A City That's Doing Something Right." Read these sentences aloud. Place emphasis on the words in italics.

7 **Understanding Contrast.** Sometimes writers use contrast to express an idea. In other words, they begin with the opposite of the point that they want to make. The reading selection "A City That's Doing Something Right" can be divided into two parts. What is the first part? What is the second part? How do these parts show contrast?

8 **Making Inferences.** Writers usually state information clearly. However, they also often imply information. In other words, they just suggest an idea without actually stating it. It is important for students to be able to make inferences—that is, to "read between the lines" and understand information that is not clearly stated.

Here is information about Jaime Lerner. Which information is stated in the reading? Put *S* on those lines. Which information is implied but not clearly stated? Put *I* on those lines. Look back at Paragraphs B and E to decide.

1. _____ Jaime Lerner was the mayor of Curitiba.

2. _____ Under his leadership, the city established a new mass-transit system.

3. _____ Jaime Lerner was mayor for a long time.

4. _____ Under his leadership, city planners established priorities.

5. _____ Jaime Lerner was an architect.

6. _____ He was practical.

7. _____ He was a creative thinker.

8. _____ He talked with owners of factories and stores about street children.

9. _____ He was a persuasive person.

10. _____ He was a good leader of the city.

9 **Summarizing.** A reading may express several important ideas, but there is one main idea that sums up (summarizes) all of the important ideas.

Circle the number of the main idea of the selection "A City That's Doing Something Right."

1. Population experts predict a nightmare by the year 2025, especially in urban areas in developing countries.

2. Curitiba has a creative method of garbage collection that not only gets trash off the streets but also provides food and jobs for poor people.

3. Curitiba's mass-transit system consists of buses, not a subway, but offers an efficient new way for people to get on and off.

4. Curitiba has laws to protect the environment and to make the city more beautiful.

5. Curitiba is an example of how careful planning and creative thinking can lead to solutions to urban problems.

10   Turn back to page 24 and answer the question immediately before the reading selection. Then check your answers to Exercise 5 on page 26. Correct the false statements.

Discussing the Reading

11   In small groups, talk about your answers to these questions.

1.   What is the population of the major cities in your country? Is overcrowding a problem?

2.   What are some problems in your city?

3.   What kind of mass transit is available in your city? Is it clean and efficient?

4.   Does your city have a recycling program? If so, tell your group about it. How does it work?

5.   Are there homeless street people in your city? If so, is there a program to help them?

6.   What programs are there to protect the environment in your city?

PART 2   # Sick-Building Syndrome

Before You Read

1   **Skimming for Main Ideas.**   As you learned in Chapter 1, a paragraph usually tells about one topic. Often there is one sentence that tells the topic and the main idea of the paragraph. This is the topic sentence. Read these paragraphs quickly. Do not use a dictionary and don't worry about the details. When you finish, write the topic and topic sentence of each paragraph. For a short vocabulary study of this reading passage, turn to page 37.

Read

2   Read the selection again. Do you want to change the topics and topic sentences you wrote?

Sick-Building Syndrome

[A]   Elizabeth Steinberg was a healthy sixteen-year-old student on the tennis team at St. Charles High School, west of Chicago, Illinois. But in the fall of 1977, she started to have strange health problems. The same thing happened to dozens of teachers and students at the school. They went to doctors for treatment of a number of symptoms such as sore throats, tiredness, headaches, and respiratory (breathing) difficulties. Doctors treated respiratory infections with antibiotics, but the condition didn't seem to improve, except—mysteriously—on weekends and over vacations, when the symptoms disappeared. Experts came to investigate and find the cause. They discovered that St. Charles High, like thousands of other schools and office buildings nationwide, is a "sick building"—in other words, a building that creates its own indoor air pollution.

Topic: _____

Topic sentence: _____

_____

[B]   People have worried about smog for many years, and the government has spent billions of dollars to try to clean up the air of big cities. But now we find that there is no escape from unhealthful air. Recent studies have shown that air inside many homes, office buildings, and schools is full of pollutants: chemicals, mold, bacteria, smoke, and gases. These pollutants are causing a group of unpleasant and dangerous symptoms that experts call "sick-building syndrome." First discovered in 1982, sick-building syndrome most often includes symptoms similar to the flu (watering eyes, headaches, and so on) and respiratory infections such as tonsillitis, bronchitis, and pneumonia.

Topic: _____

Topic sentence: _____

_____

[C]   Although most common in office buildings and schools, the indoor pollution that causes sick-building syndrome can also occur in houses. Imagine a typical home. The people who live there burn oil, wood, or gas for cooking and heating. They might smoke cigarettes, pipes, or cigars. They use chemicals for cleaning. They use hundreds of products made of plastic or particleboard—that is, an inexpensive kind of board made of very small pieces of wood held together with a chemical. These products give off chemicals that we can't see but that we do breathe in. In some homes, carbon monoxide from cars in the garage can enter the house. And in many areas, the ground under the building might send a dangerous gas called radon into the home. The people in the house are breathing in a "chemical soup."

Topic: _____

Topic sentence: _____

_____

[D]   Then what causes sick-building syndrome in an office building or school, where people don't smoke or burn oil, wood, or gas? Experts have discovered several sources of sick-building syndrome—among them mold and bacteria, synthetic products, and lack of ventilation—a system of moving fresh air. In many buildings, rain has leaked in and caused water damage to walls and carpets. This allows mold and bacteria to grow. Air conditioning systems are another place where mold and bacteria can grow. Synthetic (that is, unnatural) products such as paint, carpeting, and furniture can be found in all offices and schools. These products release toxic (poisonous) chemicals into the air. Perhaps the most common cause of sick-building syndrome, however, is lack of ventilation. Most modern office buildings are tightly sealed; in other words, the windows don't open, so fresh air doesn't enter the building. In a building with mold, bacteria, or toxic chemicals, lack of ventilation makes the situation more serious.

Topic: _____

Topic sentence: _____

_____

[E]   There are several solutions to the problem of sick-building syndrome, among them cleansing the building. First, of course, experts must determine the specific cause in any one building. Then workers probably need to take out carpets, wallpaper, and ceiling tiles in order to remove mold and bacteria. Also, they need to clean out the air conditioning system and completely rebuild the system of ventilation. They should remove synthetic products and bring in natural products, instead, if they are available.

Topic: ____Solution to Problem_____

Topic sentence: _____

_____

[F]   All of this sounds difficult and expensive. But there is another possible solution that is simple and inexpensive. NASA (the National Aeronautics and Space Administration) was trying to find ways to clean the air in space stations. One scientist with NASA discovered that houseplants actually remove pollutants from the air. Certain plants seem to do this better than others. Spider plants, for example, appear to do the best job. Even defoliated plants (without leaves) worked well! In another study, scientists found that the chemical interaction among soil, roots, and leaves works to remove pollutants.

Topic: ____Plant to clean_____

Topic sentence: _____

_____

[G]   This seems like a good solution, but we don't know enough yet. There are many questions. For instance, which pollutants can plants remove? Which can't they remove? How many plants are necessary to clean the air in a room—one or two or a whole forest of plants? When we are able to answer these questions, we might find that plants offer an important pollution-control system for the 21st century.

Topic: _____

Topic sentence: _____

_____

After You Read

After you write the topic and topic sentence of each paragraph, exchange your answers with another student. Are your answers the same? Are your topics the same but perhaps in different words? Do you agree about the topic sentences? If you don't agree, give reasons for your answers. One of you might want to change an answer!

3   **Understanding Pronoun Reference.**   Look back at the reading selection "Sick-Building Syndrome" to find the meaning of the following pronouns. What does each pronoun refer to?

1.   they (Paragraph A, line 4)   _____

2.   they (Paragraph C, line 4, twice)   _____

3.   they (Paragraph C, line 5)   _____

4.   them (Paragraph D, line 3)   _____

5.   them (Paragraph E, line 2)   _____

6.   they (Paragraph E, line 4)   _____

7.   they (Paragraph G, line 3)   _____

Discussing the Reading

4   In small groups, talk about your answers to these questions.

1.   Is there a problem with smog in your city? When is it the worst? What are the causes?

2.   Have you ever experienced sick-building syndrome? If so, what were your symptoms?

3.   How many possible pollutants can you find in your home and classroom? Make a list.

4.   In your home country, do people usually have houseplants? Why or why not?

5.   In your opinion, why wasn't sick-building syndrome a problem in the past?

Talk It Over

Classifying and Evaluating.   Answer the following questions in small groups.

1.   What is the person in the cartoon worried about?
2.   In your opinion, what is the point (idea) of this cartoon? In other words, what is the writer telling us?
3.   Do you worry about any problems in modern life? If so, which ones?
4.   Do some people worry too much? If so, what should they do about this?
5.   In your opinion, why wasn't sick-building syndrome such a problem in the past?

PART 3

Building Vocabulary and Study Skills

1   **Understanding Parts of Speech (1).**   To guess the meaning of a new word from the context, you may find it helpful to know its part of speech; that is, is the word a noun, a verb, an adjective, or an adverb? Many words can be more than one part of speech.

Examples

He tried to <u>answer</u> the question. (Here, *answer* is a verb; it is part of the infinitive *to answer*.)

It's difficult to find an <u>answer</u> to the problem. (Here, *answer* is a noun.)

In some cases, different parts of speech (usually a noun and a verb) have the same spelling but different pronunciations.

Examples

> We can <u>contrast</u> the problems of rural and urban areas. (*Contrast* is a verb; the emphasis—the syllable stress—is on the second syllable, -*trast*.)
>
> The situation in Curitiba is a <u>contrast</u> to the situation in many other cities. (*Contrast* is a noun; the emphasis is on the first syllable, *con-*.)

Study and pronounce the words in this chart.

Noun	Verb	Noun	Verb
answer	answer	focus	focus
cause	cause	house	house*
change	change	increase	increase**
contrast	contrast**	study	study
crowd	crowd	worry	worry

* The singular noun ends in a voiceless sound /s/; the verb ends in a voiced sound /z/.
** The noun has an accent on the first syllable; the verb has the accent on the last syllable.

Complete each sentence with words from the chart. Use the same word for both blanks of each item, and write the part of speech—(n) for noun or (v) for verb—in the parentheses after each blank as in the example.

1. What __causes__ (v) air pollution? One __cause__ (n) is traffic.

2. Some people avoid subways because of the big __crowd__ s (n) of people who __crowd__ (v) onto the trains of the mass-transit system twice a day.

3. Can we solve the problem of overcrowding? No one can __answer__ (v) this question. We don't have the __answer__ (n).

4. In some cities, people without __house__ s (n) may have to sleep in the streets. It is difficult to __house__ (v) all the people who need apartments.

5. The cost of housing doesn't go down; it __increase__ s (v) every year. Often elderly people with little money have to move because of the __increase__ (n).

6. A recent __study__ ( ) has shown that indoor air pollution is a growing problem. Experts are __worry__ ing ( ) the situation and trying to find solutions.

7. People who live in big cities often _worry_____ ( ) about crime.

  _____ ( ) can cause illness.

8. The city planners decided to _____ (v) on improving the environment and the quality of life. Their specific _Jones_____ (n) for the first year was the transportation system.

2   **Understanding Parts of Speech (2).**   Many words are related to one another; they have the same stem (base word) but different endings.

Example

Cities around the <u>globe</u> need to find solutions to similar problems, so city planners sometimes meet at a <u>global</u> conference. (*Globe* is a noun. *Global* is an adjective; it describes the noun *conference*.)

Study and pronounce the words in this chart.

Noun	Verb	Adjective	Adverb
beauty, beautification	beautify	beautiful	beautifully
creation	create	creative	creatively
crowd	crowd	crowded	
difference	differ	different	differently
difficulty		difficult	
efficiency		efficient	efficiently
pollution, pollutant	pollute	polluted	
prediction	predict	predictable	predictably
safety	save	safe	safely
solution	solve	solvable	
	worsen	worse	worse

Complete each sentence with the missing words from the preceding chart. Use forms of the base word and write the part of speech in the parentheses after each blank— (n) for noun, (v) for verb, (adj) for adjective, and (adv) for adverb. The first one is done as an example.

1. solve

  They are trying to find a _solution_____ (n) to the problem of overcrowding, but this is a difficult problem to _solve_____ (v).

2. pollute

   Most people know about air ___pollution___ ( ) in big cities, but
   they're just beginning to learn about the many ___pollutant___s ( )
   that we have inside buildings.

3. crowd

   There are ___crowd___s ( ) of people everywhere; the mass-transit
   system is especially ___crowded___ ( ).

4. safe

   The city is not ___safe___ ( ) because of crime. People can't
   leave their homes ___safely___ ( ) at night, and the police can't
   provide for their ___safety___ ( ).

5. beautify

   Many people bring plants into their homes because the plants are
   ___beautiful___ ( ). However, it's possible that these plants not only
   ___beautify___ ( ) the environment but also clean the air.

6. predict, worse

   Some people ___predict___ ( ) that urban life will get
   ___worse___ ( ); according to their ___predictions___s ( ),
   conditions will ___worsen___ ( ) every year.

7. differ

   The causes of indoor air pollution ___differ___ ( ) from area to
   area. One reason for the ___difference___ ( ) is that people heat their
   homes ___differently___ ( ). People in some areas burn wood for heat;
   in other areas, they use something ___different___ ( ).

8. efficient

   The mass-transit system in our city is not very ___efficient___ ( ),
   so we need to replace it with one that runs more ___efficiently___ ( ).

3   Looking up Parts of Speech.   You know that you don't need to look up every new word in a dictionary because you can often guess the meaning from the context. Sometimes, however, you may want to use a dictionary for other purposes—for instance, to find out the part of speech of a word or to learn related words.

A dictionary will tell you the parts of speech a word can be, usually with these abbreviations: n = noun, v = verb, adj = adjective, adv = adverb, prep = preposition, conj = conjunction. The abbreviation appears before the meanings of the word with that part of speech. This dictionary entry shows that the word *reason* can be a noun (with four meanings) or a verb (with one meaning). A related adjective is *reasonable*.

> **rea-son**[1] /ríy´zən/ *n* **1** purpose, cause (for a belief or act): *The reason for the error was clear.* **2** an excuse: *I didn't have any reason for being late.* **3** the ability to think clearly: *She is normally a person of good reason.* **4** good judgment: *He has lost all reason!*
> **reason**[2] *v* to persuade or think in a sensible way: *I tried to reason with him, but he won't listen to me.*
> **rea´son-a-ble** *adj* having reason or sense: *She is normally a very reasonable person, but today she's upset.*

a.   If possible, everyone in the class should use the same kind of dictionary for the following exercises. Work quickly. The first student with the correct answers is the winner.

Find these words in your dictionary. Write the part of speech on the lines before each word—(n) for noun, (v) for verb, (adj) for adjective, and (adv) for adverb as in the example. Some words, in different contexts, can be more than one part of speech.

1. _adj_ terrible	6. ____ water	12. ____ produce
2. ____ discipline	7. ____ expert	13. ____ enormous
3. ____ value	8. ____ commute	14. ____ mystery
4. ____ original	9. ____ farm	15. ____ individual
5. ____ pleasant	10. ____ smog	16. ____ trash
	11. ____ air	

b.   Complete the chart. Write the appropriate related words under each heading. (X means that no word corresponding to that part of speech exists.)

Nouns	Verbs	Adjectives	Adverbs
education	educate	educated	educatedly
educator	X	educated	X
belief	believe	believable	believably
infection	infect	infectious	infectiously
origin	originate	original	originally
tightness	tighten	respiratory / tight	X
			tightly

Focus on Testing

Getting Meaning from Context

Many standardized exams don't test your vocabulary, but they test how well you can guess the meaning of a new word or phrase from the context. Often on tests such as the one following, one answer is close but not close enough. One has the correct part of speech but the wrong meaning. Another is simply wrong; perhaps it is the opposite of the correct answer or has the wrong part of speech. Always keep in mind that there is only one correct answer.

Take this practice test. Guess the meaning of the underlined words from the reading selection "Sick-Building Syndrome." Circle the letter of the correct answer.

1. They went to doctors for treatment of a number of <u>symptoms</u> such as tiredness, headaches, <u>sore</u> throats, and respiratory problems.

    symptoms:
    a. syndromes
    b. pains in the head
    c. signs of a sickness
    d. kinds of medicine
    e. kinds of tiredness

    sore:
    a. well
    b. painful
    c. difficult
    d. problem
    e. in the throat

2. These pollutants are causing a group of unpleasant and dangerous symptoms that experts call "sick-building <u>syndrome</u>."
    a. polluted
    b. problem with a large building
    c. symptom
    d. combination of symptoms
    e. danger

3. In many buildings, rain has <u>leaked in</u> and caused water damage to walls and carpets.
    a. escaped
    b. entered the ventilation system
    c. come in accidentally
    d. worsened
    e. rained

4. The air was full of <u>pollutants</u>: chemicals, mold, bacteria, smoke, and gases.
    a. pollution
    b. chemicals
    c. smog inside a building
    d. things that pollute
    e. gases

PART 4

Reading in the Real World

1 **Scanning for Information.**   Most magazine articles in English may seem too difficult for you at this point in your study of the language. However, you might be surprised at how much you do understand. Here are some suggestions:

- ■ Don't worry about words that you don't understand.
- ■ Let pictures (if there are any) help you with meaning.

The following article lists predictions about urban life. Before you read the article, look over these questions about it. Then scan the article and write your answers. Don't use a dictionary.

1. According to the article, will life be better or worse in the year 2025?

   _____

2. Will people use cars and trucks more or less than they do now?

   _____

3. How will food improve?

   _____

   _____

4. How will malls (shopping centers) be different from the ones today?

   _____

   _____

5. What two sources of power will people use instead of fossil fuels such as oil?

   _____

   _____

What Would a Green Future Look Like?

[A] By the year 2025 many of us will no longer tolerate the scourges of 20th century suburban life: the marathon commutes, the maddening traffic jams, the pollution spewing from tailpipes and chimneys. We'll demand neighborhoods where the air is pristine and places to work, shop and play are close at hand.

Work/Transport

[B] Lots of us will work in our houses or apartments, telecommuting with our computers. Others will make a short hop to a nearby office park. Those who have to go downtown will prefer swift mass transit. Cars and trucks will still be used, but they will run on clean, hydrogen-powered fuel cells. To keep ourselves in shape and save money, we'll spend more time on bicycles.

Food

[C] We'll favor fruits, grains and vegetables grown close to home, either in our backyard gardens or on nearby organic farms. It won't take much energy to get the fresh produce to local markets. Since the farms will employ natural forms of pest control rather than potentially toxic chemicals, there will be much less of a buildup of suspected carcinogens in the food supply.

Shopping

[D] Even in an era of online marketing, there may still be a mall, but it will be relatively small and easy to get to, with sidewalks and bike racks instead of a mammoth parking lot. An airy place where a flood of natural light will cut down on energy use, the mall will be a two-way operation: when you're through using any product you buy there, the stores will be required to take it back for recycling.

Energy

[E] Our power will come from sources cleaner than fossil fuels. Some energy will flow from modern-day windmills, but much of it will be generated in our own homes. Rooftop solar panels will supply electricity to our appliances and to a basement fuel cell, which will produce hydrogen. When the sun is not shining, the cell will operate in reverse, using the hydrogen to make electricity.

Waste

[F] Sewage will be piped into enclosed marshes, where selected plants, fish, snails, and microbes will purify the wastewater before it enters streams and reservoirs. No longer will inadequate treatment of wastewater promote algae blooms that threaten other aquatic life.

[Source: Charles P. Alexander, "What Would A Green Future Look Like?" from *Time* (November 8, 1999): p. 114.]

2   **Getting Meaning from Context.**   Scan the article to find a word or phrase for each definition.

Paragraph A:

1. allow (something) to exist _____

2. very long (trip) _____

3. coming out of _____

4. very clean _____

Paragraph B:

5. little drive (noun); trip _____

6. fast _____

7. in good physical condition _____

Paragraph C:

8. places where people grow food to sell _____

9. adjective that means "without unnatural chemicals" _____

_____

Paragraph D:

10. a place to "park" bicycles _____

11. very large; huge _____

Paragraph E:

12. come from _____

13. adjective that means "from the sun" _____

14. machine (such as refrigerators and washing machines) in the house

_____

15. a room under the house _____

Paragraph F:

16. make pure _____

Beyond the Text

Interview as many people as you can. Ask them these two questions and take notes on their answers.

- Do you think that city life in the future will be better or worse than it is today?
- How do you think city life will be different in the future from what it is today? (Make predictions.)

Video Activities: Garbage Car

Before You Watch.   Discuss the following questions with your class or in a small group.

1. Where do you usually put the garbage from your home?
2. When trash is collected in your city, where does it go?
3. Why is it important to collect and dispose of trash properly?
4. Did you ever have a trash collection problem in the city where you live?

Watch.   Watch the video and discuss the following questions with your classmates.

1. What was left in front of Ann Porter's home?
2. What is her problem?
3. Has the city where she lives tried to help her?
4. How does she feel?
5. Why is the situation dangerous?

Watch Again.   Read the following statements. Write (T) if they are true and (F) if they are false.

1. _____   The car belongs to one of Ann Porter's neighbors.

2. _____   The car smells bad.

3. _____   The car has been in front of her house for a week.

4. _____   The police have come out to see the car.

5. _____   The car is a fire hazard.

6. _____   The city is going to take the car away tomorrow.

After You Watch.   Watch the video again. When you hear each word or phrase below, stop the tape and say its part of speech.

a.   outside

b.   station wagon

c.   in front of

d.   smelly

e.   fairness

Chapter 3

Business and Money

IN THIS CHAPTER

The first reading selection discusses organizations that are helping people escape from poverty. The second reading explores the question "Why do we buy things?" In the last section, there is a news service article about the place of money in a healthy life.

| PART 1 | # Banking on the Poor |

Before You Read

1 Look at the photos and discuss them in small groups.

Photo 1

Photo 2

Photo 3

1. The photo at the bottom takes place in a bank. What might the people be doing? (Think of as many verbs as you can for activities that usually take place in a bank.)
2. How are the people in the other two photos different from the people in the bank?
3. What might be some problems of the people in the first two photos?

2   Vocabulary Preview.   Briefly look over this list of words from the reading that follows. Which words do you already know? For the ones that you don't know, don't use a dictionary. Try to understand them from the reading.

Nouns	Verbs	Adjectives	Phrases
poverty	lift	anonymous	take the initiative
microentrepreneurs	fund	worthless	peer pressure
character	plow		social ills
capacity			
eradication			
literacy			
collateral			
subsidiary			
microlending			

3   Getting Meaning from Context.   Sometimes certain abbreviations (shortened forms of words) help you understand a new word or phrase. Here are some:

e.g. = for example
i.e. = that is = in other words

Circle the words that give clues to the meaning of the underlined word(s). Then answer the questions.

1.   This is a group of <u>microentrepreneurs</u>—i.e., people who own and run their own small business.

Who are <u>microentrepreneurs</u>?

_____

2.   Instead of collateral, there is <u>peer pressure</u>; i.e., group members make sure that each person pays back his or her loan.

What happens when there is <u>peer pressure</u>?

_____

3.   The Global Fund for Women helps find solutions to <u>social ills</u>—e.g., violence and lack of education.

What are examples of <u>social ills</u>?

_____

4 Sometimes the context has an explanation of the new word, but in order to think of a synonym, you need to change the part of speech.

Example

> For many people, there seems to be no escape from poverty; in other words, they are (poor,) and they have no hope that this will change.

In this example, you see that poverty is close in meaning to *poor*, but the two words have different parts of speech. *Poverty* is a noun, and *poor* is an adjective. (What is *poverty?* "Poorness" or the condition of being poor.)

Circle the words that mean the same or almost the same as the underlined words. Then change those words to the same parts of speech as the underlined words.

If this woman wants to borrow money, she must show that she (1) is honest (has <u>character</u>), (2) is able to run her business (has <u>capacity</u>), and (3) owns a house or land or something valuable.

1. What part of speech is *character?* _____

2. What is *character?* _____

3. What part of speech is *capacity?* _____

4. What is *capacity?* _____

5 Sometimes the context does not give a clear definition or example of a new word. You can't be sure about the exact meaning, but you can still make an intelligent guess and not waste time by going to the dictionary. First, figure out the part of speech of the new word. Then imagine in your mind what other word might be logical in that place.

Example

> Everyone in the group must <u>approve</u> the loan of every other group member, or Good Faith won't lend the money.
>
> Part of speech: verb
>
> Possible meanings: agree to; say OK about; sign

Some of your guesses might be wrong, but that's not a problem. If you see the word again, in a different context, the meaning will become clearer.

Make guesses about the underlined words. Don't worry about being right or wrong. Just try to be logical. When you finish, compare your answers with a partner.

1. A poor woman has an idea to <u>lift</u> her and her family out of poverty.

    Part of speech: _____

    Possible meanings: _____

2. The primary goal of Good Faith and other, similar programs is the <u>eradication</u> of poverty.

    Part of speech: _____

    Possible meanings: _____

3. As poverty has decreased, there have been some surprising secondary effects of microlending programs. Perhaps the main <u>subsidiary</u> effect has been a change in the social status of women.

    Part of speech: _____

    Possible meanings: _____

4. She began the Global Fund for Women. This <u>fund</u> now has more than $3 million. It has given money to over 400 women's groups.

    Part of speech: _____

    Possible meanings: _____

5. With careful planning and cooperation, most people use the money well and then <u>plow</u> both money and knowledge back into their communities.

    Part of speech: _____

    Possible meanings: _____

Read

6 As you read the selection, think about the answer to this question. How can banks help poor people to change their lives?

    Read the selection quickly. Do not use a dictionary. Then do the exercises that follow the reading.

Banking on the Poor

[A] For many people, there seems to be no escape from poverty; in other words, they are poor, and they have no hope that this will ever change. In addition, they have the social problems of poverty. Imagine this situation: a poor woman has an idea for a small business to lift herself and her family out of poverty. She needs a little money to begin this business. She goes to a bank to borrow the money, and the banker interviews her. At this bank, as at most banks, the borrower must meet three necessary conditions: character, capacity, and collateral. That is, if this woman wants to borrow money from the bank, she must show that she (1) is honest (has character), (2) is able to run her business (has capacity), and (3) owns a house, land, or something valuable (collateral) for the bank to take if she can't pay back the money. So what happens to the woman? The bank won't lend her the money because she doesn't have any collateral. In such a situation, there seems to be no way for the woman to break the cycle of poverty.

Microlending

[B] One possible solution these days is microlending. This is a system of special banks and programs that are loaning money to people in "borrowing groups." For example, an international organization called Good Faith lends small amounts of money to people who want to go into business. Each person must do two things to borrow money: take classes in business and join a borrowing group. This is a group of microentrepreneurs—i.e., people who own and run their own small business. Everyone in the group must approve the loan of every other group member, or Good Faith won't lend the money. To receive a loan from Good Faith, people still must have character. They find capacity in the business classes. But collateral is not necessary any longer. Instead of collateral, there is peer pressure; i.e., group members make sure that each person pays back his or her loan. They want to keep their "good name" and continue doing business with Good Faith. Because of the importance of peer pressure, microlending is more effective in small villages (where everyone knows and depends on everyone else) than in urban areas (where it's possible to be anonymous—unknown).

What Works, What Doesn't

[C]   Good Faith has had many successes and only a few failures. In Pine Bluff, Arkansas, a small town in the United States, one person was able to open a hair salon, another a plant shop, and another a car decorating business—all with loans from Good Faith. In a developing country such as Bangladesh, a person can buy a cow or a sewing machine and begin a small business with only $20 to $50. Because of many small loans from Good Faith, there are now 1.6 million new entrepreneurs in Bangladesh. Of course, not all these loans were a success. At first, Good Faith lent half of the money to men and half to women. Unfortunately, most of the Bangladeshi men spent the money on themselves, not the business. Now Good Faith does business mainly with women's borrowing groups in that country.

Subsidiary Effect

[D]   The primary goal of Good Faith and other, similar programs is the eradication of poverty. However, as poverty has decreased, there have been some surprising secondary effects of microlending programs. Perhaps the main subsidiary effect has been a change in the social status of women. Traditionally, in some societies such as Bangladesh, people thought of women as worthless. But when a woman has access to money and is able to demonstrate her capacity for business, she often receives more respect than before from the male members of her family and from the entire village.

Global Fund for Women

[E]   In any country, women are the poorest of the poor. They produce more than half of the world's food, but they own just 1 percent of the world's land. They are 51 percent of world's population, but very, very little money goes to programs to help them. In the late 1980s, Anne Firth Murray took the initiative and began the Global Fund for Women. This fund now has more than $3 million. It has given money to over 400 women's groups in 94 countries. Unlike Good Faith, which helps people begin businesses, the direct focus of the Global Fund for Women is to help find solutions to social ills—e.g., violence and lack of education. For instance, the fund has helped a group of Palestinian and Jewish women who are working together to stop violence against women. It is giving money to a woman in a village in southern India; she has started a literacy program to teach poor women to read.

Breaking the Cycle

[F]   Good Faith and the Global Fund for Women have a lesson for banks around the world: it's a "safe bet" to lend money to the poor. With careful planning, education, and cooperation, most people use the money well and then plow the money and knowledge back into their communities. There is hope that they can begin to break the cycle of poverty for themselves, their families, and society.

After You Read

7 **Getting the Main Ideas.**   Write T on the lines before the statements that are true, according to the reading. Write F before the statements that are false.

1. _____ Poor people can't borrow money from most banks.

2. _____ Good Faith lends money to poor people in borrowing groups.

3. _____ Good Faith has always been successful.

4. _____ The Global Fund for Women is another fund that lends money so that people can start businesses.

5. _____ It's a good idea to lend money to the poor.

8 **Understanding Conclusions.**   Often, a sentence in the conclusion to a reading selection will refer back to a sentence in the introduction. This gives the reading a feeling of completion. Find a sentence in the conclusion to "Banking on the Poor" that refers back to a sentence in the introduction.

9 **Making Inferences.**   In Paragraph D, you read this information:

> In some societies such as Bangladesh, people thought of women as worthless. But when a woman has access to money and is able to demonstrate her capacity for business, she often receives more respect than before from the male members of her family and from the entire village.

What might be some specific ways in which a woman with her own business "receives more respect"? In other words, make inferences about how this changes her life.

Turn back to page 47 and answer the question immediately before the reading selection. Then check your answers to Exercise 7 on page 49. Correct the false statements.

10 **Summarizing.**   Circle the number of the one main idea of the reading selection.

1. There seems to be no escape from poverty for many people.

2. Microlending is a system of banks and programs that are loaning money to people in borrowing groups.

3. It's possible to break the "cycle of poverty" with planning, education, cooperation, and some money.

4. Good Faith and the Global Fund for Women give money to poor people.

Discussing the Reading

11   In small groups, talk about your answers to these questions.

1. In your country, do banks require collateral before they loan money to someone? What kinds of things are used for collateral?

2. In your country, do people sometimes join a cooperative group to borrow money? If so, what are these groups called? How do they work?

3. What are some social problems in your country? What are people doing to solve them?

Talk It Over

Understanding Irony.   What idea is the cartoonist expressing? Do you agree?

PART 2   # Consumerism and the Human Brain

Before You Read

1   It always helps to have ideas—or questions—in mind before you read. The more you know about a topic before reading, the more you will understand of the reading. The reading passage will confirm some of your ideas (tell you they are right), answer some of your questions, and correct some of your mistaken ideas.

Before you read the following paragraphs, talk about your answers to these questions. Work in small groups.

1. Who are consumers? What do they do?

2. What are some reasons that people choose one brand of a product instead of a similar brand of the same product?

3. How does advertising influence people?

4. Look at the photo. Why might a person choose to buy this brand of cigarette?

Read

2 **Skimming for Main Ideas.**   Read these paragraphs quickly. Do not use a dictionary and don't worry about the details. When you finish, write the topic and topic sentence of each paragraph.

Consumerism and the Human Brain

[A] We are all consumers. We all buy and use products and services; that is, we consume. The word comes from the Latin *consumere*, which means "to use up, to waste or destroy." Most of us don't think of ourselves as wasteful or destructive, but the world economy is based on consumerism. Today, people worldwide have greater access than ever before to a huge variety of products—and, often, to dozens of brands of the same product. What makes us decide to buy Brand A instead of Brand B, when the two items are really identical? Why do we buy things that we don't actually need? The answer lies in marketing—the advertising and selling of products. Successful marketers use their knowledge of psychology—and, increasingly, of recent studies of the human brain—to persuade us to consume more and more.

Topic: _____

Topic sentence: _____

_____

[B]   A good understanding of human weakness is essential if a company wants to sell a product. One way that advertisers persuade us to buy a product is by targeting our dissatisfaction with ourselves, our fears. Consider for a moment a typical fear—fear of being offensive to other people. Advertisers persuade us, for example, that if we don't buy their mouthwash, we'll have bad breath and offend other people. Dentists tell us that mouthwash is actually unnecessary; they explain that we need only simple dental hygiene—regular, correct use of a soft toothbrush and of dental floss. But we continue to spend money on mouthwash, breath freshener, and breath mints. Our fear of offending people outweighs our dentists' logic.

Topic: _____

Topic sentence: _____

_____

[C]   In a similar way, advertisers also take advantage of our need for a good self-image, our desire to appear attractive, successful, and even exciting. Take the example of the Marlboro cowboy. For years, this famous image has appeared everywhere, in even the smallest rural villages. Many men see it and think that's the kind of person they would like to be—strong, handsome, and adventurous—a person with an exciting life. Although it's irrational—impossible to explain rea-sonably—they buy the cigarettes because they want to be like the Marlboro man. It's common knowledge that the original model for these advertisements was a man addicted to smoking who died of lung cancer. However, this brand of cigarette remains very popular. Another example is the recent popularity in the United States of SUVs—sports utility vehicles. These vehicles are more expensive than most cars. They use more gas and create more pollution than most cars. They take up more space than most cars. But TV commercials show them climbing rocky mountain roads and crossing rivers, which seems exciting to many people. Most people who buy an SUV never get out of the city. They spend their morning commute in gridlock, not driving up and down mountains. Although it may seem irrational, advertisers persuade them that SUV owners are people with an exciting life.

Topic: _____

Topic sentence: _____

_____

[D]   With so many different (but almost identical) brands of the same product, what causes us to choose one brand instead of another? According to Dr. Alan Hirsch, our sense of smell actually influences our opinion of a product and our decision to buy it. A scientist at the Smell and Taste Treatment and Research Foundation in Chicago, Hirsch ran a careful, well-organized study. There were two identical rooms with an identical pair of Nike sneakers in each room. There was only one difference: he sprayed one of the rooms with a scent of flowers. Volunteers entered each room and answered questions about the sneakers. The result was that 84 percent of the people preferred the sneakers in the room with the floral smell—even though they were exactly the same as the ones in the other room!

Topic: _____

Topic sentence: _____

_____

[E]   There is also the effect of self-fulfilling prophecies. A self-fulfilling prophecy is a situation in which people cause a prediction to come true. (For example, a teacher tells a class that they are especially intelligent, and that semester the class does especially well on exams.) In marketing, a successful advertisement persuades consumers that a product works well; their belief causes them to use the product in such a way that it does work well. For example, the ads for Brand X of a diet pill say, "Take this pill, and you will lose weight because you won't be hungry." So people buy Brand X. Because they believe it will cause weight loss, they begin to eat less. They establish a new habit of eating less. The result? They lose weight. Is this because of the pill or because they are eating less?

Topic: _____

Topic sentence: _____

_____

[F]   Most of us like to think that we are reasonable, independent thinkers. We like to believe that we have a good reason for our choices. We don't want to buy products because of some strange compulsion—some irrational desire that we can't control. The truth is, however, that—with their increasing knowledge of what goes on in the human brain—marketers might have more power over us than we realize.

Topic: _____

Topic sentence: _____

_____

_____

After You Read

3   After you write the topic and topic sentence of each paragraph, exchange your answers with another student. Are your answers the same? Are your topics the same but perhaps in different words? Do you agree about the topic sentences? If you don't agree, give reasons for your answers. One of you might want to change an answer!

4   **Understanding Pronoun Reference.**   Look back at the reading selection "Consumerism and the Human Brain" to find the meaning of the following pronouns. What does each pronoun refer to?

1.   their (Paragraph A, line 9)   _____

2.   they (Paragraph B, line 7)   _____

3.   they (Paragraph C, line 10)   _____

4.   it (Paragraph D, line 4)   _____

5.   he (Paragraph D, line 8)   _____

6.   their (Paragraph E, line 5)   _____

Cross-Cultural Note: Fighting Consumerism

In Japan, as in many other countries, advertising influences people to buy more and more. However, the Seikatsu Club is fighting against this. The Seikatsu Club is a consumers' cooperative group with over 400,000 members who don't like to call themselves "consumers." They are working to reduce the influence of marketing in their lives. They hold meetings at which they discuss the actual ingredients, value, and cost of various products. They do not buy any products (such as synthetic detergents) that harm the environment. They do not buy any food products that contain harmful or inessential chemicals. They buy products in reusable or recyclable bottles and cans but not in plastic containers. They own several dairy farms so that members have access to fresh milk products without any added ingredients. Most important, they are working to educate people to think for themselves.

    Are there organizations or movements similar to this in other countries?

Discussing the Reading

5   In small groups, talk about your answers to these questions.

1.   Describe your spending habits. In your opinion, does advertising influence your choice of products?

2.   Make a list of products that you buy. Do you always buy the same brand of each product? If so, can you give a reason for your choice?

Beyond the Text

In small groups, choose one of the following products: toothpaste, cars, laundry detergent, or cigarettes. Look through magazines for advertisements on your product. Bring as many ads as you can to your group. Together, study them. What kind of psychology is the advertiser using? (Fear? Desire for a good self-image? Self-fulfilling prophecy?)

PART 3

Building Vocabulary and Study Skills

1 **Finding Related Words.** Which word in each group does not belong? Cross it out as in the example. Explain your reasons for your answers.

1. psychologist	scientist	~~company~~	hygienist
2. stores	shops	markets	checks
3. compulsive	irrational	addicted	valuable
4. cash	credit	center	money
5. car	vehicle	SUV	drive
6. shopping	salesclerk	advertiser	businessperson
7. entrepreneur	lender	borrower	microlending
8. complete	power	influence	strength
9. values	accounts	beliefs	opinions
10. spend	claim	waste	save

2 **Understanding Parts of Speech.** To guess the meaning of a new word from the context, you might find it helpful to know its part of speech; that is, is the word a noun, a verb, an adjective, an adverb, and so on? Sometimes you can tell the part of speech from the suffix (the word ending). Here are some common suffixes, listed by the parts of speech that they usually indicate.

Nouns		**Adjectives**	
-er/-or	-ee	-ive	-ful
-ist	-(i)ty	-able/-ible	-ant/-ent
-sion/-tion	-ance/-ence	-(u)al	-ous
-ment	-ure	-ic(al)	-ar(y)
-acy		-ate	

Are the following words nouns or adjectives? The suffixes will tell you. On the lines, write *n* or *a* as in the examples. (In a few cases, both answers may be correct.)

1. __a__ compulsive	12. ____ influence	23. ____ pleasure
2. __n__ spender	13. ____ compulsion	24. ____ enormous
3. ____ successful	14. ____ violence	25. ____ scientist
4. ____ marketer	15. ____ computer	26. ____ basic
5. ____ psychologist	16. ____ pressure	27. ____ failure
6. ____ literacy	17. ____ society	28. ____ special
7. ____ identical	18. ____ addition	29. ____ consumer
8. ____ violent	19. ____ expensive	30. ____ public
9. ____ influence	20. ____ different	31. ____ floral
10. ____ information	21. ____ poverty	32. ____ logical
11. ____ offensive	22. ____ addiction	33. ____ culture

3   Complete each sentence with words related to the underlined words. Then look back at the list of suffixes to check your answers. The first one is done as an example.

1. __Marketer_____s use their knowledge of psychology to <u>market</u> their

   products. They hope that _____s will buy their goods,

   <u>consume</u> them, and feel the need to soon buy more.

2. That _____ TV commercial was _____ to

   many people. They were <u>offended</u> by its <u>violence</u> and didn't see the need

   for it.

3. Advertising is a kind of _____ that has a strong

   _____ on consumers; it should not only <u>influence</u> people to

   buy products, but also <u>inform</u> them.

4. This organization has been _____ in solving some serious

   <u>social</u> problems in that _____. Their <u>success</u> is due to hard

   work and the cooperation of many people.

Focus on Testing

Paying Attention to Phrases

To do well on standardized reading exams, you need to have a good vocabulary. In recent years, linguists (experts on language) have been emphasizing the importance of learning new words in phrases instead of individually. Learning phrases instead of single words will help you in three ways:

■ It will help you acquire the new word.

■ It will allow you to use the new word correctly in both everyday language and on standardized writing exams.

■ It will help you read faster, which allows you not only to finish exams faster but also to understand more of what you read.

Certain words belong together in phrases. For example, a noun phrase can include adjectives and other words before or after the noun. A verb phrase may include noun objects, adjectives, or adverbs. A prepositional phrase includes an object after a preposition, and an infinitive phrase may include an object after the verb. Examples include the following:

Noun Phrases	**Verb Phrases**
greater access	spend money
access to information	educate people to spend wisely

Prepositional Phrases	**Infinitive Phrases**
in a similar way	to save money
with exciting lives	to buy Brand X

It is important when you read to begin to notice words in phrases—their immediate context. Look just before and just after a word to see if it is part of a phrase. For example, if the word is a verb, is it followed by an object or by a preposition? If it is followed by a preposition, which one?

4 Read this paragraph from Part 1. Notice the underlined phrases. (There are more than the ones underlined, but don't worry about this.) When you finish reading, go back and decide what type of phrase each one is: noun, verb, prepositional, or infinitive.

For many people, there seems to be no escape from poverty; in other words, they are poor, and they have no hope that this will ever change. In addition, they have the social problems of poverty. Imagine this situation: a poor woman has an idea for a small business to lift herself and her family out of poverty. She needs a little money to begin this business. She goes to a bank to borrow the money, and the banker interviews her. At this bank, as at most banks, the borrower must meet three necessary conditions: character, capacity, and collateral. That is, if this woman wants to borrow money from the bank, she must show that she (1) is honest (<u>has character</u>), (2) is able <u>to run her business </u>(has capacity), and (3) <u>owns a house</u>, land, or something valuable (collateral) for the bank to take if she can't <u>pay back the money</u>. So what happens to the woman? The bank won't <u>lend her the money </u>because she doesn't have any collateral. <u>In such a situation</u>, there seems to be no way for the woman <u>to break the cycle</u> of poverty.

5 Which words belong together in phrases in the following paragraphs? Underline them. Notice what type of phrase each one is. When you finish, compare the phrases that you've underlined with those of another student.

1. A good understanding of human weakness is essential if a company wants to sell a product. One way that advertisers persuade us to buy a product is by targeting our dissatisfaction with ourselves, our fears. Consider for a moment a typical fear—fear of being offensive to other people. Advertisers persuade us, for example, that if we don't buy their mouthwash, we'll have bad breath and offend other people. Dentists tell us that mouthwash is actually unnecessary; they explain that we need only simple dental hygiene—regular, correct use of a soft toothbrush and of dental floss. But we continue to spend money on mouthwash, breath freshener, and breath mints. Our fear of offending people outweighs our dentists' logic.

2. In a similar way, advertisers also take advantage of our need for a good self-image, our desire to appear attractive, successful, and even exciting. Take the example of the Marlboro cowboy. For years, this famous image has appeared everywhere, in even the smallest rural villages. Many men see it and think that's the kind of person they would like to be—strong, handsome, and adventurous—a person with an exciting life. Although it's irrational—impossible to explain reasonably—they buy the cigarettes because they want to be like the Marlboro man. It's common knowledge that the original model for these advertisements was a man addicted to smoking who died of lung cancer. However, this brand of cigarette remains very popular. Another example is the recent popularity in the United States of SUVs—sports utility vehicles. These vehicles are more expensive than most cars. They use more gas and create more pollution than most cars. They take up more space than most cars. But TV commercials show them climbing rocky mountain roads and crossing rivers, which seems exciting to many people. Most people who buy an SUV never get out of the city. They spend their morning commute in gridlock, not driving up and down mountains. Although it may seem irrational, advertisers persuade them that SUV owners are people with an exciting life.

| **PART 4** | # Reading in the Real World |

One way to deal with reading material that seems above your level is to focus on finding just the important information. A technique that helps many students is to highlight (mark with a light color) the reading with a highlighter (any color except black). Keep a question in mind and mark the answer when you find it.

1   Scanning for Information.   Scan the following article from the Knight-Ridder/ Tribune News Service. Keep this question in mind and mark everything that answers it:

What can (or should) we do to have a healthy life?

The Price of a Healthy Life Has Little to Do With Money

by Tim O'Brien

[A]   Have you ever thought about it? Have you ever wondered, "What is the price I must pay to live a healthy life?" Most of us want to live a long, prosperous life, free of mental and physical disability, right? Well, what does it take to increase our chances of doing that?

[B]   Heredity plays a part in creating tendency, not destiny. So, we'll admit the role it plays. Then we'll work to reduce its negative effect and optimize its benefits.

[C]   Must money play a significant role in living a healthy life? No. Avoiding smoking or tobacco products is a top priority for someone who wants a long life. Cigarettes cost money. So, if you don't smoke it saves you money up front, and long term in reduced medical expenses and sick days.

[D]   Research shows that optimists live longer and happier than pessimists. A positive attitude doesn't cost money. It is our free choice to be an optimist or a pessimist.

[E]   The diet we choose to eat strongly affects our likelihood of developing heart disease, the No. 1 killer in America. A diet low in red meat and other saturated fats and high in complex carbohydrates is inexpensive. This puts proper eating within the reach of everyone.

[F]   Ignorance might be the most costly part of trying to live a healthy life. What we don't know can certainly hurt us. However, is it expensive to learn about good health, diet and stress management? No. Libraries are free and open to everyone. And, most people now have access to the Internet, either directly, through friends or at the library.

[G]   Practicing proactive, preventive healthcare is a good idea. Getting annual physicals, including blood scans, chest X-rays, age related pap smears for women and PSA tests for men, can be expensive. If their health insurance policies don't cover routine physicals, many people do nothing. Your health is your responsibility. Does your health insurance cover going to the movies, or out to dinner, or an extended weekend vacation? No. You pay for these yourself. Isn't your health something worth paying for? Ask your doctor how often you should have a physical. Ask what the total cost will be for a thorough exam, including all tests appropriate for your age. Then, find the money and get the physical. Remember, "An ounce of prevention is worth a pound of cure."

[H]   Relaxing regularly can help reduce blood pressure and stress levels. Stress and high blood pressure are risk factors for many disorders, both mental and physical. Studies show that laughing regularly produces hormones that strengthen the immune system. And, a stronger immune system fights off disease better. If you had to drop an income producing activity to make time to relax in your life, laughing and relaxing could cost you money. However, if you're that busy, shouldn't you cut back anyway? And, if you need that much time to "make ends meet," shouldn't you consider changing to a simpler lifestyle?

[I]   What is the price of a healthy life? Little of the price involves money. Most of the price relates to changes in attitude, perception and our approach to life. After thinking about it, isn't it worth it for the chance to have a happier and healthier life?

[Source: Tim O'Brien, "The price of a healthy life has little to do with money" from Knight-Ridder/Tribune News Service, Dec. 6, 1999. Distributed by Knight-Ridder/Tribune Information Services.]
   (Tim O'Brien writes continuing-education courses and presents seminars on stress management. Readers may write to him at 2938 Wellington Circle East, Tallahassee, Fla. 32308 or send e-mail to him (at) hyperstress.com. He also has a Website at www.hyperstress.com.)

2 Compare the answers that you marked in the article with the markings of another student. Did you mark the same sentences or phrases? How many suggestions does the author make?

3 **Getting Meaning from Context.**   Scan the article to find a word or phrase for each definition.

Paragraph C:

  1. immediately, before anything _____

Paragraph D:

  2. people with a positive attitude _____

  3. people with a negative attitude _____

Paragraph E:

  4. probability _____

Paragraph F:

  5. expensive _____

Paragraph G:

6. every year _____

7. doctors' exams of a patient's body _____

Paragraph H:

8. sicknesses; diseases _____

9. make strong _____

10. find enough money to pay the bills (idiom) _____

Beyond the Text

Take a survey of students in another class. Ask each person to rate the five things listed in order of importance, 1 being the most important. Write their answers. When you finish, compare the results of your survey with the results of other students. Can you come to any conclusions about the importance of money in the lives of the people you interviewed?

- relationships
- health
- money
- work
- leisure

Video Activities: A Teenage Stockbroker

Before You Watch.   Discuss the meanings of the following words and expressions with your classmates. Check the meanings in a dictionary if necessary. Then complete the definitions below.

1. Stocks and shares

   Stocks and shares are kinds of _____

2. Stock exchange

   A stock exchange is _____

3. Investor

   An investor is a person who _____

4. Risk

   For an investor, a risk means _____

Watch.   Discuss the following questions with your classmates.

1. Talk about Dan. How old is he? What is unusual about him?
2. Where is Dan standing at the beginning of the video?

Watch Again.   Read the following statements. Write (T) if they are true and (F) if they are false.

1. _____ Dan has been trading stocks for six years.

2. _____ Dan has never lost money on the stock market.

3. _____ Dan dropped out of high school and now spends all his time trading stocks.

4. _____ Dan publishes all his wins and losses on his Website.

5. _____ Dan plans to buy a house in Malibu (California) when he is 19.

After You Watch.   Find the investments section of a newspaper and look at the stock quotations. Then answer the following questions.

1. Do you recognize any of the companies?
2. How much do the stocks of these companies cost?
3. Can you tell if the stocks increased or decreased in value?
4. What stocks would you like to own? Why?

Chapter 4

Jobs and Professions

IN THIS CHAPTER

The first reading discusses how the world of work is changing at the beginning of the twenty-first century, due to globalization and technology. The second selection is about ways people are finding jobs these days. The last reading, a textbook selection, mentions several economic revolutions of the past and compares them to the great change taking place today—the transformation into "the knowledge society."

Changing Career Trends

Before You Read

1 **Getting Started.** Look at the photos and discuss them in small groups.

Photo 1

Photo 2

1. When was the first photo taken? Where is the man, and what is he doing?
2. When was the second photo taken? Where is the woman, and what is she doing?
3. Can you think of some ways in which work has changed in the past twenty to fifty years?
4. Are these photos similar to photos from your country?

2 **Vocabulary Preview.** Briefly look over this list of words from the reading that follows. Which words do you already know? For the ones that you don't know, *don't* use a dictionary. Try to understand them from the reading.

Nouns		Verbs	Adjectives	Phrase
livelihood	cell phone	vary	secure	job security
post	beeper	upgrade	flexible	
stress	drawback	distract	rigid	
identity	millennium		passionate	
self-confidence	workaholism			
construction	pleasure			
globalization	overwork			
challenge	ulcer			
telecommuting				

Read

3   **Reading About Career Trends.**   As you read the following selection, think about the answer to this question: what are some ways in which work is changing? Read the following selection quickly. Do not use a dictionary. Then do the exercises that follow the reading.

Changing Career Trends

[A]   A hundred years ago in most of the world, people didn't have much choice about the work that they would do. If their parents were farmers, they became farmers. The society—and tradition—determined their profession. Twenty years ago in many countries, people could choose their livelihood. They also had the certainty of a job for life, but they usually couldn't choose to change from one employer to another or from one profession to another. Today, this is not always the case. Career counselors tell us that the world of work is already changing fast and will change dramatically in the next twenty-five years.

Job Security

[B]   Increasingly, people need to be prepared to change jobs several times in their lifetime. The situation varies from country to country, but in general there is less job security worldwide. In Europe, the unemployment rate is 10 percent, and many people have to accept part-time jobs while they wait to find full-time employment. The United States has the fastest-changing job market. In 1994, 6 million Americans quit their job to take a different post. In 1999, the number rose to 17 million. Even in Japan, where people traditionally had a very secure job for life, there is now no promise of a lifetime job with the same company.

The Effect of Insecurity

[C]   On the surface, it may seem that lack of job security is something undesirable. Indeed, pessimists point out that it is certainly a cause of stress. Many people find an identity—a sense of self—through their work. When they lose their job (or are afraid of losing it), they also lose their self-confidence, or belief in their own ability. This causes worry and depression. In Japan, for example, the daily newspaper *Asahi* reports a sudden rise in the number of businessmen who need psychological help for their clinical depression. However, this decrease in job security may not necessarily be something bad. It is true that these days, workers must be more flexible—able to change to fit new situations. But optimists claim that flexible people are essentially happier, more creative, and more energetic than people who are rigid.

Job Hopping

[D]   Jumping from job to job (or "job hopping") has always been more common in some professions such as building construction and not very common in other professions such as medicine and teaching. Today, job hopping is increasingly common in many fields because of globalization, technology, and a movement from manufacturing to services in developed countries. For example, people with factory jobs in industrial nations lose their jobs when factories move to countries where the pay is lower. The workers then need to upgrade their skills to find a new job. This is stressful, but the new job is usually better than the old one. Because technology changes fast, workers need continuing education if they want to keep up with the field. Clearly, technology provides both challenge and opportunity.

Telecommuting

[E] In many ways, technology is changing they way people work. There are advantages and disadvantages to this. In some professions, for instance, telecommuting is now possible. People can work at home for some—or all—of the week and communicate by computer, telephone, and fax. An advantage of this is that it saves them from the stress of commuting to the workplace. It also allows them to plan their own time. On the other hand, it is difficult for some people to focus on work when they are at home. The refrigerator, TV, and their children often distract them. Telecommuters must have enormous discipline and organizational skills. Technology is changing the way people work in another way—in the use of cell phones,  beepers, and pagers. There is an advantage: customers and clients have access to businesspeople at any time, anywhere. However, there is also a drawback: many businesspeople don't *want* to be available day and night. They prefer to have a break from their work life.

Workaholism

[F] In the new millennium, as in the 1990s, workaholism will continue to be a fact of life for many workers. Workaholics are as addicted to their work as other people are to drugs or alcohol. This sounds like a problem, but it isn't always. Some people overwork but don't enjoy their work. They don't have time for their family, friends, or leisure activities such as hobbies, sports, and movies. These people become tired, angry, and depressed. The tension and stress often cause physical symptoms such as headaches and stomach ulcers. However, other people love their work and receive great pleasure from it. These people appear to be overworking but are actually very happy. Psychologists tell us that the most successful people in the changing world of work are flexible, creative, disciplined, and passionate about their work. But they are also people who make time for relaxing activities and for other people. They enjoy their work and enjoy time away from it, too.

After You Read

4   Getting the Main Ideas.   Which statements are *true* about work today, according to the reading? Check (✔) them.

1. ___✓___ People probably need to be prepared to change jobs several times in their lifetime.

2. _____ Japan is one country where people keep the same job for a lifetime.

3. _____ Lack of job security is always a bad thing.

4. _____ People who can change to fit a new situation are usually happier than people who can't.

5. _____ Many people find a sense of self through their work.

6. _____ People in some professions move from job to job more often than people in other professions.

7. _____ Technology is making work life better for everyone.

8. _____ Telecommuters don't need to drive to the office every day.

9. _____ All workaholics have problems with stress.

10. _____ The most successful people work harder than other people.

5   Getting Meaning from Context.   Use both specific clues in these sentences and your own logic to determine the meanings of the underlined words and expressions. Then write your guess about the meaning.

1. Twenty years ago, in many countries, people could choose their <u>livelihood</u>, but they couldn't usually choose to change from one profession to another.

   ___own money to live life___

2. In 1994, 6 million Americans quit their job to take a different <u>post</u>.

   ___different job___

3. Even in Japan, where people traditionally had a very <u>secure</u> job for life, there is now no promise of a lifetime job with the same company.

   _____

4. When they lose their job, they also lose their <u>self-confidence</u>, or belief in their own ability.

   _____

5. They usually need to <u>upgrade</u> their skills to find a new, better job.

   _____

6. Because technology changes fast, workers need continuing education if they want to <u>keep up with the field</u>.

_____

7. In many professions, <u>telecommuting</u> is now possible. People can work at home for some—or all—of the week and communicate by computer, telephone, and fax.

_____

8. It's difficult for some people to focus on work when they are at home. The refrigerator, TV, and their children often <u>distract</u> them.

_____

9. There is an advantage: customers and clients have access to businesspeople at any time and anywhere. However, there is also a <u>drawback</u>: many businesspeople don't *want* to be available day and night.

_____

10. They don't have time for their family, friends, or <u>leisure</u> activities such as hobbies, sports, or movies.

_____

11. The tension and stress often cause physical symptoms such as headaches and stomach <u>ulcers</u>.

_____

6 Find a word or expression in the reading for each definition. The letters in parentheses refer to paragraphs in the reading.

1. people who give advice about professions, careers (A) _____

_____

2. changes, differs (B) _____

3. the feeling that a worker will never lose his or her job (B) _____

_____

4. percentage of people without jobs (B) _____

5. changing from one job to another (D) _____

7 The prefix *over-* can appear as part of a noun, verb, or adjective. In some words, it indicates that there is *too much* of something or that someone is doing too much of a certain action.

Example

Some people <u>overwork</u> and don't enjoy their work.

(overwork = work too much)

What might be nouns and verbs for the following definitions? Write words that begin with *over-*. When you finish, compare your answers with another student's.

1. (verb) **do** something too much _____

2. (adjective) with too many people, a **crowd** that is too big

   _____

3. (verb) give an **estimate** that is too high _____

4. (adjective) left unpaid, undone, or unreturned too long, past the **due** date

   _____

5. (noun) too many people in an area; a **population** that is too high

   _____

8 In various countries, people have different terms for a portable telephone. In some countries, this is a *cell phone*. In other countries, it's a *hand phone* or a *mobile phone*. What do you call it in your country?

9 **Understanding Details.** Try to answer these questions without looking back at the reading.

1. What are several effects of lack of job security?

   _____

2. What do many people need to do if they want to keep their job or find a better job?

   _____

3. What is one advantage to telecommuting? What is one disadvantage?

   _____

4. What is one advantage to the use of cell phones and beepers? What is one disadvantage?

   _____

5. In what situation is workaholism a problem? In what situation is it not a problem?

   _____

10 **Understanding Main Ideas.**   Circle the number of the one main idea of the reading selection.

1. Workaholism can lead to serious problems, but it can also create a happy life.

2. Job hopping is a new trend that causes stress but can also lead people into good work experiences if they learn new job skills.

3. It is important for people to be flexible in this changing world of work and to continue their education because they may need to change jobs several times in their lifetime.

4. Globalization is causing many changes in the way people work today.

5. In the workplace today, there are dramatic changes in areas such as job security, the need for flexibility, the use of technology, and the importance of passion for one's work.

11 **Checking Your Understanding.**   Turn back to Exercise 3 on page 65 and answer the question.

Discussing the Reading

12 In small groups, talk about your answers to these questions about your country.

1. What is the unemployment rate? Is it difficult for people to find jobs?

2. Do most people have job security, or is there a lot of job hopping?

3. Is it possible for people to change professions?

4. How is the employment situation different from what it was twenty years ago?

5. Is telecommuting common? If so, in what professions?

6. Do people talk about workaholism? If so, do they consider it a problem?

7. How has technology changed the way in which people live and work?

PART 2

Looking for Work in the Twenty-First Century

Before You Read

1 **Thinking Ahead.**   Before you read the following paragraphs, talk about your answers to these questions. Work in small groups.

1. In your country, where do people find out about job openings? Make a list of the places.

2. How do people prepare for a career? What steps do they need to take?

2 **Skimming for Main Ideas.**   Read these paragraphs quickly. Do not use a dictionary and don't worry about the details. When you finish, write the topic and topic sentence of each paragraph.

Looking for Work in the Twenty-First Century

[A]   Not very long ago, when people needed to find a job, there were several possible steps. They might begin with a look through the classified ads in the back of the newspaper. They could go to the personnel office at various companies and fill out an application, or they could go to an employment agency. They could even find out about a job opening through word-of-mouth—from another person who had heard about it.

JOBS OFFERED	CHEF, Sushi - Select, clean,	REAL ESTATE

JOBS OFFERED

Jobs Domestic   **8200**

AUPAIR L/I 2 kids 8 & 9 Housekeeping & driving. H-(818)762-1890; w-(310)245-5445

Accounting Manager
Mountain Plumbing Contractor looking for an Asst to Controller. Ideal Candidate will have 3- 5 Yrs. Const. Acctng/Job Costing Exp. Handling Revenues $5MM & grater. Proficiency in Windows based-computer enviroment w/Exp. in Excel/Word a must. Fax Resume to 714-555-5870 Attn: Oscar

ACTORS Comedians and great personalitites to teach fun traffic school 16-24hrs/wk. $12/hr. 800-535-6463

Administrative Assistant
City office of nat'l org dedicated to helping low-income communities find creative solutions to problems of

CHEF, Sushi - Select, clean, carve, & prepare traditional Japanese sushi & sashimi incl. tuna, yellowtail, salmon, albacore, octopus, snapper, mackerel, eel, shrimp, squid, scallops, sea urchin, smelt roe, lobster, rice, seaweed, & vegetables. Requires 2 yrs exp. in job offered. $2002/mo. 11a-2p & 5-10p Wed-Sun. Interview & job in Long Beach, CA. Send this ad and your resume/letter of qualifs to Job #MM057000, PO Box 1256, Sacramento, CA 95826-1256

AUTOMOBILES

Automobiles   **9000**

'98 M Roadster Z-3 $37,988 Silver cert. to 100K 15K Mi. (vinLC90000) Exp. 12/31 Bob's BMW (818)554-1352

'95 Camaro Z28 Convertible auto, 16K mi, like new. (5487646) (562)525-1397

'92 Lumina V6, Auto, 58Kmi.

REAL ESTATE

HOMES FOR SALE   **9001**

Older home in town. Great location, schools, shops nearby. Motivated to sell. 3BR/2BA 1300sqft. $119k 910-878-7799

BAYS COVE Updated home in a great neighborhood. 3 bedrooms, 2 baths, den, fireplace with gas logs, beautiful large kitchen, over 2200 sqft, 2 car garage and large lot. Only $185,900. Call 245-767-1930 or page 245-767-1901

OWNER FINANCING. . .2BR, 1.5 BA condo, eat-in kit., deck, 99,900.

716 DOVER...3BR, 2BA custom built , great rm w/stone F/P, FR, 2 car gar., wooded lot. $119,900.

B&S REALTY AND AUCTION
753-644-1967

Topic: _____

Topic sentence: _____

_____

[B]   These days, job hunting is more complicated. The first step is to determine what kind of job you want (which sounds easier than it is) and make sure that you have the right education for it. Rapid changes in technology and science are creating many professions that never existed until recently. It is important to learn about them because one might be the perfect profession for you. The fastest-growing areas for new jobs are in health services and computer science. Jobs in these fields usually require specific skills, but you need to find out exactly *which* skills and *which* degrees are necessary. For example, it may be surprising to learn that in the sciences, an M.S. is more marketable than a Ph.D.! In other words, there are more jobs available for people with a Master of Science degree than for people with a doctorate. (However, people who want to do research still need a Ph.D.)

Topic: _____

Topic sentence: _____

_____

Cross-Cultural Note: The Pace of Life

In which countries do you think speed is most important? A recent study compared the pace of life in thirty-one countries. Researchers based their conclusions on three specific areas: work speed, walking speed, and the accuracy of public clocks. The results? Pace of life is fastest in Switzerland, Ireland, and Germany. Japan ranked fourth. The United States ranked sixteenth. The slowest countries included Brazil and Indonesia.

If your country is not listed here, what ranking do you think it received? In other words, what is the pace of life in your country?

[C]   How do people learn about "hot" new professions? How do they discover their "dream job"? Many people these days go to a career counselor. In some countries, job hopping has become so common that career counseling is now "big business." People sometimes spend large amounts of money for this advice. In Canada and the United States, high school and college students often have access to free vocational counseling services on campus. There is even a career organization, the Five O'Clock Club, which helps members to set goals. Members focus on this question: what sort of person do you want to be forty years from now? The members then plan their careers around that goal. All career counselors—private or public—agree on one basic point: it is important for people to find a career that they *love*. Everyone should be able to think, "I'm having such a good time. I can't believe they're paying me to do this."

Topic: _____

Topic sentence: _____

_____

[D]   After people have determined what their dream job is, they need to find it. The biggest change in job hunting these days is the use of the Internet. More and more employers are advertising job openings on their computer Websites. More and more job hunters are applying for jobs online. There are also several *thousand* job boards, among them HotJobs.com, Jobsjobsjobs.com, and Monster.com. Some people think that online job hunting is only for people in technology fields, but this isn't true. Over 65 percent of online job seekers are from nontechnical fields. Even truck drivers now find jobs on the Internet!

Topic: _____

Topic sentence: _____

_____

[E]   So how does this work? A job seeker can reply to a "Help Wanted" notice on a company's Website. This person can also post his or her resume (page with information about education and work experience) on one—or many—of the online job boards. If a company is interested, the person still has to take the next step the old-fashioned way—actually go to the job interview and perhaps take a skills test. However, even this might soon change. In the near future, companies will be able to give the person a skills test and check his or her background (job history and education) online. But what about the interview? Companies will soon be able to interview the person by videolink, so people can interview for jobs in other cities—or even other countries—without leaving home. Clearly, job hunting is not what it used to be.

Topic: _____

Topic sentence: _____

_____

_____

After You Read

3 **Checking Your Answers.** After you write the topic and topic sentence of each paragraph, exchange your answers with another student. Are your answers the same? Are your topics the same but perhaps in different words? Do you agree about the topic sentences? If you don't agree, give reasons for your answers. One of you might want to change an answer.

4 **Understanding Pronoun Reference.** Look back at the reading selection "Looking for Work in the Twenty-First Century" to find the meaning of the following pronouns. What does each pronoun refer to?

1. they (Paragraph A, line 2) _____

2. it (Paragraph B, line 3) _____

3. it (Paragraph D, line 1) _____

4. them (Paragraph D, line 5) _____

5. this (Paragraph E, line 6) _____

6. it (Paragraph E, line 11) _____

Discussing the Reading

5 In small groups, talk about your answers to these questions.

1. Have you ever gone job hunting? If so, what steps did you take?

2. Do you already know what your "dream job" is? If so, what will you need to do to get it?

3. In your country, do people go to career counselors? Are there vocational counseling services in high schools and colleges? Have you ever gone to a career counselor for advice?

4. Have you ever visited an online job board? If so, tell your group about it.

Talk It Over

Understanding Proverbs and Quotations.   Here are two English proverbs and three quotations about work. In small groups, discuss your answers to these questions about each of them.

1.   What does the proverb (or quotation) mean? (You might need to use a dictionary for a few words.)

2.   Do you agree with it?

3.   What are some proverbs about work in your language? Translate them into English and explain them.

Proverbs and Quotations

■   All work and no play makes Jack a dull boy. (proverb)

■   Ninety percent of inspiration is perspiration. (proverb)

■   Work expands to fill the time available. (from C. Northcote Parkinson)

■   Laziness travels so slowly that poverty soon overtakes him. (from Benjamin Franklin)

■   It is neither wealth nor splendor, but tranquility and occupation, which give happiness. (from Thomas Jefferson)

Beyond the Text

Here are some online job boards. Do some sound interesting to you? If you have access to the Internet, check out some of them. Report to the class what you discover.

Job Boards

overseasjobs.com

bilingual—jobs.com

spacejobs.com

jobsinthemoney.com

MBAfreeagents.com

asia—net.com

PART 3 Building Vocabulary and Study Skills

1 **Adjective and Noun Phrases.**   Some words often appear together in phrases. In some phrases, there is a hyphen (-).

Example
    Many people have to accept part-time jobs.

The last word of a phrase is usually a noun or an adjective. The first word may be a noun, an adjective, or an adverb. When a noun comes before another noun, it usually functions as an adjective.

Examples
    city life (= noun + noun)
    social sciences (= adjective + noun)
    especially interesting (adverb + adjective)

Complete each sentence with the missing words as in the example. Choose from the following:

personnel	job	computer	city
self	career	mass	dream
classified	shopping	unemployment	part
traffic			

1. He looked through the _____classified_____ ads and hoped to find his
    _____ job.

2. In that country, the _____ rate is very high, and many people
    have to accept _____-time jobs temporarily. This sometimes
    causes depression and loss of _____-confidence.

3. Some advantages of _____ life are the _____
    centers and _____-transit systems. A disadvantage, though, is
    the problem of _____ jams.

4. Her _____ counselor told her about the many possible jobs in
    _____ science.

5. When I began _____ hunting last year, I put in my application
    at the _____ office of many companies.

2 Match the pairs of words by writing the letters on the lines as in the example.

1. _d_ old-   a. administration
2. ____ business   b. openings
3. ____ cell   c. agency
4. ____ public   d. fashioned
5. _b_ job-   e. transportation
6. ____ charge   f. fulfilling
7. _c_ employment   g. account
8. ____ self-   h. phone

3 **Compound Words.** Some words belong together in "compounds" (long words that consist of smaller words).

Examples

I talked to a <u>salesclerk</u> at the <u>supermarket</u>.

Draw a line between the two words of each compound. Then match the words with the definitions by writing letters on the lines. The first one is done as an example.

1. _h_ overseas   a. terrible traffic jam
2. ____ drawback   b. too much work
3. ____ overcrowding   c. television pictures on the computer
4. ____ gridlock   d. using the Internet
5. ____ worldwide   e. disadvantage
6. ____ overwork   f. improve
7. ____ videolink   g. one's experience and education
8. ____ upgrade   h. in another country across an ocean
9. ____ online   i. everywhere in the world
10. ____ background   j. too many people in one place

4 How many compound words or phrases can you make from these words, in any order? Work as fast as you can for five minutes. Write them on the lines and then check them in your dictionary. The student with the most correct words or phrases is the winner.

high	work	network
lab	exam	security
office	public	market
college	interview	department
self	tuition	confidence
science	school	job
Website	service	computer
life	city	planning

1. _____

2. _____

3. _____

4. _____

5. _____

6. _____

7. _____

8. _____

9. _____

10. _____

11. _____

12. _____

13. _____

14. _____

15. _____

Focus on Testing

Increasing Reading Speed—Left-to-Right Eye Movement

Slow readers look at the same words several times. Their eyes move back and forth over each sentence. Fast readers usually move their eyes from left to right one time for each line. They don't look back very often. A fast left-to-right eye movement increases reading speed. The following exercises will help you improve your reading speed. You will feel less nervous during tests if you can read quickly.

Your teacher will tell you when to begin each section and when to stop. Look at the underlined word at the left of each line. Read across the line, from left to right, as fast as you can. Some words in the line are the same as the underlined word. Quickly underline each one. At the end of each section, write down your time (the number of seconds it took you to finish). Try to read faster with each section.

banking	banks	banking	bank	banking	banking
challenge	challenges	challenging	challenge	challenge	challenged
savings	savings	save	savings	saving	saver
benefit	benefits	beneficial	benefited	benefit	benefit
employer	employ	employment	employee	employ	employed

Time: _____

experience	experience	experienced	expertise	experience	expert
opening	opening	opening	opened	open	opened
excellent	excel	excelled	excellent	excellent	excellent
identity	indent	identity	identify	identity	indent
account	account	accounting	account	accounts	account

Time: _____

part-time	part-time	partly	party	part-time
position	possible	position	positive	position
public	public	publicity	public	publicize
appointment	appoint	appointed	appoints	appointment
personnel	person	personal	personnel	personable

Time: _____

salary	salary	celery	salaries	salaried	sales
apply	applied	apply	apply	apply	application
pleasure	pleasure	pleasant	pleasurable	pleased	pleasant
skills	skilled	skill	skills	skills	skillful
ability	ability	able	capable	ability	capability

Time: _____

| **PART 4** | # Reading in the Real World |

1 **Vocabulary Preview.** Here are some words from the textbook passage that follows. Match them with their meanings. Write the letters on the lines. Use a dictionary if necessary.

1. _g_ transformation
2. _____ rearrange
3. _____ invention
4. _____ printing press
5. _____ wealth
6. _____ income
7. _____ significant
8. _____ founded
9. _____ emerged
10. _____ accruc
11. _____ dominant

a. machine that prints newspapers and books
b. established; begun
c. put in different order
d. with power or high position
e. the thinking of and producing of something for the first time
f. salary
g. complete change
h. appeared; came out
i. main
j. money and possessions; riches
k. gain; collect

2 **Preparing to Read.** Students often need to read material that seems too difficult, and they may need to remember it several weeks in the future, for an examination. One way to deal with both of these challenges is to make a chart that includes main ideas and important details. Making charts of reading material requires you to read *actively.* Active readers understand more and remember it longer than passive readers do.

The textbook selection is about three important periods of transformation in Western history. Before you read, look over the chart that follows the reading. Then, as you read, mark information that you will need for the chart.

The Knowledge Society

According to American economist Peter Drucker (1993), every few hundred years in Western history a sharp transformation takes place in which society rearranges itself. One such period happened between 1455 and 1517, beginning with the invention of the printing press, and included the Renaissance, the European discovery of America, a reawakening of science, and the Protestant Reformation. All these events had significant effects on the development of Western society. The next period lasted from the American Revolution and the perfection of the steam engine in 1776 until Napoleon's defeat at Waterloo in 1815. During this time, the Industrial Revolution took place, public school systems were established on a large scale, the first modern university was founded in Berlin in 1809, and both capitalism and communism emerged as economic and political ideologies. Again, society had been altered.

Drucker suggests that another such transformation is taking place today. He claims it began around 1960 with the introduction of computers and the emergence of the first non-Western country—Japan—to be a global economic power. The period is predicted to end sometime around 2010 or 2020, when what Drucker calls the "post-capitalist" era will have produced the knowledge society. The major characteristic of this new society will be the use of knowledge as an economic resource. That is, knowledge, not labor, will be the basis of wealth. The leading social group will be "knowledge workers" who know how to make specialized knowledge productive and innovative in a free-market system.

Drucker warns that this situation may create class conflict, as knowledge workers accrue much higher status and income than service workers. Recognizing that these two groups of workers are not social classes in the traditional sense, he nonetheless feels that people who provide various types of services—food, finance, leisure, and the like—must not be socially and economically disadvantaged. Otherwise, the old conflict outlined by Marx between capitalists and workers will be transformed into one between the two new dominant groups: those who create and work with knowledge and those who provide various services to them.

[Source: "The Knowledge Society" from William C. Cockerham, *The Global Society: An Introduction to Society,* p. 300. Copyright © 1995 by McGraw-Hill, Inc.]

3   **Scanning for Information.**   Complete the chart with information from the first and second paragraphs of the reading.

1st Period	2nd Period	3rd Period
Years: _____	Years: _____	Years: _____
What happened?	What happened?	What happened?
1.	1. Am. Revolution	1.
2.	2. steam engine	2.
3.	3.	3. knowledge as econ. resource
4.	4.	
5.	5.	
	6.	
	7. Napoleon's defeat	

4 **Checking Your Understanding.**   Look back at the second and third paragraphs to find the answers to these questions.

1. What does Drucker call the period that we are living in now?

2. What will be the basis of wealth in this new society? What will *not* be the basis of wealth?

3. What will be the two groups of workers?

4. What might cause class conflict?

Video Activities: I Love My Job

Before You Watch.   Discuss these questions in a group.

1. Have you ever had a job? If you have, did you like it? If you've had many jobs, which one was your favorite? Why?

2. Describe your ideal job. Why does this kind of job appeal to you?

3. Do you know anyone who is retired? What are the advantages and disadvantages of being retired?

Watch.   Watch the video one time. Then discuss the following questions with your classmates.

1. Describe Lu. What does she look like? How old is she, probably?

2. Why do customers love Lu?

3. How does Lu feel about her job?

4. What kind of restaurant is Nicolosi's, probably?

Watch Again.   Write answers to the following questions.

1. What skills does Luella have that make her good at her job?

2. What does it mean to "kill people with kindness"?

3. Have you ever known a wonderful waiter or waitress like Lu?

4. Why do you think Luella is still working?

After You Watch.   Italian food is very popular in the United States. The dishes below are very well-known. Do you know them? Use a dictionary to find out what they are. Do they sound tasty to you?

a. pizza

b. pepperoni

c. ravioli

d. spaghetti

e. lasagne

Chapter 5

Lifestyles Around the World

IN THIS CHAPTER

The first selection discusses the ways and the reasons our lives are influenced by fashion. The second reading explores interests that people have now, at the beginning of a new millennium. The last part of the chapter is a newspaper article about aromatherapy, which might have an effect on how we relax, work, sleep, and even think.

PART 1

Trendspotting

Before You Read

1   **Getting Started.**   Look at the pictures and discuss them in small groups.

1. What are the people in these pictures wearing? What are they doing?
2. What else do you see in each picture? What do you know about these things?
3. About when (what general time) does each picture take place?
4. How are these scenes similar to (or different from) scenes in your country?

2   **Vocabulary Preview.**   Briefly look over this list of words from the reading that follows. Which words do you already know? For the ones that you don't know, *don't* use a dictionary. Try to understand them from the reading.

Nouns	Verbs	Phrase
lifestyle	distinguish	competitive edge
slang	invest	
gourmet	enroll	
fad	spot	
trend		
trendspotting		
profit		

Read

3   As you read the following selection, think about the answer to this question: what are fads and trends, and why are they important? Read the following selection quickly. Do not use a dictionary. Then do the exercises that follow the reading.

Trendspotting

Urban Lifestyle

[A]   These days, urban lifestyles seem to change very fast. It is more than just clothing and hairstyles that are in style one year and out of date the next; it's a whole way of living. One year people wear sunglasses on top of their heads and wear jeans and boots; they drink white wine and eat sushi at Japanese restaurants; for exercise they jog several miles a day. However, the next year everything has changed. Women wear long skirts; people drink expensive water from France and eat pasta at Italian restaurants; everyone seems to be exercising at health clubs. Then, suddenly, it has changed again. Men shave their heads and wear earrings; people wear only natural fabrics (safe for the environment); they drink gourmet coffee and eat Thai food; for both leisure and exercise, they go inline-skating.

Fads

[B]   Almost nothing in modern life escapes the influence of fashion: food, sports, music, exercise, books, slang words, movies, furniture, places to visit, even *names* go in and out of fashion. For a while, it seems that all new parents are naming their babies Heather, Dawn, Eric, or Adam. These names are "in." Then, suddenly, these same names are "out," and Tiffany, Amber, and Jason are "in." It's almost impossible to write about specific fads because these interests that people enthusiastically follow can change very quickly.

The Essence of a Fad

[C]   This is the essence, the central quality, of a fad: it doesn't last long. Some fads disappear before we have all even heard of them. How many people remember Green Peace swimsuits? (They changed color to indicate polluted water.) And

then there was "Beethoven Bread." Popular in Japan in 1994, it was expensive—
$20 for one loaf. It was made while classical music played in the kitchen. The
woman who created this bread emphasized that "bread doesn't like rock music."

The Reason for Fads

[D] What causes such fads to come and go? And why do so many people follow
them? Although clothing designers and manufacturers influence fads in fashion
because they want to make a profit, this desire for money doesn't explain fads
in other areas, such as language. For example, why have English-speaking
teenagers in the past twenty-five years used—at different times—the slang
words *groovy, boss, awesome, rad,* or *tubular* instead of simply saying *"wonderful"*? According to Jack Santino, an expert in popular culture, people who follow
fads are not irrational; they simply want to be part of something new and creative, and they feel good when they are part of an "in group." Dr. Santino believes that fads are common in any country that has a strong consumer
economy—for example, Britain, Japan, Germany, and the United States. However, due to TV and the Internet, fads are now common worldwide and spread
very fast. Increasingly, they seem to begin in Asia, especially in Hong Kong,
Japan, and Korea.

Fads and Trends

[E] Dr. Santino points out that it's sometimes difficult to see the difference between
a *fad* and a *trend.* A fad, he says, lasts a very short time and is not very important.
A trend lasts much longer. A recent trend is the interest in good health, but many
fads come from this trend: aerobic exercise, kickboxing, special diets, cholesterol counting, organic vegetables, and the like. A trend in the 1980s was the
use of personal computers; certain computer games were fads. However, these
days we can't really continue to call computers a "trend" because now they have
become an essential part of everyday life.

Trendspotting

[F] Trendspotting is the ability to identify a trend at an early stage—an extremely
important skill in the business world. The first company that can correctly identify a new trend (and do something with it) has a competitive edge—an advantage—over other companies. The person who founded the Starbucks chain of
coffeehouses was able to spot a trend—interest in quality and variety in coffee.
Today, people buy Starbucks products in shopping centers, airports, and super-
markets everywhere. But when a development in popular culture is new, it's
difficult to distinguish between a fad and a trend. Trendspotters need to ask
themselves: will this become an important global trend, or is it just a passing
fad? People who invested their funds in Green Peace swimsuits probably regret
their decision. Clearly, they mistook a fad for a trend.

Popular Culture and the University

[G] Possibly because of the importance of trendspotting in business, more and
more universities are offering classes in popular culture. Parents of students at
New York University are sometimes surprised to find their children taking such
classes as "Inside the Mouse" (about the influence of Disney), "Golden Arches
East" (about McDonald's in Asia), or "Hope in a Jar" (about the cosmetics industry). At Bowling Green State University, in Ohio, students can take a course
on Pokemon in Japanese culture. At other schools, students might enroll in "The

History of Rock 'n' Roll," "Addiction in Literature," and "Smoking and Advertising." Many people don't take such classes seriously. However, companies are seeking out graduates of Bowling Green, which actually offers a master's degree in popular culture. These graduates find jobs in advertising, television, publishing, and manufacturing. With an understanding of popular culture, these graduates are becoming the new trendspotters. The question now becomes this: are courses in popular culture just a fad or a real trend?

After You Read

4 **Getting the Main Ideas.**   Write T on the lines before the statements that are true, according to the reading. Write F on the lines before the statements that are false.

1. _____ Fashion influences many things in addition to clothing and hairstyles.

2. _____ Fads come and go very quickly.

3. _____ People who follow fads are irrational.

4. _____ *Trend* is a synonym for *fad*.

5. _____ When a trend becomes an essential part of everyday life, it isn't called a "trend" any longer.

6. _____ Successful businesspeople are probably good at recognizing new trends.

5 **Getting Meaning from Context.**   Sometimes the definition is clearly stated in the reading, so it's easy to determine. Sometimes you need to make an inference about the meaning. Look back at the reading passage to find the meaning of each of these words. On each line, write a definition or synonym—either one from the reading passage or in your own words. Do this exercise without a dictionary. (Letters in parentheses indicate paragraphs.)

lifestyles (A): _____

fads (B): _____

essence (C): _____

profit (D): _____

slang (D): _____

trend (E): _____

trendspotting (F): _____

competitive edge (F): _____

distinguish (F): _____

enroll (G): _____

6 **Checking Your Understanding.**   Turn back to Exercise 3 on page 85 and answer the question.

7 **Understanding Main Ideas.**   Circle the number of the *one* main idea of the reading selection.

1. Fads in fashion are common because clothing manufacturers make more money if styles change every year.

2. Trends are basically "long-lasting fads."

3. Fads usually last a very short time, but they can be a lot of fun.

4. People follow many different kinds of fads because they like to be part of something new and creative.

5. The ability to distinguish between fads and trends is increasingly important in the business world.

Discussing the Reading

8 What are some fads these days? Are these fads part of any trend? To help you answer these questions, fill in this chart. Then compare your charts in small groups and discuss your answers.

Clothing	Hairstyles	Food	Music	Activities
_____	_____	_____	_____	_____
_____	_____	_____	_____	_____
_____	_____	_____	_____	_____
_____	_____	_____	_____	_____
_____	_____	_____	_____	_____
_____	_____	_____	_____	_____
_____	_____	_____	_____	_____
_____	_____	_____	_____	_____
_____	_____	_____	_____	_____
_____	_____	_____	_____	_____
_____	_____	_____	_____	_____

PART 2   Fads and Trends at the Turn of the Twenty-First Century

1   **Marking a Book for Skimming.**   Students—especially college students—often need to read so much material that they don't have time to reread it before an important exam. For this reason, it's necessary to learn how to mark a book. If you mark the topics, main ideas, and important details as you read, you can go back later and look over your markings to study for a test—without reading the whole passage again. It's important to note that there is no one "right" way of marking a book. You need to find a style that is comfortable to you.

Read these paragraphs quickly. As you read, mark the topic, main idea, and important details. (The first paragraph is marked for you, as an example.) Do not use a dictionary. When you finish, write the topic and the topic sentence of each paragraph.

Fads and Trends at the Turn of the Twenty-First Century

[A]   The nineteenth-century American philosopher Henry David Thoreau was famous for saying, "Simplify, simplify." Unfortunately, the trend these days seems to be "complicate, complicate" instead. Many people are working longer hours, spending more money, and getting in more debt than ever before. They are also relaxing less and spending less time with family and friends. However, there is also a countertrend—a trend toward voluntary simplicity. People in the voluntary simplicity movement take various steps to make their lives both simpler and more enjoyable. Some people work fewer hours each week. Some move close to their workplace, to avoid a long daily commute; they walk or ride a bike, instead. Some plant a vegetable garden; this gives them fresh air, exercise, and time with their families—not to mention organic produce. But all people in the voluntary simplicity movement try to cut back—to buy less; they cut up their credit cards and stop buying unnecessary items. In short, the priority for people in the voluntary movement is to follow Thoreau's suggestion: simplify.

Topic: _voluntary simplicity_

Topic sentence: _People in the voluntary simplicity movement take various steps to make their lives simpler and more enjoyable._

[B]   In the 1990s, a popular fad for many teenagers was tattooing. Parents were usually horrified by these permanent designs on their children's skin, but the young people saw them as a fashion statement. In the new millennium, parents were greatly relieved when their teenage children found a new fad, a temporary form of decorating the hands, feet, neck, or legs—*mehndi,* a method of painting beautiful designs that last only about three weeks. This "new" fad is actually very old: for hundreds of years in India, a woman's friends have painted her to celebrate her wedding day. Another fad from India, however, causes parents more worry—*bidis.* Children and young teens are attracted to these thin cigarettes in candy flavors such as orange, chocolate, mango, and raspberry. The problem?

Bidis contain more nicotine than regular cigarettes. Unfortunately, many children think these are "cool"—fashionable. So until a new fad comes along, "Indian chic is hot," as one radio commentator observed.

Topic: _____

Topic sentence: _____

_____

[C]   Another ancient art—aromatherapy—is also popular today. Of course, people have always used perfume to make them more attractive to other people. And we all have experience with the power of smell in a different way—memory. When we smell something for the first time in many years, a sudden rush of memories comes to us. We remember where we were and how we felt all those years ago when we first smelled it. In aromatherapy, floral scents and the smell of such things as lemon, pine, and mint are used to make people feel better in a variety of ways. Some scents make people more relaxed. Other scents make them more alert, more awake. As you might imagine, the market reflects interest in this trend. Businesspeople are happy to make scents available to their customers, for a price.

Topic: _____

Topic sentence: _____

_____

[D]   Another fad from the 1990s—dangerous sports—seems to be turning into a trend in the new millennium. People began to make traditional sports such as skiing and bicycling more challenging and dangerous. Some thrill seekers—people who want more and more excitement and danger—have actually created new "extreme sports." One of these, sky-surfing, combines sky-diving

Sky-surfing

Waterfall-running

(jumping out of an airplane with a parachute) with surfing. In another, waterfall-running, a person rides a kayak off a high waterfall. The thrill seekers who are addicted to such sports don't seem to feel fear. They say they need to "focus 100 percent" in order to survive their experience. But they also say they feel "100 percent alive" only in those few moments of falling through air or water.

Topic: _____

Topic sentence: _____

_____

_____

After You Read

2 **Learning to Summarize.** Marking a book is an essential study skill. It is also good preparation for *summarizing,* one of the most important types of writing that most college students need to do. When you can summarize reading material well, you show your understanding of the material. To write a summary, you retell the main ideas and the important details, in *shorter* form than the original. You do not include the less important details. You can use some words from the reading and some of your own words. *There is never just one "perfect" way to summarize any material.* Different people might have equally good summaries that have different words.

Read these two summaries of Paragraph A. Compare them to the original paragraph. Notice which points are included and which are omitted (left out). Also, notice what is similar about the two summaries and what is different.

Summary 1:

In a countertrend to the complexity of modern life, people in the voluntary simplicity movement take different steps to simplify their lives. Some may work fewer hours weekly; some walk or ride a bike to work. Others plant their own vegetable gardens. But all attempt to cut back—to buy less.

Summary 2:

Voluntary simplicity is a countertrend to the complexity of modern life. The priority for people in this movement is to follow Thoreau's famous suggestion: "Simplify, simplify." These people focus on working less and spending less.

3 In a small group, compare the way that you marked Paragraphs B, C, and D with the way that other students marked them. Which important points do you all agree on?

4 Choose one paragraph—B, C, or D. Write a short summary of it. Then compare your summary with those of other students who summarized the same paragraph.

Discussing the Reading

5 In small groups, talk about your answers to these questions.

1. In your country, is there a countertrend toward simplicity? If so, what do people do to simplify their lives?

2. What "extreme sports" are popular these days? Have you tried any of these? Do you know anyone who has tried one? If so, tell your group about this sport. Why is it so thrilling—so exciting?

3. Are there any scents that cause you to experience a "sudden rush of memories"?

Cross-Cultural Note: Fads in Korea

The strong consumer economy in Korea may explain the burst of fads—or are they trends?—at the turn of the twenty-first century. Here are some.

Among Teenagers

- *Computer game rooms were very popular. Students discovered that some computer games could be extremely addictive. Especially popular in the year 2000 was DDR—Dance Dance Revolution—an L-shaped machine with a computer that instructs the dancer where (and how fast) to move his or her feet.*

- *Photo machines allowed people to take their own picture (or a picture with friends) and choose a special background for it—for example, the cover of Vogue magazine. The machine made these photos into stickers, which people put in all sorts of different places.*

Among Tired Working People

- *At lunchtime, a person who had to stand all day could have a thirty-minute foot massage. A person who spent a lot of time on a computer could have a finger and arm massage. And for a person in the service field, there was a head and neck massage.*

- *For people who put in long hours at work, there was the "capsule"—a very small room in a new kind of inn. In these hotels, there were perhaps fifty capsules on each floor. Tired workers could take a short nap at a low price.*

- *There were also saunas that stayed open all night. A businessman could relax in the sauna and have his shirt washed and ironed while he did so.*

Talk It Over

Breaking Stereotypes.   People worldwide who don't know much about another culture may have oversimplified ideas—stereotypes—about it. Some stereotypes are positive and some are negative, but all are somewhat dangerous—or untrue—because they are too general. Although stereotypical ideas are partly right, they are also partly wrong. A stereotype often begins with the word *all:* "All people from that country are poor." Sometimes the word *all* is not said, but it is implied (suggested): "The people in this city are impolite." People who believe a certain stereotype usually do so because they lack knowledge. Before going to another country or after being in that country for only a short time, people often carry many stereotypes with them; they believe that they "know" about the country. However, after living there for a *long* time, meeting many people and having many different experiences there, they change their opinions about stereotypes. As people learn more about another culture, they begin to see and appreciate the great variety of customs, educational levels, beliefs, and lifestyles.

Here are some common stereotypes of people in the United States.

- Most people are rich.
- It's important to these people to be fashionable and "trendy."
- They have big cars.
- They go to baseball games all the time.
- The diet in the United States consists of hamburgers and hot dogs.
- Everyone owns a gun.
- A lot of people are poor and homeless.
- A lot of people have psychological problems.

As with all stereotypes, these ideas are oversimplified. For example, most Americans are actually middle-class. The majority of people do not own a gun. Many people rarely eat hamburgers or hot dogs; in fact, the number of vegetarians is growing.

1. On this chart, make a list of stereotypes that people from other cultures have about *your* culture.
2. Is there another culture that you know about? If so, make a list of common stereotypes of people from that culture.
3. For each stereotype, write a brief note about it. How, in your opinion, is this stereotype correct, incorrect, or both? If it is incorrect, in what way?

	Stereotypes	**How These Are Correct or Incorrect**
My Culture		
Other Culture		

| PART 3 | # Building Vocabulary and Study Skills |

1   **Suffixes and Prefixes.**   Suffixes (word endings), such as *-er, -sion,* and *-ive,* often indicate the part of speech of a word (see the list on page 55). Here are some more suffixes, listed by the parts of speech that they usually indicate.

Nouns	Verbs	Adjective	Adverb
-ess	-ate	-less	-ly
-ship	-ize		
-ism	-en		

Write *n* on the lines before the nouns, *v* on the lines before verbs, *adj* before adjectives, and *adv* before adverbs. In some cases, two answers are correct.

1. _____ attention
2. _____ entertainment
3. _____ organization
4. _____ international
5. _____ worthless
6. _____ visitor
7. _____ simplicity
8. _____ hopeless
9. _____ general
10. _____ typical
11. _____ pleasure
12. _____ individualism

13. _____ identity
14. _____ exactly
15. _____ worsen
16. _____ frequently
17. _____ workaholism
18. _____ indicate
19. _____ essence
20. _____ participate
21. _____ hostess
22. _____ experience
23. _____ seeker
24. _____ flexible

25. _____ enjoyable
26. _____ positive
27. _____ description
28. _____ concentrate
29. _____ marketable
30. _____ socially
31. _____ friendship
32. _____ memorize
33. _____ dangerous
34. _____ impatiently
35. _____ characteristic
36. _____ competitive

2   The prefix (beginning) of a word sometimes gives a clue to its meaning. Some prefixes create a word with an opposite meaning.

Examples

We've discovered many unusual hotels in our travels.

(Discover means to "uncover" information—i.e., to find out something that we didn't know before. Unusual means "not usual"—i.e., out of the ordinary.)

The following prefixes can have the meaning "no" or "not."

un-   in-   im-   dis-   ir-

Use one of the preceding prefixes to change each word into its opposite as in the examples. Use your dictionary, if necessary. (The prefixes -in and -im have another meaning; they can both mean "in" or "into.")

1. __un__ pleasant   5. _____ avoidable   9. _____ desirable

2. __im__ patient   6. _____ rational   10. _____ advantage

3. _____ expensive   7. _____ safe   11. _____ possible

4. _____ characteristic   8. _____ frequent   12. _____ interesting

3 Here are some other prefixes with their usual meanings.

con-/com- = with, together   pre-   = first, before
counter-   = opposite   re-   = again, back
ex-/e-   = out of, from   sur-   = over, above
inter-   = between, among   trans- = across
mis-   = wrong

The definitions on the right are based on the meanings of prefixes. Match them with the words on the left by writing the letters on the lines as in the example.

1. __g__ reflect

2. _____ survive

3. _____ transit

4. _____ international

5. _____ invest

6. _____ experience

7. _____ replace

8. _____ prevent

9. _____ combination

10. _____ counterclockwise

a. among other countries

b. get knowledge from life (not books)

c. moving people or things across places

d. stop something before it happens

e. provide something again

f. in the opposite direction to the hands of a clock

g. throw back; give back an image of

h. joining together of people or things

i. continue to live or exist

j. put money into a business in the hopes of making a profit

4 **Dictionary Entries.**   Some words have only one meaning. You can find the meaning in a dictionary entry, which sometimes includes an example. Read these two
dictionary entries and answer the questions about them.

> **en·roll, enrol** /in'ro^wl/ v **-ll-** [I;T *as, in*] to
> make (oneself or another person)
> officially a member of a group, school,
> etc. **–enrollment** n [C;U *as, in, of*] : *his*
> *enrollment as a member of the club*

> **fad,** /fæd/ *n* a short-lived interest or
> practice: *Her interest in photography*
> *is only a passing fad.*

1. What part of speech is *enroll*? _____

2. What is the dictionary definition of the word? _____

    _____

3. What word is related to it? _____

4. What part of speech is *fad*? _____

5. What is the dictionary definition of the word? _____

    _____

5 Most words, however, have more than one meaning. Often the same word can be
more than one part of speech, and each part of speech can have different meanings.

Example

The word *style* is most
commonly a noun. In the
first dictionary entry, it
has five meanings; the
last meaning is part of a
hyphenated phrase. *Style*
can also be a verb, with
two other forms.

> **style**[1] /stail/ *n* **1** a general way of doing
> something: *the modern style of building|a*
> *formal style of writing* **2** fashion, esp. in
> clothes; *the style of the 30's* **3** a type of sort,
> esp. of goods: *They sell every style of*
> *mirror|a hair style* **4** high quality of social
> behavior,appearance, or manners: *She gives*
> *dinner parties* **in style** (= in a grand way), *with*
> *the best food and wine.* **5** **-style** in the manner
> of a certain person, place, etc.: *He wears his*
> *hair short, military-style.*
>
> **style**[2] *v* **styled, styling** to form in a certain
> pattern, shape, etc.: *The dress is carefully*
> *styled.*

Refer to the previous dictionary entries to answer these questions.

1. What part of speech is the word *style* when it means "fashion, especially in clothes"? _____ Give an example of this use of the word in a phrase.

   _____

2. How many meanings does the word *style* have as a noun? _____
   As a verb? _____

3. Write the part of speech of the word *style* in each of these sentences.

   a. When they travel, they go in *style*. _____

   b. The couple preferred a modern *style* of life. _____

   c. All the people in the house *styled* their own hair. _____

4. Write the dictionary definition of the word *style* in each of these sentences.

   a. When they travel, they go in *style*.

      _____

   b. The couple preferred a modern *style* of life.

      _____

   c. All the people in the house *styled* their own hair.

      _____

   d. In my travels, I saw many *styles* of furniture, clothing, and so on.

      _____

6   Read the following dictionary entries, paying close attention to the parts of speech, the different meanings, and the examples for each meaning. Then write the part of speech and the meaning of the underlined word in each sentence as in the example.

1. I hope the dry cleaner can remove this <u>spot</u> from my jacket.

   _____

   _____

   _____

   He got lost in the crowd at the soccer game, and I couldn't <u>spot</u> him anywhere.

   _____

   _____

   _____

> **spot**[1] /spat/ *n* **1** [C] a usu. round part or area different from the main surface, e.g. in color: *a white dress with blue spots* **2** [C] a particular place: *Spain is our favorite vacation spot* | *Wherever she's needed she's quickly* **on the spot.** (= at the place of action) **3** [C] a dirty mark: *to clean off ink spots with soap and water*
> **spot**[2] *v* -tt- [T] **1** to pick out with the eye; recognize: *to spot a friend in a crowd* **2** to mark with spots: *white cloth spotted with green* | *a spotted dog*

2. It's important to get enough sleep so that you can be <u>alert</u> on the exam tomorrow.

_____

_____

_____

She <u>alerted</u> us about the new computer virus.

_____

_____

_____

a·lert[1] /əlɜrt/ *adj* quick to see and act; watchful –**allertness** *n* [U]

alert[2] *n* **1** a warning to be ready for danger –compare ALL CLEAR **2 on the alert (for)** in a state of watchfulness for danger, as after a warning

alert[3] *v* [T] **1** to put (esp. soldiers) on the ALERT[2] **2** to warn: *The doctor alerted me to the danger of not getting enough sleep*

3. I very much <u>value</u> the friendships I made on my travels.

_____

_____

_____

That hotel has comfortable rooms for the money; it is an excellent <u>value</u>.

_____

_____

_____

What is the present <u>value</u> of the house where you live?

_____

_____

_____

value[1] /ˈvælyuʷ/ *n* **1** [U] the degree of usefulness of something: *You'll find this map of great value/of little value in helping you to get around the city.* | *The government sets a higher value on defense* (= considers it more important) *than on education.* **2** [C;U] the worth of something in money or as compared with other goods for which it might be change: *Because of continual price increases, the value of the dollar has fallen in recent years.* | *I bought this old painting for $50, but its real value must be about $500.* | *The thieves took some clothes and a few books, but nothing of great value.* **3** [U] worth compared with the amount paid: *We offer the best value in the city: only three dollars for lunch with coffee and dessert.* | *You always get value for your money at that store.* (= the goods are always worth the price charged) -see also VALUES; WORTHLESS (USAGE) -**valueless** *adj*

value[2] *v* **-ued, -uing** [T] **1** to calculate the value, price, or worth of (something): *He valued the house and its contents at $75,000.* **2** to consider to be of great worth: *I've always valued your friendship very highly.*

4. He nailed the sign to a wooden post.

_____

_____

_____

They <u>posted</u> the job opening on the Internet.

_____

_____

_____

post[1] /poʷst/ *n* **1** [C] a strong upright pole or bar made of wood, metal, etc., usu. fixed into the ground: *The fence was made of posts joined together with wire.|a gate post|a signpost* **2** [*the* S] the starting or finishing place in a race, esp. a horse race: *My uncle's horse was* **first past the post.**|*the* **finishing post**

post[2] *v* [T] **1** to make public or show by fixing to a wall, board, post, etc.: *The names of the members of the team will be posted today.* **2** [T usu. pass.] to make known (as being) by putting up a notice: *The ship was posted missing.*

PART 4	# Reading in the Real World

1 **Scanning Scientific Articles.** The following passage is part of an article from the *Los Angeles Times.* It is about recent research that is the basis for the new interest in aromatherapy. First, read the questions that follow the article. Then read the article, marking the answers to the questions as you find them. Don't worry if you don't understand every word. Work as quickly as you can, as you would on a test.

Scientists Say Aromas Have Major Effect on Emotions

Perhaps it has always been apparent. As plain as the nose on your face. But nobody was paying much attention.

"From an evolutionary point of view, we typically don't think of the nose as very important," said Dr. Gary Schwartz, professor of psychiatry and psychology at the University of Arizona. "But it is stuck square in the middle of the face. Why would something that was less relevant to normal activities be so prominent? It implies there is something more important there than we may have realized."

Indeed, scientists are learning that fragrance affects us more than previously thought. New research indicates that smells influence our minds, our moods and our bodies.

But smell remains one of the least-understood senses. Although we know a great deal about the eyes and ears, we only partly understand smell. According to Charles Wysocki, an olfactory scientist at the Monell Chemical Senses Center in Philadelphia, we do know that an odor is first detected by the olfactory epithelium, a sort of receptor sheet located in the nose. This starts a chain of events that leads to an information flow to the olfactory bulb and limbic system of the brain, which plays a key role in regulating body functions and the emotions.

Smell, Wysocki said, is the only sensory system to directly project into the limbic system, making it perhaps our most basic, primitive sense. (Other senses reach the limbic system, but travel first to other brain regions.)

Some of the most significant new findings about smell and scent come from William Dember and Joel Warm at the University of Cincinnati. They recently presented their findings at the annual meeting of the American Assn. for the Advancement of Science and concluded that scents can keep people more alert and improve performance of a routine task.

Subjects tackled a 40-minute vigilance test, which required them to watch a video screen and press a button whenever a certain line pattern appeared. While performing the task, some were intermittently given a whiff of peppermint or muguet (lily of the valley) through oxygen masks. Dember said that those workers receiving the fragrances performed 25% better than those given only whiffs of pure air. A replication study conducted by Raja Parasuramen at Catholic University, using only peppermint, achieved the same findings.

Although it isn't clear exactly *how* fragrance works, Dember believes his study may soon have practical applications. "Truck drivers, even passenger car drivers, who need to keep alert while traveling long distances, could find it helpful," he said. An industry group, International Flavors and Fragrances, selected the scents and sponsored this study.

In Japan, fragrance is already used in the workplace. Shimizu, Japan's largest architectural, engineering and construction firm, has developed an environmental fragrancing system that uses computerized techniques to deliver scents through air-conditioning ducts. The Japanese have found that scents enhance efficiency and reduce stress among office workers.

In one experiment in Japan, 13 key-punch operators were monitored eight hours a day for a month. When the office air was scented with lavender, errors per hour dropped 21%. They dropped by 33% with a jasmine fragrance, and a stimulating lemon aroma reduced errors by 54%. Junichi Yagi, vice president of Shimizu's Boston subsidiary S. Technology Center-America, said the key-punchers enjoyed the fragrances. "They reported feeling better than they did without it," he maintains.

Yagi said that fragrances were selected based upon the principles of aromatherapy, an ancient form of herbal medicine. Aromatherapists believe that "essential oils," the distilled "essences" of flowers, herbs and plants, can be used to make people feel better. Oils such as lavender and chamomile are considered relaxing; lemon and jasmine, stimulating; pine and eucalyptus, invigorating. Aromatherapy is widely practiced in England, France, Belgium, Germany and Switzerland.

"These ideas have been around for a long time," said Yagi, "and now [we're] applying it in Japan."

Other research is still in the laboratory phase. Peter Badia, a professor at Bowling Green State University, is finding that even when you are sleeping, your nose is wide awake. He's worked with about 100 college subjects in the university sleep lab. Electrodes on test participants monitored brainwave activity, heart rate, respiration and muscle tension.

"What we've determined is that we respond to odors in sleep," Badia said. "Tests clearly showed subjects are able to detect the odors; typically their heart rate would increase slightly and their brain waves quicken slightly."

But Schwartz thinks that while he was at Yale University he may have found a relaxing scent: apple spice. Schwartz conducted the experiments over a five-year period, testing more than 400 subjects.

In 1989, Schwartz published findings that he terms "quite remarkable." "We found spiced apple had relaxing effects as measured in brain waves, within a minute of [a subject's] smelling the fragrance."

In a separate study, respiration, muscle tension, heart rate and blood pressure were measured as a group of healthy volunteers were asked a series of stressful questions such as: "The kind of person I find sexually attractive is . . . ?" They received whiffs of spiced apple aroma, while a control group was given bursts of plain air. The spiced apple produced a drop in blood pressure, on average of 5 millimeters per person, Schwartz said.

"It's not a big decrease, but could be the difference between taking medication and not taking medication; or reducing the dosage in medication."

Schwartz, now at the University of Arizona, continues his work on scent. In one of his current studies, Schwartz is looking at "subliminal scent," scent below the level of awareness.

"I think one of the reasons taking trips to pine forests makes us feel so good is the presence of the mixture of molecules in pine," Schwartz said. "Equally important—if not more important—may be the absence of . . . smog molecules, gasoline, carpet, paint . . . putting a great strain on our nervous system."

Schwartz points to so-called "sick" buildings as an example. They inhibit the circulation of fresh air, so people instead breathe a veritable soup of man-made chemicals. "The idea is that the nose can detect those molecules and that that information is fed to the brain and does activate brain centers to make us feel queasy or uncomfortable," Schwartz said. "Yet we wouldn't be able to attribute it to any scent we're aware of it."

It is clear that the study of scent is positively blossoming. "It's definitely on the increase," Wysocki said. "We've learned a lot, but we're a long way from fully understanding smell. We're still on a great adventure."

[Source: Carla Kallan, *Los Angeles Times,* May 13, 1991.]

1. Another word that means *smell* is _____.

   a. odor

   b. scent

   c. fragrance

   d. aroma

   e. all of the above

2. People who deal with scent as an important part of their profession are
    _____.

    a. olfactory scientists
    b. subjects
    c. aromatherapists
    d. A and B
    e. A and C

3. Smell might be the most basic, primitive sense because it _____.

    a. plays a key role in body functions
    b. influences our moods
    c. reaches the limbic system after traveling first to other brain regions
    d. reaches the limbic system directly, without traveling first to other brain
        regions
    e. none of the above

4. If people are doing a difficult job in which it's important not to make any
    errors, it would be *best* for them to smell _____.

    a. spiced apple
    b. lemon aroma
    c. lavender
    d. jasmine
    e. none of the above

5. If people are tense and want to relax, it would be *best* for them to smell
    _____.

    a. spiced apple
    b. lemon aroma
    c. lily of the valley
    d. jasmine
    e. all of the above

6. Taking a trip to a pine forest might make us feel good because of _____.

    a. the presence of the mixture of molecules in pine
    b. the absence of other molecules from smog, gasoline, carpet, and paint
    c. the strain on our nervous system
    d. A and B
    e. none of the above

Video Activities: Telecommuting

Before You Watch.   Discuss the following questions with your class or in groups.

1. Is traffic a problem in your area?
2. What can people in your area do to avoid sitting in traffic on the way to work?
3. Are businesses in your area doing anything to help workers who have to travel a long time to get to work?

Watch.   Discuss the following questions with your classmates.

1. How does David Carroll reduce his commuting time?
2. Where does Marty Barrazo work?

Watch Again.   Read the statements below. Say if they are true (T) or false (F). Then watch the video again and check your answers.

1. _____   David Carroll spends an hour commuting to work.

2. _____   David's company allows flexible work hours.

3. _____   Marty Barrazo works for an Internet company.

4. _____   He commutes three hours a day to the community computer center.

5. _____   Many people don't know that the community computer center exists.

6. _____   The computer center has very modern computers.

7. _____   Marty Barrazo is always grumpy when he gets home.

After You Watch.   One way to make new words is to combine two words or to combine a word with a prefix. Here are three examples from the video clip:

a. tele + commute = telecommute
b. god + send = godsend
c. flexible + time = flextime

Sit in small groups. You will need a dictionary. Choose one person to be the writer for your group. Your teacher will give you a time limit (5 or 10 minutes). In that time, your group should find and list as many combined words as you can. Share your lists and discuss the new words.

Chapter 6

Global Connections

IN THIS CHAPTER

The first reading selection discusses some obstacles to global trade. The second selection looks at some recent exciting changes in global travel. Finally, the last part of the chapter, a magazine article on global crime, reviews suggestions on reading difficult material.

PART 1

Global Trade

Before You Read

1 **Getting Started.**   Look at the photos and discuss them in small groups.

1. What might be some reasons for the economic success of some cities (such as Hong Kong) and countries?
2. What might be some reasons for economic failure in other countries?
3. Which of the workers in these photos probably has the highest yearly income?
4. How can geography help—or hurt—a country's economy?

Boats and ships in Hong Kong harbor

Agricultural workers

Factory workers

Infotech workers in Bangalore, India

2   **Vocabulary Preview.**   Briefly look over this list of words from the reading that follows. Which words do you already know? For the ones that you don't know, *don't* use a dictionary. Try to understand them from the reading.

Nouns	Verbs	Adjectives	Phrases
benefit	share	landlocked	goes without saying
harbor	reduce	tropical	in turn
geography	contribute	startling	protectionist policies
tide			
consumer			
gap			
nutrients			
subsidy			
goods			
soil			
standards			
fuel			
obstacle			
infrastructure			

Read

3   As you read the following selection, think about the answer to this question: what seems to be the main key to a country's economic success? Read the following selection quickly. Do not use a dictionary. Then do the exercises that follow the reading.

Global Trade

Open Trade

[A]   For the first time in history, almost the entire world is now sharing the same economic system. Communism began to fall in the late 1980s, and since then, capitalism has spread to most corners of the world. The basis of a "pure" capitalist economy is free trade, also called "open trade." There are benefits of open trade for both rich and poor countries. For developed countries such as Japan and England, free trade brings with it more competition, which in turn brings advantages such as lower prices and more choice of products for consumers. For developing countries, open trade means that people have access to essential goods such as food, clothing, and fuel (for transportation and heat). An open economic system can be a key to improving the lives of people in both poor and rich countries because it can reduce poverty and improve living conditions.

"Leaking Boats"

[B]   This is apparently very good news. Optimists often say that "the rising tide lifts all the boats." What do they mean by this? Imagine a harbor filled with boats—some small ones, some medium-sized, and some huge ships. As the ocean tide comes in every eight hours, the water rises and literally lifts all the boats—both large and small. In economics, this expression means that in good economic times, poor countries benefit as much as rich countries do. However, pessimists point out that many of the "small boats" seem to be "leaking"—have holes in them—and so are going down instead of up. In other words, the gap between rich and poor—the economic difference between them—is wider than it was in the past. The contrast can be startling. According to *The Nation* magazine, "the wealth of the world's 200 richest people is greater than the combined incomes of the poorest 41 percent of humanity."

The Influence of Geography

[C]   Why is this happening? What is causing this widening gap between rich and poor? Many of the poorest countries are at a disadvantage because of geography, which is the root of several problems. First, a country that is landlocked, with no access to an ocean, has a disadvantage because it cannot easily transport its products to other parts of the world. Second, many—but not all—countries in tropical regions (near the Equator) have the disadvantage of heavy, heavy rains that often wash nutrients from the land. Without these nutrients in the soil, agricultural development is more difficult. Another obstacle for many countries is the problem of infectious diseases such as malaria, schistosomiasis, and dengue fever, which are found only in tropical climates. It goes without saying that people weak with disease cannot contribute to the economy of the country.

Protectionist Policies

[D]   Another cause of the growing gap between rich and poor countries is protectionist policies. In other words, many rich countries have governmental plans that give special help to their own people, so trade isn't actually completely "open." One example of a protectionist policy is an agricultural subsidy. This is money that a government gives to farmers; unfortunately, governments in poor countries can't pay these subsidies to their farmers. Therefore, the farmers in rich countries have a competitive edge in the global market. Other protectionist policies are "hidden." For example, Country X (a rich nation) might *say* their trade is open. However, it will not buy products from Country Y (a poor nation). Why? It says that Country Y does not have high enough health or safety standards.

A Way Out

[E]   It may sound as if the situation is hopeless for developing countries ever to have a competitive edge in global trade—but perhaps not. East Asia, for example, has found far more economic success than Africa has. The key to success seems to lie in each government's economic policy. Malaysia, Indonesia, and Thailand have the same tropical climate as many African countries, but their economies—unlike those of Africa—are growing fast. The reason? Their governments have created an economic climate in which people can move from agriculture to manufacturing. Geography is not the terrible obstacle to manufacturing that it is to farming. To help new entrepreneurs, these governments pay careful attention to areas such as infrastructure (harbors, railroads, and so on) and telecommunication. In other countries, such as India, information technology is driving the economy in some cities. Computer technology doesn't depend on geography, but it *does* require educated workers. Therefore, education must be a priority. In addition, governments of developing countries must work with developed countries and persuade them to drop protectionist policies. Clearly, it is possible for government policy to prepare a path out of poverty in even landlocked, tropical countries.

After You Read

4 **Getting the Main Ideas.** Write T on the lines before the statements that are true, according to the reading. Write F on the lines before the statements that are false.

1. _____ Open trade has advantages for both developed and developing countries.

2. _____ The economic difference between rich and poor is narrower than it was in the past.

3. _____ Tropical countries without access to the ocean usually are at a disadvantage in the global economy.

4. _____ Protectionist policies help to keep global trade open.

5. _____ Some countries have more economic success than others because of their governments' policies.

5 **Getting Meaning from Context.** Many words with one basic literal meaning have other figurative meanings.

Example

The woman with the sad <u>face</u> is worried about how to <u>face</u> the future.

(Literally, *face* is a noun and means "the front part of the head." However, figuratively, the verb *face* means "to meet a difficult situation.")

Words with figurative meanings can cause problems for a student who doesn't realize that the meaning is figurative and thinks, "Oh, this word is easy. I know this word. I don't have to use a dictionary."

The underlined words express figurative meanings. For each item, circle the words that give clues to the meaning of the underlined word. Then circle the letter of the appropriate meaning *for this context.*

1. Information technology is <u>driving</u> the economy in some cities.

   a. guiding and controlling a car, bus, or truck

   b. taking someone in a car, bus, or truck

   c. forcing (someone) to leave

   d. providing the power for

   e. good

2. Communism began to <u>fall</u> in the late 1980s.

   a. lose power

   b. come down from a standing position

   c. become lower in level

   d. be killed in a battle

   e. become lower in quantity

3. Capitalism has spread to most <u>corners</u> of the world.

    a. points where two walls meet

    b. points where two roads meet

    c. distant places

    d. difficult positions from which there is no escape

    e. edges

4. Geography is the <u>root</u> of several problems.

    a. feeling of belonging to one place

    b. part of a plant that grows in the soil

    c. part of a tooth or hair that holds it to the rest of the body

    d. cause

    e. solution

5. An open economic system can be a <u>key</u> to improving the lives of people in developing countries.

    a. a metal instrument to unlock a door

    b. something that helps to find an answer

    c. important

    d. part of a piano, typewriter, or computer

    e. a list of answers to exercises in a textbook

6. Heavy rains <u>wash</u> nutrients from the land.

    a. clean with water

    b. water

    c. rain on

    d. cause to be carried off by water

    e. clean oneself in a bathtub

7. Pessimists <u>point out</u> that many poor countries are doing worse than before.

    a. hold out a finger to show direction

    b. accuse or blame

    c. aim at or direct

    d. look at

    e. draw attention to (a fact or idea)

8. Their governments have created an economic <u>climate</u> in which people can move from agriculture to manufacturing.

   a. weather

   b. average weather condition in an area over a long time

   c. urban area

   d. condition, situation

   e. temperature

9. It's possible for government policy to prepare a <u>path</u> out of poverty.

   a. road for walkers

   b. open space for people to move through

   c. way

   d. line that something (e.g., an arrow) moves along

   e. road for runners

6 Find words and expressions in the reading selection "Global Trade" with the following meanings and write the words on the lines. The letters in parentheses indicate the paragraphs in which the words appear.

1. advantages (A): _____

2. after (another step) (A): _____

3. people who buy things (A): _____

4. things that people buy (A): _____

5. something that produces heat or power (A): _____

6. make less (A): _____

7. area of water where ships and boats are safe (B): _____

8. movement of the ocean toward the beach and away from the beach (B):

   _____

9. difference (B): _____

10. becoming wider (C): _____

11. area with no access to an ocean (C): _____

12. natural chemicals that help plants grow (C): _____

13. something that prevents success (C): _____

14. obviously (idiom) (C): _____

15. governmental plans that give special help to a country's own people (D):

    _____

16. money that the government gives people so that they can sell their products at a low cost (D):

    _____

17. not similar to (D): _____

18. system of roads, trains, harbors, and so on. (D): _____

7   **Checking Your Understanding.**   Turn back to Exercise 3 on page 107 and answer the question.

8   **Understanding Outlines.**   Many reading selections follow an *outline*. The outline is the plan, or the organization, of the material. It shows the relationship of the topics and ideas. You can outline reading material to help yourself see clearly the relationship of ideas; you can also write an outline when you organize your ideas for a composition. In an outline, the *general* ideas begin on the left. The more *specific* ideas are indented to the right.

Example

   I. Introduction: Benefits of Open Trade
      A. For developed countries
         1. More competition
         2. Lower prices
         3. More consumer choice
      B. For developing countries—access to essential goods
      C. For both
         1. Reduce poverty
         2. Improve living conditions
  II. Disadvantages for Poor Countries
      A. *Apparent* advantage: "Rising tide lifts all the boats"
      B. Problems with this idea
         1. "Leaking boats"
         2. Gap widening between rich and poor
 III. The Disadvantage of Geography
      A. Landlocked countries
      B. Problems of tropical countries
         1. Rain washes nutrients from agricultural soil
         2. Diseases that weaken workers
 IV. Protectionist Policies
      A. Definition
      B. Examples
         1. Agricultural subsidies
         2. "Hidden" protectionist policies
  V. Government Policies—Key to Economic Success
      A. East Asia (contrasted with Africa)
      B. Good Economic Climate
         1. Geography not obstacle
         2. People move from agriculture to
            a. Manufacturing
            b. Information technology
         3. Help from government
            a. Infrastructure
            b. Education
            c. Persuade developed countries to drop protectionism
      C. Conclusion: Path out of poverty

Answer these questions about the outline.

1.   What is the topic of the whole outline?

_____

2.   What are three benefits of open trade for developed countries?

_____

3.   What are two problems with the idea that "the rising tide lifts all the boats"?

_____

4.   What are two examples of protectionist policies?

_____

5.   In what two ways can government policies help people in poor countries?

_____

9   Now circle the number of the *one* main idea of the reading selection "Global Trade."

1.   Almost the entire world now shares the same economic system—capitalism—which is based on the idea of open trade.

2.   Good economic times benefit poor countries, as well as rich ones, because "the rising tide lifts all the boats."

3.   Geography is a serious disadvantage for many landlocked, tropical countries.

4.   The result of protectionist policies of rich countries is that "open" trade isn't actually open, and poor countries are at a disadvantage.

5.   Many developing countries are at a disadvantage in global trade, but they can find success with good government policies.

10   In your opinion, does the writer of "Global Trade" have more sympathy (agreement and understanding) for developed or developing countries? Why do you think this?

Discussing the Reading

11   In small groups, talk about your answers to these questions.

1.   In your country, is geography an obstacle to economic success? If so, is government policy moving the economy toward manufacturing or info tech?

2.   In your country, is the economy better or worse than it was five or ten years ago? Why?

Making Inferences

On tests and in general reading, it is important to be able to make inferences. A reading selection often gives information from which a reader can *infer* (figure out) other information.

Example

> Communism began to fall in the late 1980s, and since then, capitalism has spread to most corners of the world.
>
> This sentence does not say, but it *implies* or suggests, that capitalism is more successful than communism.

Complete each sentence by circling the letters of all the information that the reading selection "Global Trade" on pages 107–108 either states or implies.

1. Landlocked countries are at a disadvantage because _____.
   a. they have no access to the ocean
   b. they are in tropical countries
   c. it is difficult for them to transport their products to other countries
   d. many products must be transported by ship
   e. their agricultural land is of poor quality

2. Protectionist policies _____.
   a. are a cause of the gap between rich and poor countries
   b. include agricultural subsidies
   c. are most common in poor countries
   d. help everyone
   e. are sometimes hidden

3. Malaysia, Indonesia, and Thailand _____.
   a. are now developed countries
   b. have a tropical climate
   c. have fast-growing economies
   d. are moving from farming to manufacturing
   e. have protectionist policies

4. Information technology _____.
   a. is important to the economy in some cities in developing countries
   b. does not depend on government policies
   c. does not depend on geography
   d. is difficult to have in landlocked countries
   e. depends on educated workers

PART 2	# Global Travel . . . and Beyond

1   **Skimming for Main Ideas.**   Read the following paragraphs quickly, without using a dictionary. After each paragraph, circle the number of the sentence that best expresses the main idea.

Global Travel . . . and Beyond

[A]   When many people think of global travel, they think of expensive cruise ships and hotels or sightseeing tours to famous places. However, global travel has changed a lot in recent years. Now, not all travel is expensive, so lack of money doesn't have to hold people back. And these days there is an enormous variety of possibilities for people of all interests. Are you looking for adventure? Education? Fun? Do you like to travel with a group? Do you prefer to travel on your own? Would you like to get "inside" another culture and understand the people better? Would you prefer to volunteer to help others? Are you in the market for something strange and different? There is something for almost everybody.

1. Global travel doesn't have to be expensive.
2. Global travel is different now from what it was in past years.
3. Global travel includes cruise ships, hotels, and sightseeing.
4. There are now group tours for people with a variety of interests.
5. Global travel can now be strange and different.

[B]   Train travel used to be simply a means of getting from one place to another. Now, for people with money, it can also offer education or adventure. The Trans-Siberian Special, for example, is a one-week tour that runs from Mongolia to Moscow. The train stops in big cities and small villages so that passengers can go sightseeing, and there is a daily lecture on board the train, in which everyone learns about history and culture. For people who are looking for fun and adventure, there is the Mystery Express, which runs from New York to Montreal, Canada. This trip interests people who love Sherlock Holmes, Hercule Poirot, and Miss Marple. It's for people who have always secretly dreamed of being a private eye and solving mysteries. The passengers on board have the opportunity to solve a murder mystery right there on the train. In the middle of the night, for instance, there might be a gunshot; soon everyone learns that there has been a "murder," and they spend the rest of the trip playing detective. They track down clues, exchange this information and their opinions, and solve the whodunit by the time the train has pulled into Montreal. Of course, no *real* crime takes place. The "murderer" and several passengers are actually actors. The trip is a very creative weekend game.

1. The Mystery Express allows passengers to solve a murder on the train.
2. The Trans-Siberian Special is a tour that offers sightseeing and lectures.
3. The Trans-Siberian Special and Mystery Express are expensive.
4. Train travel can offer education and adventure, in addition to transportation.
5. Train travel is one way to get from one place to another.

[C]   Many people don't realize that the world's largest industry is tourism. Clearly, tourists have a big impact on the environment. Perhaps, then, it's fortunate that there is growing interest in *ecotourism;* 34 percent of all international travel is now nature travel. Serious ecotourists are interested in preserving the environment and learning about wildlife. Most also want to experience a new culture. Although it's possible to be very comfortable on an ecotour, many travelers choose to rough it; they don't expect hot showers, clean sheets, gourmet food, or air-conditioned tour buses. They live as villagers do. They get around on bicycle, on foot (by hiking or trekking), or on the water (on a sailboat or river raft).

1. An increasingly popular form of travel—ecotourism—is for people who are interested in nature.
2. Ecotours are not usually comfortable.
3. Ecotourists live as villagers do and do not travel by train, bus, or car.
4. The world's largest industry, tourism, is changing.
5. Most ecotourists want to experience another culture.

[D]   For people who want a valuable experience abroad, there are exciting opportunities to study or volunteer. You can study cooking (for one day or eleven
weeks) at Le Cordon Bleu in Paris or painting at the Aegean Center for the Fine
Arts in Greece. There are classes in art collecting at Sotheby's in London or
Indonesian music at the Naropa Institute in Bali. There is marine biology in
Jamaica, archaeology in Israel, meditation in Nepal, film in Sweden. But for
those who don't have a lot of money for tuition, volunteering for a few weeks can
also offer a rich learning experience. Scientists in Costa Rica need volunteers
to help count sea turtles and check their health. Archaeologists from Ireland to
Grenada (West Indies) need people to help them with excavations. College-age
volunteers can sign up for a summer in India. The opportunities change from
year to year, but all offer the chance to learn while helping out.

1. There are exciting opportunities for people who want to study
   abroad.
2. Scientists in several fields need volunteers to help them.
3. It's possible to have a valuable experience by studying or
   volunteering in another country.
4. Volunteering can offer a rich learning experience for people who
   can't afford tuition for classes.
5. There are opportunities to learn while helping out.

[E]   Volunteering is a good way to experience another country without paying
for expensive hotels or tuition. But how can a person *get* to another country
cheaply? One possibility is courier travel. For a low fee (about $35), a person
can join an association that sends information about monthly courier opportunities. The passenger agrees to become a courier (i.e., carry materials for a
business in his or her luggage) and can then receive huge discounts on airfare—for example, $400 Miami-Buenos Aires round trip or $300 L. A.-Tokyo
round trip. People who enjoy ocean travel but don't have money for a cruise ship

might try a freighter. Although freighters carry cargo from country to country, most also carry eight to twelve passengers. For people who want to take their time, it's a relaxing way to travel and is less expensive than taking a crowded cruise ship.

1. Volunteering is a good way to experience another country.
2. Courier flights and freighters are two ways to get to another country cheaply.
3. On a courier flight, a passenger carries something in exchange for cheap airfare.
4. A trip on a freighter is both cheap and relaxing.
5. It's possible to travel cheaply.

[F]   Travelers who return from a vacation often answer the question "How was your trip?" by saying, "Oh, it was out of this world!" By this idiom, they mean, of course, that their trip was wonderful. However, people will soon be able to use this expression *literally,* but it will be expensive. Already, it's possible to enter a special plane that gives you the feeling of weightlessness that astronauts experience.  Just go to Star City, Russia, and pay $4980 for ten minutes of zero-gravity. (Gravity is the force that keeps us on the Earth.) Zegrahm Space Voyages, a company in the United States, is now accepting reservations for a 2 1/2-hour flight in a Space Cruiser. The price might be an obstacle, though: $98,000 per person. Very soon, flights to a space hotel will be possible. The main attractions will be the view (of Earth), the feeling of weightlessness, and the chance to take a hike . . . on the Moon. It goes without saying that the price will also be "out of this world."

1. People who want a space adventure need to go to Russia or the United States.
2. People pay a lot of money to experience weightlessness, or zero-gravity.
3. Soon, it will be possible to take a flight to a space hotel.
4. There are three main attractions, not available on Earth, which people can experience at a space hotel.
5. Trips into space will soon be possible—but expensive.

After You Read

2 **Understanding Idioms.**   An idiom is a phrase that means something different from the individual words in it. Idioms are most common in informal English but are found everywhere. The reading selections in this chapter contain several. Some phrases have both a literal meaning and an idiomatic meaning.

Example

Our trip was <u>out of this world</u>. We spent a fabulous week on the island of Bali.

In this case, <u>out of this world</u> is an idiom that means "wonderful." The context usually helps you figure out if the expression has a literal meaning or is an idiom, and you can often guess the meaning of an idiom from the context. Sometimes, as in the preceding example, it helps to visualize ("see" in your mind) the literal meaning of the expression.

For each of the following items, find an idiom in the reading selection "Global Travel . . . and Beyond" that has a similar meaning and write it on the line. The letters in parentheses indicate the paragraphs where the idioms appear.

1. cause to stay in one place (A): _____

2. alone; not with a group (A): _____

3. looking for; hoping to find (A): _____

4. travels; goes (B): _____

5. on a train (B): _____

6. detective (B): _____

7. look for and find (B): _____

8. mystery (B): _____

9. arrived in (B): _____

10. travel in a simple and not comfortable way (C): _____

_____

11. go from place to place (C): _____

12. agree to participate in (D): _____

13. travel slowly (E): _____

3   **Making Inferences.**   Turn back to "Global Travel . . . and Beyond" to answer this question: what can you infer from each paragraph? On the short lines, put a check mark next to each statement that you can infer from the paragraph. Do not check the other statements, even if you think they are true. On the line after each statement you check, write the phrases from which you inferred the information. The first one is done as an example.

Paragraph A

1. __✔__ You don't have to be rich in order to travel.

   Global travel doesn't have to be expensive.

   _____

2. _____ It costs a lot of money to take a cruise.

   _____

   _____

3. _____ There is greater variety today in types of travel than there used to be.

   _____

   _____

4. _____ It's better to travel on your own than in a group.

   _____

   _____

Paragraph B

1. _____ Today, train travel is more than just a way to get from place to place.

   _____

   _____

2. _____ The Trans-Siberian Special is a lot of fun.

   _____

   _____

3. _____ The Mystery Express is expensive.

   _____

   _____

4. _____ The Mystery Express is fun.

   _____

   _____

Paragraph C

1. _____ Ecotourism is becoming more popular.

   _____

   _____

2. _____ Ecotours are often not very comfortable.

   _____

   _____

3. _____ Serious ecotourists care about animals.

   _____

   _____

4. _____ Ecotourists don't enjoy comfortable hotels.

   _____

   _____

Paragraph D

1. _____ It's more expensive to study film in Sweden than meditation in Nepal.

   _____

   _____

2. _____ There is a variety of subjects that people can study in different countries.

   _____

   _____

3. _____ Rich people prefer to take courses, and people without money prefer to volunteer.

   _____

   _____

4. _____ Volunteering can be a very good learning experience.

   _____

   _____

Paragraph E

1. _____ Cruise ships are expensive.

   _____

   _____

2. _____ A freighter is a kind of ship.

   _____

   _____

3. _____ Freighters are as exciting as cruise ships.

   _____

   _____

4. _____ Travel by freighter is probably not good for people who are in a hurry.

   _____

   _____

Paragraph F

1. _____ The expression *out of this world* has both a literal and a figurative meaning.

   _____

   _____

2. _____ The feeling of weightlessness is always enjoyable for all people.

   _____

   _____

3. _____ Some people might not be able to afford a flight in a Space Cruiser.

   _____

   _____

4. _____ Space hotels will be comfortable.

   _____

   _____

4 **Summarizing.**   Choose one paragraph—A, B, C, D, E, or F. Write a short summary of it. In your summary, include only the main idea and *important* details. Then compare your summary with those of other students who summarized the same paragraph.

Discussing the Reading

5 In small groups, talk about your answers to these questions.

1. What kinds of travel are most interesting to you? Why?
2. Is tourism important in your country? If so, what kind of tourism?
3. Think of one trip that you've taken. (It could have been fun, exciting, boring, terrible, etc.) Tell your classmates about it.

PART 3   # Building Vocabulary and Study Skills

1 **Expressions and Idioms.**   Complete each sentence with the missing words. Choose from these expressions.

out of this world	private eye
goes without saying	in the market for
on board	get around
track down	on your own
whodunit	pull into
hold back	rough it

1. A fear of flying will _____ many people from traveling into space. Lack of money will cause many more to stay on Earth.

2. We're going to fly to Europe. Then, while we're there, we'll _____ by train.

3. I love to read mystery novels. Someday maybe I'll become a _____ and solve crimes myself.

4. She spent hours in the library, but she wasn't able to _____ the information that she needed.

5. His old car breaks down all the time, so he's _____ a new car.

6. I don't enjoy camping trips. I've never liked to _____.

7. It _____ that people who travel into space will need to enjoy the feeling of weightlessness.

8. Let's go to that new Thai restaurant next Saturday. The food is absolutely _____.

2   Participles as Adjectives. There is a group of adjectives that comes from verbs. Present participles (*-ing*) are used for the *cause* of an emotion. Past participles (*-ed*) are used for the *result* or *effect*.

Examples

> The contrast between rich and poor is <u>startling</u>.
>
> You might be <u>startled</u> to learn that "the wealth of the world's 200 richest people is greater than the combined incomes of the poorest 41 percent of humanity.

These participles come from the verb *to startle.*

Fill in the blanks with the present or past participles of the verbs on this list. (Use a dictionary if necessary.)

Verbs:	addict	excite	horrify	relax	thrill
	challenge	frighten	interest	terrify	tire

1. Ecotourism is a type of travel for people who are _____ in preserving the environment. They enjoy a _____ hike through a tropical rainforest and don't mind roughing it.

2. My job has been very stressful and _____ this year. I've been working too hard and not sleeping enough. I'm so _____! I need a _____ vacation someplace restful, where I can just lie on a beach and do absolutely nothing. After two weeks, when I come back to work, I want to be completely _____ and free of stress.

3. I guess most people think that a trip into space would be _____. They would sign up for such a trip right now, if they could afford it. But I couldn't get _____ about a trip like this. I don't even like to fly on a regular airplane. I'm _____ by planes, so I'm pretty sure that space travel would be _____ to me.

4. Dangerous sports are _____ to some people, who love excitement and are _____ to danger. They are _____ to be able to jump out of a plane or off a waterfall. Other people are just the opposite. They're _____ at the thought of doing anything so dangerous.

3   Increasing Reading Speed. The following exercise will help you to improve your left-to-right eye movements and to increase your reading speed. Your teacher will tell you when to begin each section. Look at the underlined phrases to the left of each line. Read across the line, from left to right. Quickly underline the phrases that are the same as the underlined phrase. At the end of each section, write down your time (the number of seconds it took you to finish). Try to read faster with each section.

break up	break out breakfast	break up break off	break into break up
out of this world	out of the world other worlds	outer world out of this world	out of this world underworld
pulled into	pulled into pulled up	pulled over pulled for	pulled out pulled into
in a hurry	hurry up in a hurry	no hurry hurry over	in a hurry in a hurry
private eye	private eye private eye	private life private car	private school private eye

Time: _____

by train	train track by train	by train in the rain	by train buy a train
take your time	take much time take some time	take your time take your time	time after time behind the times
see the sights	see the sights keep sight of	sightseeing see the sights	eyesight sight something
in the market	on the market to the market	in a market at the market	in the market in the market
get around	get around get over	get over get under	get up to get around

Time: _____

open trade	open trade open track	opening trade opened trade	open trading open trade
on your own	on the town on your own	of your own in your town	your own on your own
sign up for	sign over sign away	sign in sign up for	sign up for sign for
above board	above board overboard	on board above board	across the board above board
hold back	hold over hold down	hold up hold out	hold back hold onto

Time: _____

global crime	global travel global crisis	global crisis global crime	global warming global crisis
point out	point out point at	point to point out	point out point toward
take place	take part take place	take place take parts	take turns take over
social order	social studies social order	social work social studies	social science social order
child care	child care child care	child's play child care	childhood childbirth

Time: _____

PART 4

Reading in the Real World

1   **Reading Difficult Material.**   As you've seen in previous chapters, students often need to read material that seems too difficult. As with all reading, it will help to remember the following suggestions.

1.   Consider what you already know about the topic before you read.

2.   Have questions in mind as you read. When you *scan* for specific information, have a pencil or felt-tip marking pen in hand and your questions in mind. Mark the information as soon as you find it.

3.   Try not to worry about new words. You may see some of them several times in the same reading selection. Each time you see one, it will probably add to your ability to guess the meaning.

Consider these questions before you read "The Global Crime Wave."

1.   What are some countries with a lot of crime (high-crime cultures)? What are some low-crime cultures?

2.   Why do you think some cultures have more crime than others?

3.   Which might have more crime—a homogeneous country (with one main ethnic group) or a heterogeneous one (with many ethnic groups)?

2   **Scanning for Information.**   As you read, scan for information to help you fill in the chart. Mark the information when you find it. When you finish reading, complete the chart. This reading selection will probably seem very difficult, but *don't worry* about what you don't understand. If you can fill in the chart when you finish, it means that you understand the main ideas. After you finish filling in the chart, compare your chart with those of other students. Were your answers the same? Were they similar (but perhaps in different words)?

Characteristics of High-Crime Cultures	Characteristics of Low-Crime Cultures
Culture	
Parenting	
Wealth	
Social Order	

The Global Crime Wave

Crime is increasing worldwide, and there is every reason to believe the trend will continue through the 1990s and into the early years of the twenty-first century.

Crime rates have always been high in multicultural, industrialized, democratic societies such as the United States, but a new phenomenon has appeared on the world scene—rapidly rising crime rates in nations that previously reported few offenses. Street crimes such as murder, assaults, rape, robbery, and auto theft are clearly rising, particularly in some formerly communist countries such as Hungary and in western European nations such as Scandinavia and the United Kingdom.

What is driving this crime explosion? There are no simple answers. Still, there are certain conditions associated with rising crime: increasing heterogeneity of populations, greater cultural pluralism, higher immigration, changing national borders, democratization of governments, greater economic growth, and the rise of anomie—the lack of accepted social ideas of "right" and "wrong."

These conditions are increasingly observable around the world. For instance, cultures that were previously isolated and homogeneous, such as Japan, Denmark, China, and Greece, are now facing the sort of cultural variety that has been common in the United States for most of its history.

Multiculturalism can be a rewarding, enriching experience, but it can also lead to a clash of values. Heterogeneity in societies will be the rule in the twenty-first century, and failure to recognize and plan for such diversity can lead to serious crime problems.

The connection between crime and culture cannot be overemphasized: there are high-crime and low-crime cultures around the world. In the years ahead, many low-crime cultures may become high-crime cultures because of changing world populations and politicoeconomic systems. In general, heterogeneous populations in which people have lots of economic choice (capitalism) are prime candidates for crime. Why? The very nature of crime is culturally defined. What is legal and desirable in one culture may be viewed as a serious crime in another.

A culture in which the citizens are very similar—sharing similar ethnicity, religious beliefs, income levels and values, such as Denmark—is more likely to have laws that represent the wishes and desires of a large majority of its people than is a culture where citizens come from diverse backgrounds. For this reason, homogeneous cultures normally have a lower level of law violation than heterogeneous cultures.

In addition, some cultures have a tradition of discipline—a belief that laws ought to be obeyed. In cultures where individualism is strong, and belief and respect for law is low, laws are often broken. Usually these are heterogeneous cultures, where citizens disagree about the laws and are poorly socialized to obey them.

Critical to crime rates in any culture are the parenting and child-care philosophies and methods. Most street crimes such as burglaries and robberies in all societies occur among adolescents and young adults. In some societies, parents are seen as primarily responsible for their children, but all citizens share in that responsibility. In other societies the child is treated as chattel—the property of the parents. The first type of society assures that parents receive preparation for infant care and provides support for parents in caring for their children. In the second type, no such support system exists. In these societies, nothing is required to be a parent—no knowledge, no skills, no income—and the parent is on his or her own to care for the child. It is not difficult to determine which system is more likely to produce a law-abiding young adult.

The disparity between the richest and poorest citizens is narrow in some cultures. People may be poor by world standards, but the little available wealth is shared fairly equally. In other societies, the differences between the wealthy and the poor are enormous: the people at the top may have hundreds, even thousands, of times more wealth than those at the bottom. This disparity between rich and poor may lead to a high crime rate.

Currently, much of the world is in a state of what French sociologist Emile Durkheim called *anomie*—a situation where people don't have clear ideas about the difference between "right" and "wrong." In most societies, the traditional social order has broken down, and there is a lack of clear-cut, well-established laws and limitations on behavior. Some nations, such as the United States, face widespread anomie due to their lack of restraints on human desires. In the United States, people feel that anyone can become a millionaire or president. With the fall of communism, dictatorships, and colonialism and the beginning of democracy in different forms around the world, many peoples are now experiencing huge expectations. Cultural differences increase this anomie. Moving from an authoritative society to a democracy also creates anomie because old rules and ideas are abandoned before new laws and ideas have become accepted.

Anomie results from a breakdown in the "bonding" process (which holds people in a society together). The individual who is closely in agreement with social expectations over a long period of time probably won't commit a serious crime because he or she has developed a "bond" with society.

The United States was the first industrialized, democratic, heterogeneous nation and thus the first to face the crime problems associated with anomie. We can imagine that crime will be a growth industry in many countries as they find themselves gripped by the same social forces that have long affected the United States.

Source: "The Global Crime Wave" from Gene Stephens, *The Futurist*, July–August, 1994.

3   **Discussion.**   In small groups, answer these questions.

1. This article was written in 1994. Which of the author's predictions have been realized (come true) in the new millennium?
2. Is crime increasing in many countries where there wasn't much crime in the past?
3. Are there countries where crime is decreasing?

Talk It Over

Applying the Death Penalty.   Some countries and some states in the United States have capital punishment (the death penalty), and others do not. Capital punishment means that if a person has been found guilty of a very serious crime, such as murder, he or she might receive death as a punishment. People often argue about this. Some believe that capital punishment is necessary to keep the crime rate down. Others disagree and say that it does not result in less crime. What's your opinion—and why?

Video Activities: Teen Talk

Before You Watch.   Discuss these questions in a group.

1. What are the most common problems that teenagers have?

2. How do teenagers get help when they have a problem?

3. If you have a problem, do you think it's easier to talk to a stranger or to someone you know?

Watch.   Discuss the following questions in a group.

1. What is "Teen Talk"?

    a. a magazine

    b. a Website

    c. a school group

2. On Teen Talk, teenagers can . . . (Choose 2 answers)

    a. talk to other teens about their problems

    b. see advertisements for products they might like

    c. get help with homework

    d. learn about resources to help them with their problems

Watch Again.   Fill in the answers.

1. List three examples of problems that the users of Teen Talk discuss.

    a. _____

    b. _____

    c. _____

2. The teen girl believes that just _____ about something can help teens to solve problems.

3. The "number 1 goal" of Teen Talk was to give teens a place to go to find _____ .

After You Watch.   Look at the advice columns in an English language newspaper. Read one of the letters and then write a brief paragraph of advice. When you are finished, look at the advice columnist's real answer. See if yours is similar or different.

Chapter 7

Language and Communication

IN THIS CHAPTER

The first reading selection discusses recent research in animal communication. The second selection looks at how we humans learn our first language. Finally, the last part of the chapter, a newspaper article on the use of English as an international language, gives you an opportunity to practice reading difficult material.

PART 1   If We Could Talk With the Animals . . .

Before You Read

1   Look at the photos and discuss them in small groups.

1. What might be some ways in which these animals communicate?
2. What might whales need to communicate with each other?
3. In your opinion, what is the difference between communication and language?
4. Do you think animals can learn language? Can they learn grammar?

A trail of ants

Whale

Primatologist Jane Goodall with chimps in the wild

Dolphins at the University of Hawaii

2   **Vocabulary Preview.**   Briefly look over this list of words and expressions from the reading that follows. Which words do you already know? For the ones that you don't know, *don't* use a dictionary. Try to understand them from the reading.

Nouns		Verbs	Adjective	Adverb	Phrases
prey	grin	claim	clicking	upright	shed light on
colony	mammal	vocalize			feel like
gender	degree	acquire			head back
mate	whale	reassure			
pod	species	hug			
swagger	creature				
primate	gesture				
brain	chatter				
honeybee	coyote				

Read

3   As you read the following selection, think about the answer to these questions: how do animals communicate? do animals have the capacity to learn language? Read the following selection quickly. Do not use a dictionary. Then do the exercises that follow the reading.

If We Could Talk With the Animals . . .

Do Animals Communicate?

[A]   In a famous children's story, Dr. Doolittle is able to talk to—and understand—animals. This has long been a dream of many people—to be able to communicate with animals and know what they're thinking. For almost as long, scientists have wondered if animals actually have language. It seems clear to anyone who has a dog or cat or who closely observes animals that there is certainly communication going on. But *how* do animals communicate? What do they "say"? And is it truly language? Recent research into everything from ants to chimpanzees is shedding light on animal communication.

The "Language" of Smell

[B]   Many animals produce chemicals called pheromones, which send "smell-messages" to other animals of the same species. These odors have different meanings. One odor attracts a mate. Another sends a warning. Another marks a territory. A honeybee, for example, makes over thirty-six different pheromones to communicate such information as where to find good flowers. An ant that has found food will take a bit of it and then head back "home" to the anthill. As it carries the food, it wipes its stomach on the ground. This leaves a chemical trail or path so that other ants will know where to go for more food.

Body Language

[C]   Just as humans do, animals communicate with body language and sometimes gestures. In addition to using odors, for example, a honeybee uses its entire body in a complex "dance" to give other bees exact directions to flowers. A dog expresses happiness by wagging his tail, as most people know. But what is the dog in the picture "saying"? His stomach is on the floor; his rear end is up in the air, and his tail is wagging. This means "I want to play." Chimpanzees in the wild communicate a wide variety of gestures and facial expressions, as we learn from the research of primatologist Jane Goodall. To express anger, for example, a chimp stands upright on two legs, moves with a swagger—a proud walk, swinging from side to side—and waves her arms or

throws branches. A nervous chimp who is afraid of a more powerful chimp will lower himself to the ground. Then he either holds out his hand or shows his rear end to the other chimp. Interestingly, when a chimp "smiles," it is not a smile of happiness. Instead, it is an expression similar to the nervous, fearful grin that a human makes in a tense or stressful situation. A powerful chimp will reassure a nervous, fearful chimp by touching, hugging, or kissing him.

Vocalizations

[D] Like humans, many animals vocalize, but we are only beginning to understand the meaning of these sounds. As they move through the ocean, some whales make use of echolocation—the ability to make clicking noises in order to locate and identify objects (such as boats) or prey (such as fish) even in cloudy water, where it's difficult to see. Some whales also produce mysterious "songs." These are probably calls to communicate with other members of their pod, or group, and to know where each member is. So far, we don't know much more than that. Research into whale communication is especially difficult because different populations of whales have different songs—even if those whales are of the same species.

Which chimp is nervous?

[E]   We have a better understanding of the chatter of prairie dogs. A professor at Northern Arizona University, Con Slobodchikoff, has spent over ten years studying one colony of prairie dogs in the wild. He records their sounds. He also carefully observes their actions and all events that happen at the same time as the sounds. He then feeds the data into a

computer. The computer puts together the chatter—the "talking"—and the actions. By utilizing the computer in this way, Slobodchikoff claims that he has identified about fifty words. So what are these prairie dogs talking about? They often alert each other when they spot danger—from such creatures as a human, dog, or coyote. Surprisingly, in their chatter, they can apparently distinguish shapes, colors, and sizes: "There's a tall blue human coming from the north." Slobodchikoff believes that they can distinguish gender (a man from a woman) and a dog from a coyote. Their chatter also varies according to the degree of danger: is this creature *very* dangerous or just something to be careful about?

Symbols

[F] Many scientists wonder about animals' capacity to understand a system of symbols, such as language. At the University of Hawaii, studies with dolphins have been going on since 1979. Researchers are teaching these ocean mammals a language of hand signals that includes nouns (*ball, basket, pipe*), adjectives (*big, small, red*), directions (*left, right*), verbs (*go, take*), and prepositions (*in, under*). The dolphins prove that they understand by following commands such as "Go to the ball on your right and take it to the basket." There is even clear evidence that dolphins understand the grammatical difference between subjects and objects. The head of the research program, Dr. Louis Herman, says that with a vocabulary of about fifty words, the dolphins demonstrate their intelligence by following new commands that they have never before experienced or practiced.

Primate Studies

[G] Since the 1970s, other researchers have been studying the capacity for language among primates—especially among chimpanzees. Because chimps don't have vocal organs that allow them to form spoken words, researchers decided to teach them other types of language. One of the earliest subjects, a chimp named Washoe, began to learn ASL (American Sign Language, the hand signals of deaf Americans) when she was less than a year old. By age four, she understood and used 132 ASL signs. In other studies, researchers have been communicating with chimps by using a keyboard with special symbols called lexigrams. One chimp named Kanzi picked up this language naturally; in other words, he watched as people tried (unsuccessfully) to teach this language to his mother.

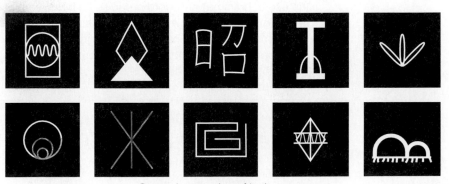

Several examples of lexigrams

[H]   How much can chimps under-stand? And what can they do with these words? They understand the difference between "take the potato outdoors" and "go outdoors and get the potato." They understand adjectives such as *good*, funny, hungry, and stu-pid. They can combine words into short sentences: "You me out"; or "Me banana you banana me you give." Perhaps most interestingly, they can

coin new words or phrases when they don't know a word—for example, "water bird" for a swan and "green banana" for a cucumber. And they can express emotion: "Me sad."

Language?

[I]   But is this language? What distinguishes communication from true language? Do chimps actually have the capacity for language? There is much disagree-ment about this. Some people argue that chimps can acquire only the vocabu-lary of a 2 1/2-year-old human. They also point out that a sentence such as "Lana tomorrow scare snake river monster" is not exactly Shakespearean English. It goes without saying that there is a gap between the language ability of chimps and humans. But clearly, this gap is not as wide as we used to think it was. Recent research is now focusing on the structures and activity of the brain. Biologists have looked at one small area of the brain, the *planum temporale,* which humans use to understand and produce language. In chimps, this is larger on the left side of the brain than on the right. In the journal *Science,* researchers tell us that this is "essentially identical" to the *planum temporale* in humans. This is not surprising to people who believe that chimps *do* have the capacity for language. After all, they say, 99 percent of the genetic material in chimps and humans is identical, making chimps our closest relative.

Conclusions

[J]   It is clear, then, that animals certainly communicate in various ways. The ques-tion "Is it language?" is still open. The famous linguist Noam Chomsky believed that what distinguishes communication from true language is *syntax*—that is, the use of grammar and word order, so he believed that only humans can have language. However, now we know that some animals (dolphins, chimps) have at least simple syntax. Louis Herman suggests, "Some people think of language like pregnancy—you either have it or you don't." But he and other researchers prefer to see language as "a continuum of skills." In other words, some animals simply have more than others.

After You Read

4 **Getting the Main Ideas.** Write T on the lines before the statements that are true, according to the reading. Write F on the lines before the statements that are false. Write I before the statements that are impossible to know from the reading.

1. _____ Some animals communicate by producing odors for other animals to smell.

2. _____ Chimpanzees, like humans, smile when they are happy.

3. _____ We know a lot about the communication of whales.

4. _____ With their vocalizations, prairie dogs can warn each other of specific dangers.

5. _____ Dolphins can understand only sentences that they have memorized.

6. _____ Chimps can understand much more vocabulary and grammar than researchers now realize.

7. _____ Researchers agree that all animals communicate but that only humans have a capacity for language.

5 **Getting Meaning from Context.** (Exercises 5 to 9 summarize the ways the context of a reading can give clues to the meaning of vocabulary items.) There can be a definition of the item in the text—usually after the verb *be*—between commas, dashes, or parentheses; or after connecting expressions such as *in other words, that is, (i.e.),* and so on.

On the lines, write the words and expressions from the reading selection "If We Could Talk With the Animals . . ." that fit these definitions. The letters in parentheses refer to the paragraphs of the reading where the items appear. The first one is done as an example.

1. a place where ants live (B): _anthill_ _____

2. path or "road" (B): _____

3. straight up; standing on two feet (C): _____

4. move proudly, from side to side (C): _____

5. a method of locating objects or prey by producing noises (D):

   _____

6. group of whales (D): _____

7. male or female (E): _____

8. the use of grammar and word order (J): _____

6 On each line, write the category that the items are examples of. The letters in parentheses refer to the paragraph where the category appears.

1. human, dog, coyote (E): _____

2. chimpanzees (G): _____

7 Use the context and your own logic to find a word or expression for each of these definitions.

1. return (B): _____

2. moving a tail (C): _____

3. make someone feel better (C): _____

4. animal that another animal hunts for food (D): _____

8 Use information in another sentence or sentence part to find a word for each definition.

1. smile (C): _____

2. make sounds (D): _____

9 On each line, write a word from the reading that fits both definitions as in the example.

1. gives food to; puts (information) into (E): _feeds_____

2. part of the body; director or leader (F): _____

3. musical instruments in a church; parts of the body (G): _____

4. topic; person or animal in an experiment (G): _____

5. lift from a lower place; learn (G): _____

6. piece of metal money; create (a word or term) (H): _____

10 **Understanding Punctuation.** Writers use italics in English for several reasons:

- ■ for emphasis—to stress an important word
- ■ to mean "the word _____"
- ■ for the title of a magazine, newspaper, or book
- ■ for words in foreign languages

Writers use quotation marks for two main reasons:

- ■ to quote direct speech—someone's exact words
- ■ when the word in quotation marks really means something different

Examples

There is certainly communication going on. But *how* do animals communicate? What do they "say"?

(The word *how* is in italics for emphasis. The word *say* is in quotation marks because the writer believes that animals don't really say anything.)

Look through the reading on pages 133–136, beginning with Paragraph B. With a felt-tip pen, mark every example of italics and quote marks. In each case, decide the reason for this punctuation. Then compare your answers with other students'.

11 **Checking Your Understanding.** Turn back to Exercise 3 on page 133 and answer the questions.

12 **Understanding Outlines.** The following outline shows one possible organization of the information in the reading selection. Notice that the more general topics are on the left, and the more specific topics are indented to the right. Some topics have been left blank. Go back to the reading selection, find these topics, and add them to the lines.

If We Could Talk With the Animals . . .

    I. Do Animals Communicate?

        A. How?

        B. What?

        C. Truly language?

   II. The "Language" of Smell

        A. Chemicals called pheromones

            1. Attract a mate

            2. _____

            3. _____

            4. _____

B. Examples

    1. Honeybee

    2. _____

III. _____

A. Bee—"dance" to give directions

B. _____

    1. Wagging tail = _____

    2. Stomach on floor, rear end up, tail wagging = _____

C. _____

    1. _____

    2. _____

    3. _____

    4. _____

IV. Vocalizations

A. _____

    1. Echolocation: to locate and identify objects and prey

    2. _____

B. Prairie dogs

    1. Chatter to _____

    2. Are able to

        a. _____

        b. _____

        c. _____

V. Symbols—Dolphin Studies

A. _____

    1. Nouns—_____

    2. _____

    3. _____

    4. _____

    5. _____

    B. Dolphins can

        1. Follow commands

        2. _____

        3. _____

VI. Primate Studies

    A. Chimps

        1. Washoe—ASL

        2. _____

    B. Chimps can

        1. Understand adjectives

        2. _____

        3. _____

        4. _____

VII. Language?

    A. No

        1. _____

        2. _____

    B. Yes

        1. Studies of brain

        2. Genetic material: _____

VIII. Conclusions

    A. Animals communicate

    B. Language?

        1. Noam Chomsky—"no"

        2. Louis Herman—"yes," but some more than others

Discussing the Reading

13   In small groups, talk about your answers to these questions.

1. Do you have a pet (animal)? Have you ever had one? If so, what kind? How does—or did—this animal communicate with you? Could you understand each other?

2. Did anything in the reading surprise you? If so, what?

3. You read that whales make a "clicking" sound. The word click actually imitates the sound itself. Say this word aloud several times. Can you hear it?

Cross-Cultural Note: Animal Sounds

In every language, we imagine that animals make certain sounds. We create words for these sounds. These are words that you often see in children's books.

Example
   "Meow," said the cat.

Here are some in English.

Animal	What This Animal "Says"
cat	*meow*
dog	*bow-wow (or woof-woof)*
pig	*oink*
small bird	*cheep! cheep!*
duck	*quack*
owl (night bird with large eyes)	*whoo*
rooster	*cock-a-doodle-doo*

It's sometimes fun to compare these in different languages. What do animals say in other languages?

PART 2   # "Parentese"

Before You Read

1   **Preparing to Read.**   Before you read, discuss your answers to these questions with a classmate.

1. In your opinion, who talks more—men or women? In school, who is better at language skills—boys or girls?

2. Do parents talk differently with their sons than they do with their daughters? If so, how?

3. What kind of toys do parents usually give to their sons? What kind of toys do parents usually give to their daughters?

4. In your opinion, what is more important in determining what we are— genetics (biology) or our education and environment?

2 **Skimming for Main Ideas.** The following paragraphs are about the language that parents use with their young children—what some people are calling "parentese." Read these paragraphs quickly, without using a dictionary. After each paragraph, circle the number of the sentence that best expresses the main idea.

"Parentese"

[A] Who talks more—men or women? Most people believe that women talk more. However, linguist Deborah Tannen, who has studied the communication style of men and women, says that this is a stereotype. According to Tannen, women *are* more verbal—talk more—in private situations, where they use conversation as the "glue" to hold relationships together. But, she says, *men* talk more in public situations, where they use conversation to exchange information and gain status. Tannen points out that we can see these differences even in children. Little girls often play with one "best friend"; their play includes a lot of conversation. Little boys often play games in groups; their play usually involves more *doing* than talking. In school, girls are often better at verbal skills; boys are often better at mathematics.

1. Women talk more than men.
2. It's a stereotype that women talk more than men.
3. Women talk more in private, and men talk more in public.
4. Little girls and little boys have different ways of playing.
5. Men and women have different styles of talking, which may begin in childhood.

[B] A recent study at Emory University helps to shed light on the roots of this difference. Researchers studied conversation between children age 3–6 and their parents. They found evidence that parents talk very differently to their sons than they do to their daughters. The startling conclusion was that parents use far more language with their girls. Specifically, when parents talk with their daughters, they use more descriptive language and more details. There is also far more talk about emotions, especially sadness, with daughters than with sons.

1. A study at Emory University can help to explain the differences between communication styles of boys and girls.
2. Researchers have studied the conversations of children and their parents.
3. A research study found that parents talk differently to their sons and daughters.
4. An Emory University study found that parents talk more with their daughters than with their sons.
5. Parents don't talk much about sadness with their sons.

[C]   Most parents would be surprised to learn this. They certainly don't *plan* to talk more with one child than with another. They don't even realize that this is happening. So why do they do it? Interestingly, it begins when the children are newborn babies. It is a known fact that at birth, males are a little less developed than females are. They don't vocalize—make noises—as much as girls do, and they don't have as much eye contact. Female babies vocalize, look at their parents, and remain alert longer. The result? Parents respond by talking more to the baby girls, who seem to be paying attention and "talking" back to them. Apparently, then, biology determines the amount of language that parents use.

1. Parents who talk more to their baby girls are responding to the fact that girls are a little more developed at birth.
2. Most parents don't know that they talk more with their girls and would be surprised to learn this.
3. Males are a little less developed than females are at birth.
4. Baby girls make noises and have eye contact a little more than baby boys do.
5. Baby boys don't remain alert as long as baby girls do.

[D]   There is always this question: what determines our character, personality, and behavior—nature (biology) or nurture (environment and education)? The research with babies seems to suggest that *nature* causes the amount and quality of language use. However, a study from the University of California at Santa Cruz provides evidence that the *situation* or *context* also influences the conversation. For example, parents usually give stereotyped toys to their children. A boy gets a car that he can take apart and put back together, for instance. A girl gets a toy grocery store. The type of talk depends on the toy that they're playing with. A toy grocery store naturally involves more conversation. If we consider this, we might decide that *nurture* determines language ability because we *choose* which toys to give our children.

1. The toys that parents give their son or daughter may influence the child's language ability.
2. From research with babies, we know that biology determines language use.
3. Parents usually give stereotyped toys to their children.
4. Different toys involve children in different amounts of conversation.
5. Education determines language ability.

[E]   Campbell Leiper, a researcher at the University of California, believes that the choice of toys is important. Both boys and girls, he says, need "task-oriented" toys such as take-apart cars. With these toys, they practice the language that they will need, as adults, in work situations. Both boys and girls also need "social, interactive" toys such as a grocery store. With these toys, they practice the kind of conversation that is necessary in relationships with friends and family. The data suggest that biology does not have to be a self-fulfilling prophecy. Leiper concludes that verbal ability is the result of both nature and nurture. Parents might naturally respond to their baby's biology, but they can choose a variety of toys and can choose how to talk with this child.

1. Boys usually receive toys with which they practice language that they will use in work situations.
2. Girls usually receive toys with which they practice language that is necessary in relationships.
3. Biology is not a self-fulfilling prophecy.
4. Parents can choose both their children's toys and how to talk with their children.
5. Biology influences language ability, but environment also does, so parents need to give both their boys and girls a variety of types of toys.

After You Read

3   **Getting Meaning from Context.**   For each definition, find a word in the reading selection that has a similar meaning and write it on the line.

Paragraph A

1. connected with the use of spoken language: _____

2. sticky liquid that joins things together: _____

Paragraph B

3. feelings: _____

Paragraph C

4. understand and believe: _____

5. act in answer: _____

6. it seems that: _____

Paragraph D

7. biology: _____

8. environment and education: _____

9. proof; support for a belief: _____

4   **Making Inferences.**   On the short lines, put a check mark by the statements that you can infer from the paragraph. Do not check the other statements, even if you think they are true. On the line after each statement that you check, write the phrase(s) from which you inferred the information. Look back at the reading for the information.

Paragraph A

1. _____ According to Deborah Tannen, the belief that women talk more is partly right but mostly wrong and oversimplified.

   _____

   _____

2. _____ Women talk more in some situations; men talk more in others.

   _____

   _____

Paragraph B

3. _____ Parents enjoy talking more with their daughters than with their sons.

   _____

   _____

4. _____ Girls have more practice discussing sadness than boys do.

   _____

   _____

Paragraph C

5. _____ Vocalization and eye contact are evidence of development in babies.

   _____

   _____

6. _____ Little girls, like baby girls, are more alert than little boys are.

   _____

   _____

Paragraph D

7. _____ People naturally talk more in some situations than in others.

   _____

   _____

8. _____ A toy car probably doesn't involve boys in much conversation.

_____

_____

Paragraph E

9. _____ According to Campbell Leiper, we should prepare both boys and girls for the adult world of work and relationships.

_____

_____

10. _____ If parents choose their child's toys carefully, biology won't influence the child's verbal ability.

_____

_____

5 **Distinguishing Facts from Theories.** In reading textbooks, students need to be able to determine the difference between facts (information that has been proven to be accurate) and theories (ideas that might or might not be true). *One way* to do this is to be aware of certain "signal words."

In affirmative statements, some words and expressions that indicate a fact are

found proof   a known fact   evidence

Other words that indicate a theory are

believe   suggest
apparently   may/might
seem

On the line, write *fact* or *theory* for each statement, according to the presentation of information in the reading selection "Parentese." (You'll need to look back at the selection for words that indicate fact or theory.)

1. _____ Women talk more than men.

2. _____ Parents talk very differently to their sons than they do to their daughters.

3. _____ At birth, males are a little less developed than females are.

4. _____ The situation in which conversation takes place—in addition to a child's gender—influences the amount of talk.

5. _____ The choice of toys that parents give their children is important.

6. _____ Biology does not have to be a self-fulfilling prophecy.

6 **Summarizing.** Choose one paragraph—A, B, C, D, or E. Write a short summary of it (two to three sentences). To write this summary, first make sure that you understand the paragraph well. Then choose the main idea and the most important details. In order to summarize this in your own words, *don't look at the original paragraph as you write.* When you finish writing, compare your summary with those of other students who summarized the same paragraph.

Discussing the Reading

7 In small groups, talk about your answers to these questions.

1. What might cause some schoolchildren to be better at language skills than other children?
2. Did anything in the reading surprise you? If so, what?

Talk It Over

Toys.   Make a list of the toys that you played most often with as a child. What were they? What kind of conversation did they involve you in? (Task-oriented? Social-interactive?) Do you think these toys influenced your language ability?

Beyond the Text

Go to a toy store, or contact an online toy company. Find out what the five most popular toys are these days. Which of these toys are "task-oriented"? Which are "social-interactive"? Discuss your findings with a small group.

PART 3   # Building Vocabulary and Study Skills

1 **Categorizing.**   On the lines, write the categories for the numbered groups of words. Then compare your answers with those of another student.

1. _____: touch, hug, kiss

2. _____: sadness, happiness, fear, nervousness

3. _____: primatologist, linguist, biologist

4. _____: chatter, call, click, talk

5. _____: dog, coyote, prairie dog

6. _____: whales, dolphins

7. _____: ants, bees

8. _____: point out, claim, suggest

9. _____: data, evidence, proof

10. _____: determine, decide, influence

2 **Prefixes and Suffixes.**   Here is a summary of word prefixes and suffixes and their approximate meanings.

Prefixes	Meanings
com-/con-	together; with
im-/in-/un-/dis-	not
inter-	between; among
mis-	wrong
pre-	before; first
re-	again; back

Suffixes	Parts of speech	Meanings
-al	adjective	having the quality of
-ar	adjective	of or relating to; resembling
-(i)an	noun	belonging to; characteristic of
-ed	adjective	passive participle
-en	verb	to make; to become
-ence/-ance	noun	state; quality
-ent/-ant	adjective	having the quality of
-er	adjective	comparative form
-er/-or/-ist	noun	a person who
-ess	noun	a person (female)
-est	adjective	superlative form
-ful	adjective	full of
-ible/-able	adjective	having the quality of; able to be
-ic	adjective	having the quality of; affected by
-ing	noun, adjective	active participle; gerund
-ion	noun	state; condition
-ive	adjective	having the quality of; relating to
-ly	adverb	manner (how)
-ment/-ness/-ship	noun	state; condition; quality
-(i)ous	adjective	full of
-ure	noun	state; result
-y	adjective	having the quality of; full of

In the parentheses after each word in the following list, write the part of speech (n. = noun; v. = verb; adj. = adjective; adv. = adverb). Then complete the sentences that follow with the appropriate words.

1. converse (v.), conversation (n.), conversational (adj.)

    Recent studies show that there is more _____ between parents and their daughters than with their sons. This begins at birth, when parents _____ _____ more with baby girls, who tend to have more eye contact and make more noises than baby boys do. It continues in childhood, when girls' play is more _____ than boys' is.

2. linguist (   ), linguistic (   ), linguistics (   )

    The field of _____ has several branches. In one of these, _____s study how children acquire language. In another branch, they work to discover if some animals have _____ ability.

3. reassurance (   ), reassure (   ), reassuringly (   )

    The mother chimp hugged her frightened baby to _____ him. Then she kissed him to give him further _____. These actions are similar to those of a human, who, in addition, speaks _____ to a fearful child.

4. able (   ), ability (   ), ably (   )

    Many people wonder if animals have the _____ to learn language. Studies with dolphins and chimps indicate that they are _____ to learn a certain amount of vocabulary. They also _____ follow a number of directions.

5. appear (   ), apparent (   ), apparently (   )

    _____, both nature and nurture decide a child's linguistic ability. It is _____ that boys and girls vocalize to a different degree from birth. However, it also _____s that parents can influence the amount and type of conversation that their children have.

6. simple ( ), simplify ( ), simplified ( )

When humans _~~simplify~~_ their language, chimps are able to understand a certain amount. The chimps can also use _~~simplify~~_ grammar to put together _____ sentences.

7. vocal ( ), vocalize ( ), vocalization ( )

Members of a pod of whales frequently _____ with each other. We believe they are _~~vocal~~_ in this way to make sure where each member is, but we really don't know much, yet, about their _~~vocalization~~_s.

3 **Word Roots.** Here are some word roots (also called "stems") that can combine with prefixes and suffixes to make words.

psych   sent   ist   fine   nat   dict

The words in each horizontal row are missing the same word root. Choose from those above, make necessary spelling changes, and complete the words. Use your dictionary, if necessary.

Noun	Verb	Adjective	Adverb
de_____ition	de__ _____	de_____ite	de_____itely
pre_____ation	pre_____	pre_____able	pre_____ly
_____ure	_____uralize	_____ural	_____urally
ex_____ence	ex_____	ex_____ent	
_____ology	_____ological		_____ologically
pre_____ion	pre_____	pre_____able	pre_____ably

Write sentences that show the meanings of some of the words in the preceding chart. Leave blanks for the words. Then exchange papers with a classmate. Write the appropriate words in the blanks. Exchange papers, make corrections, and discuss the vocabulary.

4   **Learning New Vocabulary.**   While you are reading, you need to understand vocabulary, but you do not need to learn it actively. Sometimes, however, you may want to remember new vocabulary for use in conversation and writing. These steps may prove useful.

1. Divide a sheet of paper into three columns. (This will become your Vocabulary Log.) Write new words or expressions in the left-hand column. Write the pronunciation under each word or expression. In the middle column, write the definitions. In the right-hand column, write sentences that illustrate the meanings of the items. (You can find these sample sentences from the readings in this book or from a dictionary.)
2. Look up and write related words, with their parts of speech, on the same piece of paper.
3. Pronounce the words to yourself. Try to fix their spelling in your mind as you learn them. Repeat the examples to yourself and make up other examples.
4. Cover the words and examples and try to remember them when you read the definitions.
5. Review your list regularly.
6. If desired, put only items that begin with the same letter on each sheet of paper, or write items on separate index cards.

Pay special attention to *how* the word is used. For example, if the word is a verb, is it transitive? (Does it need an object?) Is a preposition used after the word? If this is a noun, is it a count noun or a noncount noun?

Word	Definition	Example
respond (rĭ-spŏnd´)	(v.) answer	Parents <u>respond</u> to their baby's vocalizations.
response (rĭ-spŏns´)	(n.) answer	Her <u>response</u> was immediate.
responsive (rĭ-spŏn´sĭv)	(adj.) answering willingly with words or actions	They were <u>responsive</u> to their child's needs.

Choose a few words from each chapter so far (1–7) in this book. These should be words that are especially important for you to learn and remember. Use your dictionary to find related words. Then put these words, their parts of speech, meanings, and word forms in your Vocabulary Log. Be sure to add an example for each one of how to use the word. Each day, as part of your homework, spend a few minutes adding new words to your Vocabulary Log.

PART 4

Reading in the Real World

1 **Preparing to Read.** You're going to read a newspaper article about the spread of English. Before you read, with a small group, discuss your answers to these questions.

1. English seems to be the *lingua franca*—the international language—of the world today. In your opinion, why is *English* (and not another language) the lingua franca?
2. What is good about having English as the international language? What is bad about it?
3. Is English influencing your native language in any way? For example, are any English words creeping into (beginning to appear in) your language?
4. Are words from your language creeping into English?

2 **Vocabulary Preview.** Because this article is rather difficult, you might need some help with vocabulary. Here is a glossary of some words from the article. Look it over briefly now. You can refer back to it as you read.

Words for Communication and Language

Esperanto	=	a language that was created to be a lingua franca
dialect	=	a variety of a language; it is usually spoken in one area of a country
pidgin	=	a language that is a combination of two languages
jabber	=	talk fast and not clearly
blunt	=	honest (in speech) but without being polite or kind (Note: This *doesn't* mean "stupid," as in many languages.)

Words for War

blitzkrieg	=	sudden attack
genocide	=	killing an entire group of people
take by storm	=	take sudden and complete control

Words for Botany (the science of plants)

germination	=	the beginning of growth
hybrid	=	combination of two or more plants, animals, or languages
offshoot	=	a branch of a plant (or language)

Idioms

keep on our toes	=	stay alert and aware
cut a deal	=	reach a business agreement

Others

morph	=	change
dominate	=	have the most important position
frenetic pace	=	very fast speed
impromptu	=	without preparation
bemoan	=	complain about
degradation	=	reduction in quality
exasperated	=	irritated or frustrated
lash out at	=	speak very angrily to
launching	=	beginning
preserve	=	keep; save
eradicate	=	destroy; end
outmoded	=	old fashioned; out-of-date
thrive	=	live well
halted	=	stopped
inevitable	=	not avoidable

Focus on Testing

Comprehension Questions on Reading Tests

Standardized tests often give a reading passage followed by questions about it. You'll be able to answer some from memory, after one quick reading. You'll need to look back and scan for the answers to others. The items are usually in the same order that they appear in the selection, so look for the answer to No. 1 near the beginning. Some questions ask about information that the passage *states* (says directly). Others ask about information that the passage *implies*. These questions will be harder. Hint: It usually helps to look over the questions before reading.

3 **Scanning for Information.**   First, read the questions (pages 157–158) that follow the article. Then read the article. Try to keep some of the questions in mind as you read and mark the answers with a felt-tip pen. Don't worry if you don't understand every word. When you finish reading, answer the questions. Work as quickly as possible, as you would on a test. Your teacher might decide to give you a time limit.

As English Spreads, Speakers Morph It Into World Tongue

. . . In Britain, . . . editors of the *Oxford English Dictionary* are struggling to keep up with the "morphing" of the mother tongue.

What centuries of British colonialism and decades of Esperanto couldn't do, a few years of free trade, MTV, and the Internet has. English dominates international business, politics, and culture more than any other language in human history, and new words are melding into English at a frenetic pace.

"English is probably changing faster than any other language," says Alan Firth, a linguist at the University of Aalborg in Denmark, "because so many people are using it."

More than 1 billion people are believed to speak some form of English. For every native speaker, there are three nonnative speakers. Three-quarters of the world's mail is in English and four-fifths of electronic information is stored in English.

As more nonnative speakers converse with each other, hundreds of impromptu varieties of English are taking on a life of their own around the world.

But the uncontrolled, global germination of so many "Englishes" has some worried. English purists, led by Britain's Prince Charles, bemoan the degradation of the language as they see it.

Multiculturalists, meanwhile, say the blitzkrieg-like spread of English effectively commits "linguistic genocide" by killing off dozens of other languages.

These differing views lead to the question: Is the world taking English by storm or is English taking the world by storm?

Tom McArthur, editor of the *Oxford Companion to the English Language,* says that in 20 to 30 countries around the world, English is merging with native languages to create hybrid Englishes.

"The tensions between standard English and hybrid Englishes are going to become very, very great," says Mr. McArthur, who calls the process neither good nor bad. "We are going to have to keep on our toes. Some standard form of English [should be maintained] . . . as a tool of communication."

Linguists see three main "Englishes" forming along with dozens of offshoots.

One includes Britain, the US, Canada, Australia, and New Zealand where distinct dialects of English are already spoken by about 350 million people.

A second includes South Asia and such African countries as Kenya and Tanzania, where pidgin Englishes—in numerous forms—are dominant.

And a third is broken English used for basic communication in the rapidly industrializing regions of East Europe, East Asia, Latin America, and the Mideast.

The spread of English has given rise to interaction between foreign peoples that would have been considered remarkable only a few years ago, according to linguists.

In a Sydney factory, Cambodian, Samoan, Maltese, Greek, and Latvian workers take orders, talk about their families, and complain about their bosses to each other in their own broken English.

In Thailand, Russians, Pakistanis, Japanese, and Germans make phone calls by shouting out mispronounced numbers in English to exasperated Thai operators.

One of the largest sources of new terms is computers, according to linguists. In more than 100 countries, Internet users jabber in English—or something like it. . . .

Prince Charles recently warned of a creeping degradation of the English language, lashing out at Americans for cheapening it with bad grammar. And French-language purists have been trying to eliminate English slang from entering the world's previous lingua franca, but with little success.

"People tend to invent all sorts of nouns and verbs and make words that shouldn't be," said Prince Charles at the March launching of a five-year British effort to preserve "English English."

"I think we have to be a bit careful, otherwise the whole thing can get rather a mess," he added.

The prince's concerns are both cultural and financial. The rapidly growing "English industry"—made up of English classes and tens of thousands of academics studying the language and its offshoots—currently produces more than $750 million in income for Britain annually.

But Britain faces competition from the United States and Australia in the crucial Asian market, where more than 200 million Chinese are studying English and where English is the main language of commerce.

As China continues to grow, meanwhile, some fear that a form of Chinese could replace English as the world's global language within three generations.

Danish Professor Firth, who studies conversations between nonnative speakers when they conduct business, says businessmen tend to be blunt, humorless, use simplified grammar, and develop and use their own English terms to cut a deal.

He cites one example where a Hungarian used the phrase "It's a little bit middle, middle power" to say things weren't going well. His Danish counterpart began to also use the phrase.

"People develop their own ways of doing business with each other, of talking and even writing . . . that native speakers might not understand," Firth says. "And native speakers join in and start to speak that way also."

But those who seek to preserve native cultures warn that in many parts of the world, English is taking more than it is giving. Some linguists attending the 1995 global Cultural Diversity Conference held in Sydney last month warned of accelerating global "linguicide."

Schools in former European colonies still use English or French to assimilate ethnic populations, eradicating dozens of native languages, they warn . . .

The problem, according to linguists at the conference, is the outmoded 19th century concept that a "nation-state" requires a single language to unify its people. Multiculturalists argue that multilingual states, such as Switzerland, can exist and thrive. Having several official languages can also reduce ethnic tensions among people lumped together by colonial mapmakers.

Oxford Companion editor McArthur says the spread of English can't be halted. The globalization of the world, mostly driven by economics, is inevitable.

"It's the [world's] need for a unified language of trade, politics, and culture," he says. "We're going to lose a lot of languages around the world, but if it's not English, it would be something else."

Source: Adapted from "As English Spreads, Speakers Morph It Into World Tongue" from David Rohde, *The Christian Science Monitor*, May 17, 1995.

4 **Checking Your Understanding.** If necessary, look back at the article to answer these questions.

1. What is the main idea of the article? _____

   a. English has spread very fast and is changing cultures worldwide, but this rapid spread is also changing the English language.

   b. English is probably changing faster than any other language.

   c. The spread of English is killing off dozens of other languages.

   d. There are three main "Englishes" and many offshoots of them.

   e. People are developing their own way of speaking English, and sometimes native speakers don't understand them.

2. English has become today's international language because of _____.

   a. capitalism and international business

   b. politics

   c. the Internet

   d. none of the above

   e. all of the above

3. How many people probably speak English? _____

   a. three-fourths of the world

   b. four-fifths of the world

   c. people in twenty to thirty countries

   d. more than 1 billion people

   e. one in three people

4. Two groups of people with differing views are _____.

   a. dictionary editors and dictionary writers

   b. purists and multiculturalists

   c. native speakers and speakers of pidgin English

   d. businessmen and linguists

   e. linguists and multiculturalists

5. People who believe that the spread of English is harming (hurting) English are _____.

    a. linguists

    b. multiculturalists

    c. purists

    d. all of the above

    e. none of the above

6. Prince Charles _____.

    a. leads the English purists

    b. does not like the changes in the English language

    c. does not appear to like American English

    d. all of the above

    e. none of the above

7. *Linguicide* (line 80) probably means _____.

    a. the teaching of languages

    b. the preservation of languages

    c. the eradication of languages

    d. the teaching of linguistics

    e. the preservation of culture

8. According to this article, the common international language before English was _____.

    a. Esperanto

    b. pidgin

    c. French

    d. Chinese

    e. Danish

9. Tom McArthur, editor of the *Oxford Companion to the English Language,* believes _____.

    a. English is joining with other languages to create something new

    b. it's not necessary to have a standard form of English

    c. the spread of English is unavoidable

    d. a and b

    e. a and c

Beyond the Text

Choose one of these projects. When you finish, report your findings to the class.

- Interview ten people who are not native speakers of English. Ask them if the spread of English is having any effect on their culture or language—and if so, *what* effect?

- Interview ten native speakers of English. Ask them if they notice any recent changes in the English language (vocabulary, grammar, etc.) due to the influence of other languages—and if so, *what changes*?

Video Activities: Technology for the Disabled

Before You Watch. Discuss the following in a group.

1. What are *disabilities*? Do you have a friend or a relative who is *disabled*?
2. Define these terms: paraplegic, quadriplegic
3. What are some of the difficulties that disabled people have in an "abled" world?

Watch. Discuss the following questions in a group.

1. Guido Corona is blind. How does technology help him to see?
2. The man in the wheelchair cannot use his hands. How can he use a computer?
3. What percentage of Americans have a disability?

Watch Again. Read the questions below. Fill in the blanks. Then watch the video again to check your answers.

1. The IBM Home Page Reader allows _____ people to access everything on the Web. It was created by a person with a _____.

2. The man in the wheelchair is able to use a computer with the help of a device called Track 2000. With this program, the man can move the computer cursor by moving his _____, and he can "right click" and "left click" a mouse by twitching his _____.

After You Watch.   Below is a list of famous people, living and dead, who accomplished great things even though they had a disability. Choose a name from the list. Use an encyclopedia or the Internet (search for "famous people with disabilities") to write a short biography of this person. Tell the facts of this person's life, and be sure to explain how this person succeeded in spite of his or her disability.

Andrea Bocelli	Franklin D. Roosevelt	Stevie Wonder
Chris Reeves	Tom Cruise	Walt Disney
Beethoven	Albert Einstein	Marlee Matlin
Van Gogh	Stephen Hawkins	Sarah Bernhardt
Ray Charles	Thomas Alva Edison	Winston Churchill
"Magic" Johnson	Robin Williams	

Chapter 8

Tastes and Preferences

IN THIS CHAPTER

The first reading selection discusses art history and what we can learn about people from their art. The second selection describes things that people do in different societies to make themselves more attractive. The last selection is a magazine article about a discovery of Stone Age cave art.

| PART 1 | # What Can We Learn from Art? |

Before You Read

1 Getting Started.   Look at the photos and discuss them in small groups.

1. What kinds of photos are these? Where might you see them?
2. Describe each photo. If you can, talk about the people and the activities.
3. Compare the photos. What are the similarities? What are the differences?
4. Which photo do you like the best? Why?

Cave art

Francisco Goya, *The Third of May, 1808,* 1814

Pablo Picasso, *Guernica,* 1937

Chiwara dancers
with headdresses,
Bambara people,
Bamako area, Mali

Statue for the front of a boat, which functions to scare sea spirits that might bring storms, Solomon Islands

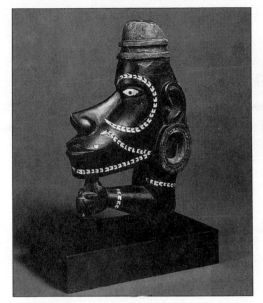

Islamic bowl with decoration of arabesques and Kufic writing

2 **Vocabulary Preview.** Briefly look over this list of words and expressions from the reading that follows. Which words do you already know? For the ones that you don't know, *don't* use a dictionary. Try to understand them from the reading.

Nouns	**Verbs**	**Adjectives**
target	worship	essential
caves	crawl	Paleolithic
arabesques	foretell	holy
destination	depict	exquisite
cliff	admire	significant
calligraphy	come upon	functional
headdress		objective
spelunkers		subjective
tunnel		
mosques		
mammoths		
spear		
statues		
archaeologists		

Read

3 As you read the selection on pages 164–166, think about the answer to this question: what can we learn from *art* history that we can't usually learn in a general history class? Read the following selection quickly. Do not use a dictionary. Then do the exercises that follow the reading.

What Can We Learn from Art?

The Study of Art History

[A] A study of art history might be a good way to learn more about a culture than is possible to learn in general history classes. Most typical history courses concentrate on politics, economics, and war. But *art* history focuses on much more than this because art reflects not only the political values of a people, but also religious beliefs, emotions, and psychology. In addition, information about the daily activities of our ancestors—or of people very different from our own—can be provided by art. In short, art expresses the essential qualities of a time and a place, and a study of it clearly offers us a deeper understanding than can be found in most history books.

Cave Art

[B] Art even provides us with limited access to the world of *pre*historic people. In over 100 countries, Stone Age people created amazing paintings in caves deep in the earth or under rocky mountain cliffs. This astonishing art is usually discovered by spelunkers—people whose hobby is exploring caves—who come upon it by chance. They may be crawling on hands and knees through low, narrow tunnels when suddenly the space opens and they are able to stand upright. They have the thrill of discovering exquisite paintings of startling beauty. The most famous of these cave paintings are in Lascaux, France, and Altamira, Spain. They most often depict animals that were prey (deer, woolly mammoths, horses, and so on) that Stone Age people hunted 15,000 to 30,000 years ago. The reason for the creation of this art is a mystery. However, archaeologists who specialize in the Paleolithic (Stone) Age believe that the art was part of religious ceremonies—perhaps to assure success in hunting or to worship some animal "god," such as a bear. It is primarily a study of art history that sheds light on these prehistoric people.

Art as an Expression of Political Views

[C] In history books, objective information about the political life of a country is presented; that is, facts about politics are given, but opinions are not expressed. Art, on the other hand, is subjective: It reflects emotions and opinions. The great Spanish painter Francisco Goya was perhaps the first truly "political" artist. In his well-known painting *The Third of May, 1808,* he depicted soldiers shooting a group of simple people. This depiction of faceless soldiers and their victims has become a symbol of the enormous power—and the misuse of this power—that a government can have over its people. Over a hundred years later, symbolic images were used in Pablo Picasso's *Guernica* to express the horror of war. Meanwhile, on another continent, the powerful paintings of Diego Rivera, José Clemente Orozco, and David Alfaro Siqueiros—as well as the works of Alfredo Ramos Martínez—depicted these Mexican artists' deep anger and sadness about social problems. In summary, a personal and emotional view of history can be presented through art.

Art as a Reflection of Religious Beliefs

[D] In the same way, art can reflect a culture's religious beliefs. For hundreds of years in Europe, religious art was almost the *only* type of art that existed. Churches and other religious buildings were filled with paintings that depicted people and stories from the Bible, the Jewish and Christian holy book. Although most people couldn't read, they could still understand biblical stories in the pictures on church walls. By contrast, one of the main characteristics of art in the Middle East was (and still is) its *absence* of human and animal images. This reflects the Islamic belief (from the Koran, the book of Islam) that statues are unholy. By Islamic law, artists are not allowed to copy human or animal figures except on small items for daily use (for example, rugs and bowls). Thus, on palaces, mosques, and other buildings, Islamic artists have created exquisite arabesques—decoration of great beauty with images of flowers and geometric forms (for example, circles, squares, and triangles). They have also shown great creativity and discipline in their use of Arabic calligraphy—writing—as an art form.

Traditional Art in Africa and the Pacific Islands

[E] Art also reflects the religious beliefs of traditional cultures in Africa and the Pacific Islands. In fact, religion is the *purpose* for this art and is, therefore, absolutely essential to it. However, unlike Christian art—which influences people to have religious feelings—the goal of traditional art in Africa and the Pacific is to influence spiritual powers—gods—to enter people's lives. Each tribe or village has special ceremonies with songs and dances to make sure that crops, animals, and tribal members are healthy and increase in number. The dancers in these ceremonies wear unique masks, headdresses, and costumes that they believe are necessary to influence the gods. These masks and headdresses are a very significant part of the art.

[F] In traditional tribal cultures, art objects—masks, headdresses, statues, and so on—are not created simply for beauty. They are also essential to both religion and daily life. It is impossible to separate art and religion from everyday activities: hunting, war, travel, farming, childbirth, and so on. In the Solomon Islands of Melanesia, for example, the artistic characteristics of common everyday objects are considered to be essential to the successful use of the items. A small figure on a hunter's or soldier's spear is believed to help the spear reach its target (that is, the hunted animal or the enemy in war); a small statue on the front of a boat is supposed to help the boat reach its destination. Another example of the function of traditional art is the use of headdresses in ceremonies of the Bambara people of Mali, in Africa. These headdresses are certainly decorative, but beauty is not the reason they are made. Their purpose is to help the crops grow: they were worn by the Bambara at planting time in dances to celebrate the birth of agriculture. Likewise, among the Bakongo people, there is a rich variety of functional wooden figures: small statues of ancestors foretell the future, and images of a mother and child give protection to a woman as she gives birth to a baby. To sum up, art in many cultures is believed to serve essential, practical functions.

The Way People View Art

[G] As we've seen, art depends on culture. Similarly, the way that people view art also depends on their cultural background. For most Europeans and Americans, art serves mainly as decoration. It is something on a museum wall or in a glass case. It makes homes more attractive. People look at it and admire it: "Oh, what a beautiful painting!" they might say. "I love the lines and colors." In addition to decoration, ideas are often expressed in this art. "This is a wonderful statue," an admirer might say. "It makes such a strong antiwar statement." However, in much of the rest of the world, art is not considered to be separate from everyday existence. It has a function. A person in a tribal society might look at a mask and say, "Oh, this is a good mask. It will keep my house safe." In brief, the way in which people enjoy art depends on their culture.

Art as a Reflection of Change in Society

[H]   In conclusion, art is a reflection of various cultures. But art also reflects the *changes* in society that take place when different cultures influence one another. As people from tribal societies move to urban areas, their values and beliefs change, and their ancient art forms begin to lose their function. For example, when most Bambara people turned to Islam, they gave up their ceremonies to make the crops grow; their new religion taught them that their headdresses were unholy, so they stopped using them. Now Bambara artists make these head-dresses only for foreign tourists; the headdresses have no function. On the other hand, urban artists learn a lot from traditional art: African masks and figures had a great effect on Pablo Picasso, and Paul Gauguin was deeply influenced by South Pacific culture; many American and Canadian artists study the simplicity of Japanese painting. The result is that as the world gets "smaller," the art of each culture becomes more international.

After You Read

4   **Getting the Main Ideas.**   Write W on the lines before the statements about Western political art; CH before the statements about Christian art; IS before the statements about Islamic art; T before the statements about traditional art; and P before prehistoric art.

1. _____   The reason for this art is a mystery to us today.

2. _____   Some of these paintings show the horror of war or express anger about social problems.

3. _____   According to the tribespeople, these decorative headdresses help their crops grow.

4. _____   Artistic figures on spears or boats are believed to help them reach their destinations.

5. _____   People learned about the Bible from the stories in this art.

6. _____   Tribe members believe that wooden figures predict the future and protect women in childbirth.

7. _____   Because of religious law, artists decorate buildings with flowered and geometric designs but no human or animal forms.

8. _____   There are no images of living things (people or animals) except on small items for daily use.

9. _____   This art serves a practical, everyday function.

5   **Getting Meaning from Context.**   Circle the words that give clues to the meanings of underlined words. Then answer the questions and write a definition for each word. When you finish, check your definitions in a dictionary.

1.   In his well-known painting *The Third of May, 1808,* the Spanish artist Goya <u>depicted</u> soldiers shooting a group of simple people.

What part of speech is <u>depicted</u> (noun, verb, adjective)? _____

What kind of person might depict something? _____

What does <u>depicted</u> mean? _____

2.   In history books, <u>objective</u> information about the political life of a country is presented; that is, facts about politics are given, but opinions are not expressed. Art, on the other hand, is <u>subjective</u>; it reflects emotions and opinions.

What part of speech is <u>objective</u>? _____

Where might you find objective information? _____

What is *not* part of objective information? _____

What does <u>objective</u> mean? _____

What part of speech is <u>subjective</u>? _____

What does art reflect? _____

What is the opposite of <u>subjective</u>? _____

3.   Thus, on palaces, <u>mosques</u>, and other buildings, Islamic artists have created a unique decoration of great beauty with images of flowers and geometric forms (for example, circles, squares, and triangles).

What part of speech is <u>mosques</u>? _____

Mosques are a kind of _____.

What kind of artists decorate mosques? _____

What does <u>mosques</u> mean? _____

Sometimes you need to see a word in several different forms or contexts before you can guess the meaning.

Examples

One of the main characteristics of art in the Middle East is its absence of human and animal <u>images</u>.

There is rich variety of functional wooden figures: small statues of ancestors foretell the future, and <u>images</u> of a mother and child give protection to a woman as she gives birth.

(You can guess that <u>images</u> are pictures or figures that represent people or animals.)

6 Circle the words that give clues to the meanings of the underlined words. Then write a definition on each line. When you finish, check your definitions in a dictionary.

1. This reflects the Islamic belief (from the Koran, the book of Islam) that statues are <u>unholy</u>.

    Churches and other religious buildings were filled with paintings that depicted people and stories from the Bible, the Jewish and Christian <u>holy</u> book.

    Their new religion taught them that their headdresses were <u>unholy</u>, so they stopped using them.

    What does *holy* mean? _____

2. These headdresses are certainly <u>decorative</u>, but beauty is not the reason they are made.

    For most Europeans and Americans, art serves mainly as <u>decoration</u>. It is something on a museum wall or in a glass case. It makes homes more attractive.

    What does *decoration* mean? _____

3. They have the thrill of discovering <u>exquisite</u> paintings of startling beauty.

    Islamic artists have created arabesques—<u>exquisite</u> decoration of great beauty with images of flowers and geometric forms.

    What does *exquisite* mean? _____

7 On the lines, write the words and expressions from the reading selection that fit these definitions. The letters in parentheses refer to the paragraphs where the words appear.

1. very important; necessary (A): _____

2. deep underground places (B): _____

3. the sharp sides of mountains (B): _____

4. people who explore caves (B): _____

5. find, discover (B): _____

6. moving along the ground, not upright (B): _____

7. long, narrow underground passages (B): _____

8. people who study ancient cultures (B): _____

9. show great respect for; pray to (B): _____

10. wrong or inappropriate use (C): _____

11. not being present (D): _____

12. beautiful decoration with images of flowers and geometric forms (D):

   _____

13. writing as an art form (D): _____

14. important; meaningful (E): _____

15. a long pole with a sharp point; a kind of weapon (F): _____

16. the object that someone is trying to shoot at (F): _____

17. a place someone is trying to reach (F): _____

18. decorative head coverings (F): _____

19. useful (F): _____

20. tell in advance; predict (F): _____

21. have a good opinion of; respect and like (G): _____

8 Understanding Outlines. As you saw in Chapters 6 and 7, an outline shows the organization of a composition. On page 170 there is a possible outline for the reading selection "What Can We Learn from Art?" The *general* topics are filled in. But the reading also contains many subtopics that serve as supporting material. Write these *specific* topics in the correct places as in the example. (You'll need to look back at the reading to make sure where they belong.) Use the following list of subtopics.

1. purpose—a mystery; possibilities
2. decoration
3. ceremonies to influence spiritual powers
4. Christian images in churches
5. function
6. prehistoric; Stone Age
7. Picasso's *Guernica*
8. tribal people moving to urban areas
9. art serving a practical function
10. Goya's painting *The Third of May, 1808*
11. Islamic designs and Arabic calligraphy
12. people from the Solomon Islands (figures on spears and boats to guide them)
13. assurance of success in hunting
14. the influence of traditional art on Picasso and Gauguin
15. Bambara people (headdresses to help crops grow)
16. Mexican social art
17. The effect of Japanese painting
18. Bakongo people (statues for prediction and protection)
19. worship of animal "god"

What Can We Learn from Art?

I.   Introduction: The Study of Art History

II. Cave Art

   A. _____

   B. _____

      1. _____

      2. _____

III. Art as an Expression of Political Views

   A. Goya's painting *The Third of May, 1808*

   B. _____

   C. _____

IV. Art as a Reflection of Religious Beliefs

   A. _____

   B. _____

V.   Traditional Art in Africa and the Pacific Islands

   A. _____

   B. Ceremonies to influence spiritual powers

      1. _____

      2. _____

      3. _____

VI. The Way People View Art

   A. _____

   B. _____

VII. Art as a Reflection of Change in Society

   A. _____

   B. _____

   C. _____

Here are some common connecting words that indicate a summary of material will follow.

in short	in conclusion	to sum up
in brief	in summary	as we've seen
the result is	thus/therefore	

9   Copy the sentences from the reading selection that begin with these connecting words. Then circle the number of the sentence that best expresses the main idea of the entire reading.

1. In short, _____

    _____

    _____

2. In summary, _____

    _____

    _____

3. Thus, _____

    _____

    _____

4. To sum up, _____

    _____

    _____

5. As we've seen, _____

    _____

    _____

6. In brief, _____

    _____

    _____

7. In conclusion, _____

    _____

    _____

8. The result is _____

    _____

    _____

10   **Checking Your Understanding.**   Turn back to Exercise 3 on page 163 and answer the question.

11   **Making Inferences.**   Complete each sentence by circling the letters of the information that the reading selection states or implies. More than one answer is possible.

1. Cave art _____.

   a. was created by full-time professional artists

   b. was created by people with great artistic ability

   c. was possibly created for religious reasons

   d. assured success in hunting

2. _____ expressed political opinions with pictures of people.

   a. The Spanish painter Goya

   b. Picasso

   c. Various Mexican artists

   d. Islamic painters

3. There are examples of religious images _____.

   a. on churches in Europe

   b. on Arab rugs and bowls

   c. in tribal ceremonies

   d. on headdresses

4. Traditional art might be used to _____.

   a. cover walls of large buildings

   b. help hunters and soldiers

   c. improve agriculture

   d. protect women and children

Discussing the Reading

12   In small groups, talk about your answers to these questions.

1. Tell about art in your culture. Describe typical works of art (paintings, statues, decorations on buildings, etc.). What is the function of art in your country? How do people view art?

2. Is there cave art in your country? If so, tell your group about it.

3. What kinds of art do you prefer? Why?

| **PART 2** | # Fashion: The Art of the Body |

1 **Skimming for Main Ideas.** The main idea is not always clearly expressed in a paragraph. Instead, the details may *imply* the main idea, which sums up all the information in the paragraph.

Example

> For various reasons, clothing of some type has been worn by human beings since the beginning of time. The Inuit (Eskimos) wear animal fur to protect them against the cold winter weather. Nomadic desert people wear long, loose clothing for protection against the sun and wind of the Sahara. But is clothing really essential for protection? Perhaps not. Scientists point out the absence of clothing among certain Indians of southern Chile, where the temperature is usually 43° F (7° C) and often colder. Similarly, the tribal people of Australia, where the weather is like that of the Sahara Desert, wear almost no clothing.

(The topic of the paragraph is *clothing*. The important *details* are that some groups wear clothing for protection against the weather, while others do not. Thus, the main idea of the paragraph is that protection is one function of clothing, but not an essential one.)

Read each paragraph quickly, without using a dictionary. To help you figure out the main idea, circle the letters of the correct answers to these questions. No. 1 has one answer; No. 2 has more than one; No. 3 has one.

Fashion: The Art of the Body

[A] The enormous and fascinating variety of clothing may express a person's status or social position. Several hundred years ago in Europe, Japan, and China, there were many highly detailed sumptuary laws—that is, strict regulations concerning how each social class could dress. In Europe, for example, only royal families could wear fur, purple silk, or gold cloth. In Japan, a farmer could breed silkworms, but he couldn't wear silk. In many societies, a lack of clothing indicated an absence of status. In ancient Egypt, for instance, children—who had

An outdoor café in Paris

no social status—wore no clothes until they were about twelve. These days, in most societies (especially in the West), rank or status is exhibited through regulation of dress only in the military, where the appearance or absence of certain metal buttons or stars signifies the dividing line between ranks. With this exception of the military, the divisions between different classes of society are becoming less clear. The clientele of a Paris café, for example, might include both working-class people and members of the highest society, but how can one tell the difference when everyone is wearing denim jeans?

1. What is the main topic of the paragraph?
   a. the military
   b. sumptuary laws
   c. uniforms
   d. status

2. What details about the topic does the paragraph provide?
   a. Strict laws in some countries used to regulate what people of each social class could wear.
   b. Rich people wear more beautiful clothing than poor people do.
   c. In many societies, the absence of clothing indicated an absence of status.
   d. Today, the divisions between social classes are becoming less clear from the clothing that people wear.

3. Which idea do all the answers to Nos. 1 and 2 have in common—that is, what is the main idea of the paragraph?
   a. Today, the differences between various social classes can be seen only in military uniforms.
   b. Laws used to regulate how people could dress.
   c. Clothing (or its absence) has usually indicated status or rank, but this is less true in today's world.
   d. Clothing has been worn for different reasons since the beginning of history.

[B]   Two common types of body decoration in tribal societies are tattooing and scarification. A tattoo is a design or mark made by putting a kind of dye (usually dark blue) into a cut in the skin. In scarification, dirt or ashes are put into the cuts instead of dye. In both of these cases, the result is a design that is unique to the person's tribe. Three lines on each side of a man's face identify him as a member of the Yoruba tribe of Nigeria. A complex geometric design on

a woman's back identifies her as Nuba—and also makes her more beautiful in the eyes of her people. In the 1990s, tattooing became increasingly popular among youth in urban Western societies. Unlike people in tribal cultures, these young people had no tradition of tattooing, except among sailors and criminals. To these young people, the tattoos were beautiful. But the tattoos were also a sign of rebellion against older, more conservative people in the culture and a form of identification with other youth similarly tattooed.

1.   What is the main topic of the paragraph?
     a.   the Yoruba people
     b.   geometric designs
     c.   dirt and ashes
     d.   body decoration

2.   What details about the topic does the paragraph provide?
     a.   Tattoos are more beautiful than scarification.
     b.   Tattoos and scarification indicate a person's tribe or social group.
     c.   The dye for tattooing comes from special plants.
     d.   Designs on a person's face or body are considered beautiful.

3.   Which idea includes all the details circled in No. 2—in other words, what is the main idea of the paragraph?
     a.   Everyone who wants to be beautiful should get a tattoo.
     b.   People decorate their bodies for the purposes of identification, beauty, and sometimes rebellion.
     c.   A tattoo is a design made by putting dark blue dye into cuts in the skin.
     d.   Men more often decorate their faces; women often decorate their backs.

[C]   In some societies, women overeat to become plump because large women are considered beautiful, while skinny ones are regarded as ugly. A woman's plumpness is also an indication of her family's wealth. In other societies, by contrast, a fat person is considered unattractive, so men and women eat little and try to remain slim. In many parts of the world, people lie in the sun for hours to darken their skin, while in other places light, soft skin is seen as attractive. People with gray hair often dye it black, whereas those with naturally dark hair often change its color to blond or green or purple.

1. What is the main topic of the paragraph?
    a. hair
    b. skin
    c. body shape
    d. body changes

2. What details about the topic does the paragraph provide?
    a. It is unhealthy to lose or gain too much weight.
    b. Some societies consider large people attractive; others, slim ones.
    c. Some people prefer dark hair or skin; others, light.
    d. Most wealthy people try to stay thin.

3. What is the main idea of the paragraph?
    a. Individuals and groups of people have different ideas about physical attractiveness.
    b. Lying in the sun darkens the skin.
    c. In some societies, thinness is an indication that a family is poor.
    d. Dark-skinned people usually have dark hair.

[D]   In the West, most people visit a dentist regularly for both hygiene and beauty. They use toothpaste and dental floss daily to keep their teeth clean. They have their teeth straightened, whitened, and crowned to make them more attractive to others in their culture. However, "attractive" has quite a different meaning in other cultures. In the past, in Japan, it was the custom for women to blacken, not whiten, the teeth. People in some areas of Africa and central Australia have the custom of filing the teeth to sharp points. And among the Makololo people of Malawi, the women wear a very large ring—a *pelele*—in their upper lip. As their chief once explained about *peleles*: "They are the only beautiful things women have. Men have beards. Women have none. What kind of person would she be without the *pelele*? She would not be a woman at all." While some people in modern urban societies think of tribal lip rings as unattractive and even "disgusting," other people—in Tokyo or New York or Rome—might choose to wear a small lip ring or to pierce their tongue and wear a ring through the hole.

1. What is the main topic of the paragraph?
    a. dentistry
    b. blackening or whitening the teeth
    c. changes to the human mouth
    d. *peleles* and beards

2. What details about the topic does the paragraph provide?
   a. White teeth are attractive to all cultures.
   b. In the West, people visit dentists and have their teeth straightened, whitened, and crowned.
   c. In some cultures, people blacken their teeth or file them to sharp points, and in other cultures young people wear lip rings or tongue rings.
   d. Makololo women wear a large ring in their upper lip.

3. What is the main idea of the paragraph?
   a. People can easily change the color or shape of their teeth.
   b. The word attractive has different meanings.
   c. The human mouth suffers change and abuse in many societies.
   d. Some methods of changing the appearance of the mouth are dangerous, but others are safe.

[E]   Body paint or face paint is used mostly by *men* in preliterate societies in order to attract good health or to ward off disease. It is a form of magic protection against the dangers of the world outside the village, where men have to go for the hunt or for war. When it is used as warpaint, it also serves to frighten the enemy, distinguish members of one's own group from the enemy, and give the men a sense of identity, of belonging to the group. Women have less need of body or face paint because they usually stay in the safety of the village. In modern societies, though, cosmetics are used mostly by *women,* who often feel naked, unclothed, without makeup when out in public—like a tribal hunter without his warpaint. One exception that serves to prove this rule is Victorian society in England and the United States, when women were excluded from public life. In this period, women wore little or no makeup.

Tribal man in face paint

Modern woman in "face paint"

1. What is the main topic of the paragraph?
   a. body and face paint
   b. men's warpaint
   c. modern women's cosmetics
   d. magic protection

2. What details about the topic does the paragraph provide?
   a. Body or face paint is usually worn by men in tribal societies.
   b. People wear body or face paint to make them more attractive.
   c. Makeup ("face paint") is usually worn by women in modern societies.
   d. When women are excluded from public life, they wear little or no makeup.

3. What is the main idea of the paragraph?
   a. Body paint gives men a sense of identity.
   b. Women in modern times wear makeup to be more beautiful.
   c. In the past, men wore face paint, but in modern times, women wear it.
   d. Body or face paint may be worn as a sort of protection by people who leave the home or village.

After You Read

2 **Making Inferences.**   On the short lines, put a check mark by the statements that you can infer from the example and the reading selection "Fashion: The Art of the Body." Do not check the other statements, even if you think they are true. On the line after each statement that you check, write the phrases from the section from which you inferred the information.

1. _____ All people wear clothing to keep warm.

   _____

   _____

2. _____ Fur provides warmth, while long, loose clothing is useful in hot weather.

   _____

   _____

3. _____ Rich people wear more clothing than poor people do.

   _____

   _____

4. _____ Social status might be less important now than it was in the past.

_____

_____

5. _____ Some methods of body beautification may be uncomfortable or painful.

_____

_____

6. _____ Body or face paint may make people feel protected.

_____

_____

7. _____ Women are more interested in looking good than men are.

_____

_____

8. _____ There are some similarities between tribal people and modern urban people in their views of body decoration.

_____

_____

3 Summarizing.   Choose one paragraph—A, B, C, D, or E. Write a short summary of it (two to three sentences). To write this summary, first make sure that you understand the paragraph well. Then choose the main idea and the most important details. In order to summarize this in your own words, *don't look at the original paragraph as you write.* When you finish writing, compare your summary with those of other students who summarized the same paragraph.

Discussing the Reading

4 In small groups, talk about your answers to these questions.

1. Why are people often unhappy with their bodies? Do you agree with their reasons for changing them?

2. What do you think of the methods of body beautification that are described in the reading selection? Why?

3. What methods are common in your culture? (makeup? tattoos? ear piercing? hair dyeing? etc.) What do you think of them?

**Cross-Cultural Note:
Beauty and the Past**

*In ancient Egypt, both rich and poor
people used many kinds of scented oils
to protect their skin from the sun and
wind and to keep it soft. These oils were
a mixture of plants and the fat of
crocodile, hippo, or cat. Many people
shaved their heads and wore wigs.
Other people, with their own hair, dyed
it black when it began to turn gray.
Men, women, and children all wore
kohl—black eye liner—both for beauty
and to protect their eyes from disease.
On special occasions, people wore
exquisite jewelry, especially necklaces and earrings, and on top of their wigs wore a white cone
made of sweetly scented ox fat. As the evening went on, the cone melted, and the fragrance
dripped down over their wigs, faces, and clothes.*

Talk It Over

Art and Beauty.   Here are some quotations about art and beauty. Discuss your
answers to each of these questions.

1. What does the quotation mean? (You might need to use a dictionary.)

2. Do you agree with it?

3. What are some proverbs or quotations about art or beauty in your
    language? Translate them into English and explain them.

- Less is more.—Robert Browning

- Beauty is in the eye of the beholder.—Margaret Hungerford

- Alas, after a certain age, every man is responsible for his own face.
  —Albert Camus

- Remember that the most beautiful things in the world are the most
  useless: peacocks and lilies, for instance.—John Ruskin

- Form follows function.—motto of the Bauhaus (a German school of
  design)

- Great artists have no country.—Alfred de Musset

Beyond the Text

Bring to class advertisements about beauty treatments and methods (hairstyling
salons, makeup, etc.). Discuss new vocabulary. Tell the class about the most
interesting ads and your opinions of them.

PART 3

Building Vocabulary and Study Skills

1   **Words with Similar Meanings.**   Although words with similar meanings can often be substituted for one another, they may have somewhat different definitions.

Examples

I'm taking a geography <u>course</u>. The <u>class</u> meets twice a week and there is a different <u>lesson</u> at each meeting.

(<u>course</u> = series of lessons on a subject; <u>class</u> = a meeting of a course or the students who are taking a course; <u>lesson</u> = a separate piece of material on a subject or the amount of teaching at one time)

The words in each of the following groups have similar meanings, but they are not exactly the same. Match the words with their definitions by writing the letters on the lines as in the examples. If necessary, check your answers in a dictionary.

1. _____ study   a. gain knowledge or skill in a subject

2. _*a*_ learn   b. make an effort to learn

3. _____ memorize   c. learn to know from memory

4. _____ provide   a. show; introduce

5. _____ present   b. present (something) so that it may be accepted

6. _*b*_ offer   c. give

7. _____ depict   a. show in the form of a picture

8. _____ indicate   b. point out; make known

9. _____ express   c. put (thoughts, etc.) into words

10. _____ target   a. objective; purpose

11. _____ goal   b. the place where someone is going

12. _____ destination   c. an object or mark someone tries
                                 to reach or hit

13. _____ merchandise   a. things that are made

14. _____ products   b. things that are bought and sold

15. _____ items   c. individual thing

2 The meaning of one word can *include* the meanings of many others.

Example

Beautiful art can be found in different kinds of <u>structures</u>: <u>churches</u>, <u>mosques</u>, and <u>palaces</u>.

(<u>Churches</u> and <u>mosques</u> are religious buildings, and <u>palaces</u> are buildings for royalty. The word <u>structures</u> can mean "buildings," so it includes the meanings of the three other words.)

In each of the following items, circle the one word that includes the meanings of the others. The first one is done as an example.

1. (art)   statue   painting

2. painter   designer   artist

3. actor   entertainer   musician

4. traveler   tourist   passenger

5. bus   subway   transportation

6. royalty   prince   king

7. Christianity   religion   Islam

8. murder   crime   theft

3 Sometimes words with similar meanings have different connotations (implied meanings, "feelings").

Examples

In some societies, women overeat to become <u>plump</u> because <u>large</u> women are considered beautiful. In other cultures, a <u>fat</u> person is considered ugly.

(The words <u>plump</u>, <u>large</u>, and <u>fat</u> all mean "over normal weight." To say someone is fat is an insult, however, while *plump* and *large* are more polite ways of referring to the same characteristic.)

Some dictionaries provide information on usage of words in different situations and on connotations of words with similar meanings. Read the dictionary entries on this page and complete the following exercises.

Write + before the words with positive connotations and – before the words with negative ones, as in the examples.

1. _____ slim

2. _____ emaciated

3. _____ skinny

4. _____ slender

5. _____ fat

6. _____ overweight

USAGE 1 **Thin** is a general word to describe people who have little or no fat on their bodies. If someone is thin in a pleasant way, we say they are **slim** or (less common) **slender,** but if they are too **thin** they are **skinny** (*infml*), **underweight,** or (worse of all) **emaciated:** *I wish I were as slim as you!\|She looks very thin/skinny/underweight after her illness.\|After weeks with little or no food, the prisoners were emaciated.* The opposite of **thin** in this sense is **fat,** but this is not polite. **Plump, overweight, heavy, chubby** (esp. of babies) and **matronly** (only of older women) are all more polite ways of saying the same things. A person who is very fat is **obese.** 2 Things that are long and **thin,** in the sense of having a short distance from one side to another, are **narrow** (opposite **wide**): *a narrow country road\|a long narrow room.*

beau·ti·ful /^{1}byu^{w}təfəl/ *adj* having beauty **-beautifully** adv

USAGE When used to describe a person's appearance, **beautiful** is a very strong word meaning "giving great pleasure to the senses." Its opposite is **ugly** or even stronger, **hideous. Plain** is a less *derogatory* way of saying **ugly. Pretty, handsome, good-looking,** and **attractive** all mean "pleasant to look at;" but **pretty** is only used of women and children, and **handsome** (usually) only of men. **Good-looking, handsome,** and **plain** are normally only used of people, but the other words can also be used of things: *a pretty garden/a hideous dress.*

4 Circle the words that have a polite connotation.

1. slim   3. plump   5. obese

2. emaciated   4. matronly   6. heavy

5 For each pair of words, circle the one with the stronger meaning. The first one is done as an example.

1. (beautiful)/pretty   4. ugly/plain

2. ugly/hideous   5. beautiful/good-looking

3. attractive/beautiful   6. unattractive/ugly

6 Circle the letters of *all* the words that are usually appropriate for each sentence.

1. He's a very __ _____ man.

   a. pretty

   b. handsome

   c. attractive

   d. ugly

2. What a _____ baby!

   a. beautiful

   b. handsome

   c. pretty

   d. good-looking

3. This is a very _____ garden.

   a. good-looking

   b. plain

   c. pretty

   d. attractive

7 Write words with meanings similar to the following words. Use your dictionary for help. Then write the lists of similar words on the board and discuss with your classmates differences in meanings, connotation, and usage.

1. woman   3. talk   5. old

2. thief   4. believe   6. small

8   Increasing Reading Speed.   The following exercises may help you make your eye movements faster and increase your reading speed. When your teacher tells you to begin each section, look at the word at the left of each line. Read across the line, from left to right. Circle the one word with the most *similar* meaning to that of the word at the left. At the end of each section, write down your time (the number of seconds it takes you to finish). Try to read faster with each section.

exam	culture	test	custom	identity	way
region	hunt	society	state	area	tribe
example	addition	instance	picture	difficulty	social
education	studies	school	memorize	requirement	hard
pleasant	frequent	luxurious	satisfaction	sickness	enjoyable

Time: _____

figure	art	painting	statue	mosque	design
gardening	suburbs	transportation	traffic	plants	yardwork
migrate	move	ancestor	nomadic	language	agriculture
predict	therapist	bargain	tourist	organize	foretell
battle	fight	reservation	land	court	rights

Time: _____

chance	provide	offering	presentation	opportunity	allow
rich	various	forest	expensive	wealthy	characteristic
various	different	kind	exist	groups	general
smog	sickness	problem	theory	downtown	pollution
psychologist	science	prove	therapist	artist	member

Time: _____

form	object	fact	shape	information	express
arabesque	picture	Arabic	design	dance	mosque
show	image	expression	smile	depict	match
discount	merchandise	decoration	bargain	geometric	cheap
power	political	government	war	view	strength

Time: _____

9 Follow the instructions for Exercise 8, but in each line that follows, circle the one word with the *opposite* meaning to the first word.

wonderful	advantageous	horror	result	terrible	luxurious
cities	suburbs	villages	continent	noise	entertainment
communal	group	desert	individual	absence	house
everyday	typical	essential	beliefs	unusual	quality
generally	specifically	result	therefore	thus	such

Time: _____

modern	marketing	traditional	value	economics	activity
birth	child	figure	anger	death	crime
objective	emotional	facts	sadness	reflect	history
criminal	soldier	faceless	symbol	victim	shoot
private	opinion	public	contrast	holy	image

Time: _____

valuable	beautiful	unique	useless	impossible	successful
elderly	young	people	senior	enthusiastic	ancestor
acquire	attractive	find	lose	action	win
worsen	produce	improve	influence	summarize	entire
identical	same	different	identify	similar	important

Time: _____

Focus on Testing

Using Analogies

A common activity in the vocabulary section of standardized tests is analogy. An analogy involves finding relationships and making comparisons. On a test, you show both your knowledge of vocabulary and your use of logic when you complete an analogy. An analogy on such a test has three words; the first two are related in some way. You need to (1) figure out the relationship between the two words and (2) add a fourth word that has the same relationship to the third word. Look at this analogy:

> failure:success::guilt:innocence

This means "Failure is related to success in the same way that guilt is related to innocence." (They are opposites.) On a test, you would need to supply the fourth word, *innocence*. Here are some other examples.

Analogy to Complete	Relationship of Words in Each Pair	Possible Answers
1. ability:capacity::salary:	synonyms	pay; wages
2. poverty:poor::wealth:	noun to adjective	rich; wealthy
3. loaf:bread::ear:	quantity of food	corn

Complete these analogies with words of your own. Try to do this without a dictionary. (On a test, you will not be able to use a dictionary.) When you finish, compare your answers with those of your classmates. Explain the relationship in each analogy.

1. beautiful:ugly::cheap: _expanze_ _____

2. prey:predator::deer: _____

3. addicted:addiction::compulsive: _compulsion_ _____

4. employer:employee::teacher: _student_ _____

5. city:urban::countryside: _rural_ _____

6. enormous:big::tiny: _small_ _____

7. smog:pollution::radon: _toxin, poison_ _____

8. Spain:Europe::Canada: _North America_ _____

9. archaeologist:the past::economist: _future, money_ _____

10. hug:embrace::grin: _smile_ _____

PART 4	# Reading in the Real World

1 **Scanning for Information.**   The following passage is an article from *Time* magazine. It combines adventure with science and tells about a discovery of cave art. First, read the questions that follow the article. Then read the article, marking the answers to the questions as you find them. Don't worry if you don't understand every word. Work as quickly as you can, as you would on a test.

Window on the Stone Age

At the base of a cliff in the Ardeche region in southeastern France last December, the three middle-aged spelunkers felt a breeze wafting from a pile of rock and debris. "That was a sign that there was a cave beneath it," recalls Jean-Marie Chauvet. With his companions, Chauvet cleared away an opening, then wriggled through a tunnel into a complex of large caves.

Then, in the pale glow of their head lamps, the explorers noticed two red lines on a cavern wall. Chauvet, a government employee who oversees the protection of the many historically important caves in the region, recognized the markings as "characteristic of the Stone Age." What he did not immediately realize—and the world did not know until the French Culture Ministry announced it last week—was that they had discovered an archaeological trove that may rival even the fabled drawings on the cave walls at Lascaux in France and Altamira in Spain. The spelunkers had found an extraordinarily clear window on prehistoric life.

Restraining their curiosity, the trio crawled back outside and resealed the tunnel entrance. "Not only to keep people out," Chauvet explains, "but to return the airflow to what it had been before; a change in the interior climate could ruin whatever was inside." Six days later they returned with better lighting and plastic sheets that they spread about to avoid disturbing artifacts on the cavern floors.

Probing deeper into the cavern system, they began coming upon exquisite, intricately detailed wall paintings and engravings of animals, as well as numerous images of human hands, some in red, others in black pigment. "I thought I was dreaming," says Chauvet. "We were all covered with goose pimples."

Artful Stampede: Prehistoric horses, battling bison, a rhino, wild cattle and a miniature elephant compete for space on a crowded cavern wall.

The art was in pristine condition, apparently undisturbed for up to 20,000 years, as was other evidence of the ancient artists' presence: flint knives, mounds of clay used for making paint, and charred fire pits.

Photographs of the Stone Age art show images of lions, bison, deer, bears, horses and some 50 woolly rhinos. "These paintings are more beautiful than those in Lascaux," says Patrice Beghain, the regional head of cultural affairs. "There is a sense of rhythm and texture that is truly remarkable." One mural shows several horses apparently charging—in a Stone Age mismatch—toward two rhinos.

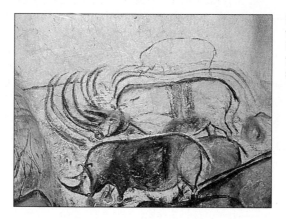

Rhinoceros: 50 drawings of woolly rhinos were discovered in the Chauvet cave, more than in all other Stone Age sites combined.

A few species represented on the walls of the Chauvet cave, as it has already been named, had never before been seen in prehistoric artwork: an owl engraved in rock and a panther depicted in red pigment. The image of a hyena, also painted in red, is only the second one discovered in Stone Age caves.

Of particular interest to Jean Clottes, France's foremost expert on prehistoric rock art, is the fact that, in contrast to previous cave artwork, images of predatory and dangerous species—bears, lions, rhinos, a panther and a hyena—far outnumber the horses, bison, deer and mammoths usually hunted by Stone Age people. "The paintings in this cave," he says, "will force us to change how we interpret Stone Age art."

Bear and Panther: While bruins were among the common subjects of cave artists, this image of the big cat is the first one ever found.

Beghain is particularly struck by the skull of a bear perched on a stone near a wall adorned by an ursine image. "What is significant," says the official, "is that some 17,000 to 20,000 years ago, a human being decided to put it in that particular place for a particular reason. I think it fair to assume that the bear did not self-decapitate on that spot to intrigue us." Was this an altar for some Paleolithic ceremony?

Stung by lessons learned at Altamira and Lascaux, where initial unrestricted access to the caves obliterated archaeological clues and led to the rapid deterioration of artwork, the French Culture Ministry has put the Chauvet cave off limits to all but a handful of experts and installed video surveillance cameras and police guards at the entrance. "Our goal," says Beghain, "is to keep the cave in this virgin state so that research can, in theory, continue indefinitely."

No further research is needed to establish one fact about the Chauvet cave art: it was created by artists of remarkable talent. "I remember standing in front of the paintings of the horses facing the rhinos and being profoundly moved by the artistry," says Clottes. "Tears were running down my cheeks. I was witnessing one of the world's great masterpieces."

Source: Leon Jaroff, "Window on the Stone Age," from *Time* v145 n4 (Jan 30, 1995) p80(2). Copyright © Time Inc. 1995.

---

2 **Checking Your Understanding.**   Complete each sentence by circling the letter of *one* answer.

1. The depictions in the Chauvet cave include _____.

   a. paintings of animals

   b. images of human hands

   c. a few species never before seen in prehistoric art

   d. a and b

   e. a, b, and c

2. The word *pigment* (line 23) probably means _____.

   a. rock

   b. paint

   c. caves

   d. a kind of animal

   e. image

3. Jean Clottes _____.

   a. discovered the cave

   b. is France's leading expert on prehistoric rock art

   c. believes that the painters of the Chauvet cave were great artists

   d. a and b

   e. b and c

4. Something different about this cave from other caves with art is the fact that _____.

   a. there are images of predatory and dangerous animals

   b. the people who used the cave hunted bears, lions, and rhinos

   c. there are more images of predatory and dangerous animals than of other animals usually hunted in the Stone Age

   d. there are more images of horses, bison, deer, and mammoths than images of predatory and dangerous animals

   e. none of the above

5. Predatory animals probably _____.

   a. hunt other animals

   b. include bears and lions

   c. are more numerous than horses, bison, deer, and mammoths

   d. all of the above

   e. a and b

6. In the Chauvet cave, they found the skull (bones of the head) of a bear that _____.

   a. was on a stone

   b. a human being had moved for a specific reason

   c. was part of a Paleolithic ceremony

   d. a and b

   e. a, b, and c

7. To protect the art in this cave, _____.

   a. the spelunkers sealed the entrance after they made the discovery

   b. the spelunkers covered the floor with plastic sheets

   c. only experts may now enter

   d. there are video cameras and police guards

   e. all of the above

3   **Distinguishing Fact from Theory.**   Which of the following statements are facts, according to the article? Write *fact* on the lines. Which are theories? Write *theory* on the lines.

1. _____   A small wind coming from a pile of rocks might indicate a cave under the rocks.

2. _____   The Chauvet cave is more important than Lascaux in France and Altamira in Spain.

3. _____   The art was in good condition when they discovered it.

4. _____   Nobody had disturbed this art for up to 20,000 years.

5. _____   The artists who created the paintings in the Chauvet cave had remarkable talent.

Video Activities: The Coffee Lover

Before You Watch.   Discuss the following questions in a group.

1. Do you like to drink coffee? Why?
2. How would you feel if you drank ten cups of coffee every day?
3. As far as you know, does coffee cause health problems for some people?

Watch.   Discuss the following questions with your classmates.

1. How many cups of coffee does Kat drink each day?
2. Does she plan to stop drinking coffee?

Watch Again.   Read the statements below. Decide if they are true (T) or false (F). Then watch the video again to check your answers.

1. _____   Kat has worked in the same place for 45 years.

2. _____   Kat doesn't drink coffee in the evening.

3. _____   Scientists now believe that coffee raises cholesterol levels.

4. _____   If you drink too much coffee, it can make your hands shake.

5. _____   If your heart is weak, drinking coffee will make it stronger.

After You Watch.   Finding Information about Coffee.

1. Use a dictionary to find the origin of the word "coffee." What language does it come from?

2. Divide the class into small groups. The first group to find the answers to all the questions below is the winner.

   ■ What kind of plant is coffee?

   ■ Where did this plant originate?

   ■ In what part of the world was coffee first used as a drink?

   ■ When and why did coffee become popular in North America?

   ■ How many varieties of coffee are there in the world?

Chapter 9

New Frontiers

PART 1   # The Human Brain—New Discoveries

Before You Read

1   **Getting Started.**   Look at the diagram and photos and answer these questions in small groups.

1.   Which areas of the brain might a person use to compose music? To throw a ball? To paint a picture?

2.   If you feel cold and want to put on a sweater, which area of the brain is probably active?

3.   It has been observed that little boys and little girls play, speak, and act differently from each other. Do you think these differences might be caused by differences in the brain?

4.   Which person might be in better health—the man in photo A or one of the men in photo B? Why do you think so?

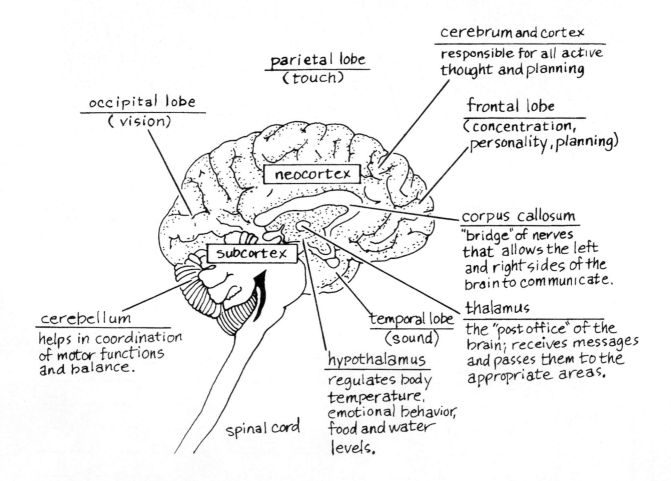

parietal lobe
(touch)

cerebrum and cortex
responsible for all active
thought and planning

occipital lobe
(vision)

frontal lobe
(concentration,
personality, planning)

neocortex

corpus callosum
"bridge" of nerves
that allows the left
and right sides of the
brain to communicate.

subcortex

thalamus
the "post office" of the
brain; receives messages
and passes them to the
appropriate areas.

cerebellum
helps in coordination
of motor functions
and balance.

temporal lobe
(sound)

hypothalamus
regulates body
temperature,
emotional behavior,
food and water
levels.

spinal cord

A.

B.

C.

D.

2   **Preparing to Read.**   In academic reading, it often helps to survey (get an overview of) the material before you begin to read it. Photos or diagrams provide useful first clues to the contents. In addition, some selections contain subheads, or lines that stand out, which give quick information about the reading. Survey the first reading selection quickly. Write the subheads here.

_____

_____

_____

_____

_____

_____

_____

_____

3   Asking yourself questions before and during reading often helps you understand and remember the material. Look again at the diagram on page 194 and at the subheads. Then check (✔) the questions on the following list that you think, from your surveying, the reading selection might answer.

1. _____ What is the function of different parts of the brain?

2. _____ How are human brains different from animal brains?

3. _____ Why do some people seem to be more creative than others?

4. _____ What is the difference between the left and right side of the brain?

5. _____ Are the happiest memories of most people's lives from their childhood?

6. _____ Is it possible to have a memory of something that never happened?

7. _____ How can we improve our memories?

8. _____ Are teenagers' brains different from adults' brains?

9. _____ How do men and women communicate with each other?

10. _____ How does the brain influence a person's ability with music?

11. _____ Can the brain cause people to get sick or become well?

4   **Vocabulary Preview.**   Briefly look over this list of words and expressions from the reading that follows. Which words do you already know? For the ones that you don't know, *don't* use a dictionary. Try to understand them from the reading.

Nouns	**Verbs**	**Adjectives**
hemisphere	exposed	consonant
neuroscientists	rotate	dissonant
origin	repressed	mature
insights		wired
maturation		
intuition		
prose		
colleague		
insomnia		

Read

5 **Reading About the Brain.** As you read the following selection, think about the answers to the questions that you checked in Exercise 3. Read the selection quickly. Do not use a dictionary. Then do the exercises that follow the reading.

The Human Brain—New Discoveries

Parts of the Brain

[A] Most of us learn basic facts about the human brain in our middle or high school biology classes. We study the subcortex, the "old brain," which is found in the brains of most animals and is responsible for basic functions such as breathing, eating, drinking, and sleeping. We learn about the neocortex, the "new brain," which is unique to humans and is where complex brain activity takes place. We find that the cerebrum, which is responsible for all active thought, is divided into two parts, or hemispheres. The left hemisphere, generally, manages the right side of the body; it is responsible for logical thinking. The right hemisphere manages the left side of the body; this hemisphere controls emotional, creative, and artistic functions. And we learn that the corpus callosum is the "bridge" that connects the two hemispheres. Memorizing the names for parts of the brain might not seem thrilling to many students, but new discoveries in brain function *are* exciting. Recent research is shedding light on creativity, memory, maturity, gender, and the relationship between mind and body.

Left Brain/Right Brain: Creativity

[B] Psychologists agree that most of us have creative ability that is greater than what we use in daily life. In other words, we can be more creative than we realize! The problem is that we use mainly *one* hemisphere of our brain—the left. From childhood, in school, we're taught reading, writing, and mathematics; we are exposed to very little music or art. Therefore, many of us might not "exercise" our right hemisphere much, except through dreams, symbols, and those wonderful insights in which we suddenly find the answer to a problem that has been bothering us —and do so without the need for logic. Can we be taught to use our right hemisphere more? Many experts believe so. Classes at some schools and books (such as *The Inner Game of Tennis* and *Drawing on the Right Side of the Brain*) claim to help people to "silence" the left hemisphere and give the right a chance to work.

Memory—True or False?

[C] In the 1980s in the United States, there were many cases of adults who suddenly remembered, with the help of a psychologist, things that had happened to them in childhood. These memories had been repressed—held back—for many years. Some of these newly discovered memories have sent people to prison. As people remember crimes (such as murder or rape) that they saw or experienced as children, the police have re-opened and investigated old criminal cases. In fact, over 700 cases have been filed that are based on these repressed memories.

[D]   However, studies in the 1990s suggested that many of these might be *false* memories. At a 1994 conference at Harvard Medical School, neuroscientists discussed how memory is believed to work. It is known that small pieces of a memory (sound, sight, feeling, and so on) are kept in different parts of the brain;

the limbic system, in the middle of the brain, pulls these pieces together into one complete memory. But it's certain that people can "remember" things that have never happened. Even a small *suggestion* can leave a piece of memory in the brain. Most frightening, according to Dr. Michael Nash of the University of Tennessee, is that "there may be no structural difference" in the brain between a false memory and a true one.

The Teen Brain

[E] Parents of teenagers have always known that there is something, well, *different* about the teen years. Some parents claim that their teenage children belong to a different species. Until recently, neuroscience did not support this belief. The traditional belief was that by the age of 8 to 12, the brain was completely mature. However, very recent studies provide evidence that the brain of a teenager differs from that of both children and adults. According to Jay Giedd of the National Institute of Mental Health, "Maturation does not stop at age 10, but continues into the teen years" and beyond. In fact, Giedd and his colleagues found that the corpus callosum "continues growing into your 20s." Because, it is believed, the corpus callosum is involved in self-awareness and intelligence, the new studies imply that teens may not be as fully self-aware or as intelligent as they will be later. Other researchers, at McLean Hospital in Massachusetts, have found that teenagers are not able (as adults are) to "read" emotions on people's faces.

Differences in Male and Female Brains

[F] Watch a group of children as they play. You'll probably notice that the boys and girls play differently, speak differently, and are interested in different things. When they grow into men and women, the differences do not disappear. Many scientists are now studying the origins of these gender differences. Some are searching for an explanation in the human brain. Some of their findings are interesting. For example, they've found that more men than women are left-handed; this reflects the dominance of the brain's right hemisphere. By contrast, more women listen equally with both ears while men listen mainly with the right ear. Men are better at reading a map without having to rotate it. Women are better at reading the emotions of people in photographs.

[G]   One place to look for an explanation of gender differences is in the hypothalamus, just above the brain stem. This controls anger, thirst, hunger, and sexual desire. One recent study shows that there is a region in the hypothalamus that is larger in heterosexual men than it is in women and homosexual men. Another area of study is the corpus callosum, the thick group of nerves that allows the right and left hemispheres of the brain to communicate with each other. The corpus callosum is larger in women than in men. This might explain the mystery of "female intuition," which is supposed to give women greater ability to "read" and understand emotional clues.

Wired for Music?

[H] It might seem logical to believe that our appreciation of music is *learned*—that nurture, not nature, determines this. However, it is now clear that nature also plays a role; recent studies indicate that the human brain is "wired" for music. At the University of Toronto, Canada, psychologists have been studying infants

age 6–9 months. Surprisingly, these babies smile when researchers play con-
sonant (pleasant) music, but they appear to hate dissonant music. As adults,
most people can remember only a few poems or pieces of prose but have the
capacity to remember at least *dozens* of musical tunes and to recognize hundreds more. Even more interesting, perhaps, is the possibility that music might
actually improve some forms of intelligence. A 1999 study proves that music can
help children do better at math—not, oddly, other subjects, just math. It is probably not surprising that much of the brain activity that involves music takes place
in the temporal lobes. It may be more surprising to learn that the corpus callosum might also be involved. Researchers at Beth Israel Deaconess Medical
Center in Boston have discovered that the front part of the corpus callosum is
actually larger in musicians than in nonmusicians.

The Mystery of the Mind–Body Relationship

[I] There is more and more evidence every day to prove that our minds and bodies
are closely connected. Negative emotions, such as loneliness, depression, and
helplessness, are believed to cause a higher rate of sickness and death. Similarly, it's possible that positive thinking can help people remain in good physical
health or become well faster after an illness. Although some doctors are doubtful
about this, most accept the success of new therapies (e.g., relaxation and
meditation) that help people with problems such as ulcers, high blood pressure,
insomnia (sleeplessness), and migraine headaches.

After You Read

6 **Getting the Main Ideas.**   Write T on the lines before the statements that are true,
according to the reading. Write F on the lines before the statements that are false.
Write I on the lines before the statements that are impossible to know from the
reading.

1. _____ Different parts of the brain control different activities or parts
   of the body.

2. _____ Most people probably don't use all their creative ability.

3. _____ Newly discovered memories from childhood are false memories.

4. _____ The human brain is mature by the age of twelve.

5. _____ There is no real difference between the brains of males and those
   of females.

6. _____ Music appears to be the result of education alone.

7. _____ Emotions may affect people's physical health.

Focus on Testing

Getting Meaning from Context

On the reading section of standardized exams, there is, of course, no opportunity to use a dictionary. Such exams are testing your ability to guess meaning from the context. Often, you need more than the information in one sentence in order to figure out what a word means. You need to consider the entire paragraph. Take this practice test. Guess the meaning of the underlined words. You may look back at the reading selection "The Human Brain—New Discoveries," but don't use a dictionary.

1. In Paragraph B, "We are <u>exposed</u> to very little music or art" probably means ____.
    a. We are not often in concert halls or museums.
    b. We are taught a little music and art.
    c. Music and art are uncovered.
    d. Music and art are not taught much.

2. In Paragraph B, <u>insights</u> are ____.
    a. dreams that we have while we're sleeping
    b. moments when we suddenly understand something
    c. logical moments
    d. vision

3. In Paragraph C, the two meanings of the word <u>cases</u> (in lines 1 and 6) are ____.
    a. examples and situations
    b. memories and crimes
    c. examples and events that need police attention
    d. situations and people who murder or rape

4. In Paragraph F, <u>rotate</u> probably means ____.
    a. read   c. understand
    b. look at   d. turn

5. In Paragraph G, <u>intuition</u> is ____.
    a. mystery   c. the power of understanding without logic
    b. the ability to read   d. female emotion

6. The word <u>read</u>, as it is used in Paragraphs E and G, probably means ____.
    a. understand the meaning of   c. show
    b. understand written language   d. see

7. In Paragraph H, <u>wired</u> probably means ____.
    a. with electrical wires   c. tense with excitement
    b. musical   d. programmed or equipped

8. In Paragraph H, <u>prose</u> is probably ____.
    a. poetry   c. language that is not poetic
    b. songs   d. music without words

7 **Distinguishing Facts from Theories.**   As you saw in Chapter 7, certain words or expressions in affirmative statements usually indicate the existence of facts—that is, information that has been proven accurate. Here are some more:

know	sure	prove
show	objective	scientific
clear	certain	positive

Other words can indicate theories—that is, ideas that are believed by some people but have not been proven to be true. Here are some:

think	subjective	doubt	possibly
(dis)agree	likely	possible	probably
claim	imply	theorize	

8   On the line, write *fact* or *theory* for each statement, according to the presentation of the information in the reading selection "The Human Brain—New Discoveries." (You'll need to look back at the selection for words that indicate fact or theory.)

1. _____   Most of us have creative ability that is greater than what we use in daily life.

2. _____   Many of us don't "exercise" our right hemisphere much.

3. _____   We can be taught to use our right hemisphere more.

4. _____   Some books help people "silence" the left hemisphere and use the right hemisphere.

5. _____   Over 700 cases have been filed that are based on newly discovered memories.

6. _____   Many newly discovered memories are false.

7. _____   Small pieces of memory are kept in different parts of the brain.

8. _____   People "remember" things that have never happened.

9. _____   There is no structural difference between a false memory and a true one.

10. _____   The brain of a teenager differs from that of both children and adults.

11. _____   Teens are not as fully self-aware as adults are.

12. _____   There is a region in the hypothalamus that is larger in heterosexual men than in women and homosexual men.

13. _____   Women have a greater ability to understand emotional clues because they have a larger corpus callosum than men do.

14. _____   Music can help children do better at math.

15. _____   Our minds and bodies are closely connected.

16. _____   Negative emotions cause higher rates of sickness.

17. _____   Positive emotions can help people remain in good physical health.

9 **Checking Your Understanding.**   Turn back to Exercise 3 on page 196 and answer the questions that are answered in the reading selection.

PART 2

Personality—Nature or Nurture?

---

1 **Skimming for Main Ideas.**   Read each paragraph quickly, without using a dictionary. To figure out the main idea, circle the letters of all the correct answers to the questions that follow. Then combine the answers to complete a sentence or two that express the main idea. Answers for Paragraph A are given as examples.

Personality—Nature or Nurture?

[A] The nature/nurture question is not a new one. Its roots go back at least several hundred years. In the 1600s, the British philosopher John Locke wrote that a newborn infant was a "blank slate" on which his or her education and experience would be "written." In other words, Locke believed that environment alone determined each person's identity. In the 1700s, the French philosopher Jean Jacques Rousseau claimed that "natural" characteristics were more important. Today, we realize that both play a role. The question now is, to what degree? To answer this question, researchers are studying identical twins, especially those who grew up in different environments.

1. What is the one main topic of the paragraph?
    a. John Locke
    b. Jean Jacques Rousseau
    c. newborn infants
    (d.) the nature/nurture question
    e. identical twins

2. What details about the topic does the paragraph provide?
    a. People have just recently begun to discuss the nature/nurture question.
    (b.) John Locke believed in "nurture."
    (c.) Jean Jacques Rousseau believed in "nature."
    (d.) Today, we know that both nature and nurture determine a person's identity.
    (e.) Researchers are studying identical twins to learn the degree to which nature and nurture determine personal characteristics.

3. The main idea of the paragraph is that <u>both nature and nurture play</u>
    <u>a role in determining a person's identity.</u>

[B] Jim Lewis and Jim Springer are identical twins who were separated five weeks after birth. They grew up in different families and didn't know about each other's existence. They were reunited at the age of thirty-nine. It is not surprising that they were physically alike—the same dark hair, the same height and weight. They both had high blood pressure and very bad headaches. But they also moved in the same way and made the same gestures. They both hated baseball. They both drank the same brand of beer, drove the same make of car, and spent their vacations on the same small beach in Florida. They had both married women named Linda, gotten divorced, and then married women named Betty. Studies of these and other separated twins indicate that genetics (biology) plays a significant role in determining personal characteristics and behavior.

1. What is the one main topic of the paragraph?
   a. a reunion
   b. twins
   c. similarities in twins who grew up in different environments
   d. genetics
   e. personal characteristics and behavior

2. What details about the topic does the paragraph provide?
   a. Jim Lewis and Jim Springer were identical twins who grew up together.
   b. Jim Lewis and Jim Springer were identical twins who grew up separately.
   c. They have similar physical characteristics, interests, and choice of specific products.
   d. They married the same woman.
   e. Their example indicates the significance of genetics in determination of identity.

3. The main idea of the paragraph is that _____

   _____

[C] Various research centers are studying identical twins in order to discover the "heritability" of behavioral characteristics—that is, the degree to which a trait is due to genes ("nature") instead of environment. They have reached some startling conclusions. One study found, for example, that optimism and pessimism are both very much influenced by genes, but only optimism is affected by environment, too. According to another study, genes influence our coffee consumption, but not consumption of tea. Anxiety (nervousness and worry) seems to be 40 to 50 percent heritable. Another study tells us that happiness does not depend much on money or love or professional success; instead, it is 80 percent heritable! Among the traits that appear to be largely heritable are shyness, attraction to danger (thrill seeking), choice of career, and religious belief.

1. What is the one main topic of the paragraph?
    a. research centers
    b. optimism and pessimism
    c. behavioral characteristics
    d. happiness
    e. heritability of behavioral characteristics
2. What details about the topic does the paragraph provide?
    a. Researchers want to understand "heritability."
    b. Researchers are studying identical twins.
    c. Most behavioral characteristics are the result of genes, not environment.
    d. A person who has money, love, and success will probably be happy.
    e. Examples of characteristics that are heritable to some degree are optimism, pessimism, happiness, thrill seeking, and choice of career.

3. The main idea of the paragraph is that _____

    _____

[D]   It is not easy to discover the genes that influence personality. The acid that carries genetic information in every human cell, DNA, contains just four chemicals: adenine, cytosine, guanine, and thymine. But a single gene is "spelled out" by perhaps a million combinations. As the Human Genome Project (which provided a "map" of human genes) was nearing completion in the spring of 2000, there were a number of newspaper headlines about specific discoveries: "Gene Linked to Anxiety," "Gay Gene!" and "Thrill Seeking Due to Genetics." The newspaper articles led people to believe that a single gene is responsible for a certain personality trait, in the same way a single gene can be responsible for a physical characteristic or disease. However, one gene alone cannot *cause* people to become anxious or homosexual or thrill seeking. Instead, many genes work together, and they *do* direct the combination of chemicals in the body. These chemicals, such as dopamine and serotonin (which affect a person's mood) have a significant influence on personality.

1. What is the one main topic of the paragraph?
    a. the Human Genome Project
    b. the effect of genes on personality
    c. chemicals
    d. DNA
    e. thrill seeking

2. What details about the topic does the paragraph provide?
    a. It's difficult to find which genes influence personality.
    b. A single gene is responsible for each personality trait such as thrill seeking.
    c. Many genes work together.
    d. Genes direct the combination of chemicals in the body.
    e. Chemicals have a significant influence on personality.

3. The main idea of the paragraph is that _____

    _____

[E]   If, indeed, personality traits are, on average, about 50 percent heritable, then environment still plays an important role. Unlike other animals, human beings have choice. If our genes "program" us to be anxious, we can choose a low-stress lifestyle or choose to meditate or do relaxation exercises. But because of the powerful influence of genes, most psychologists believe that there is a limit to what we can *choose* to do. Thomas Bouchard, a psychologist and the director of one twin study, says that parents should not push children in directions that go against their nature. "The job of a parent," he says, "is to look for a kid's natural talents and then provide the best possible environment for them."

1. What is the one main topic of the paragraph?
    a. the role of environment
    b. personality traits
    c. anxiety
    d. psychologists
    e. what parents should do

2. What details about the topic does the paragraph provide?
    a. Environment still plays an important role.
    b. Human beings have choice.
    c. Human beings can choose to do anything they want.
    d. Psychologists say that parents should not push children against their nature.
    e. Parents should provide their child with the best environment for the child's natural talents.

3. The main idea of the paragraph is that _____

    _____

After You Read

2 **Making Inferences.**   On the short lines, put a check mark next to each statement that you can infer from the reading selection. Do not check the other statements, even if you think they are true. On the line after each statement that you check, write the phrases from the selection from which you inferred the information.

1. _____ The philosophical question of nature/nurture is an old one.

_____

_____

2. _____ The environment in which Jim Springer and Jim Lewis grew up had no effect on their behavior or personality.

_____

_____

3. _____ The goal of twin studies is to determine the amount of influence from genes and the amount from education and experiences.

_____

_____

4. _____ Our possibility of being happy is mostly a result of our genes—not our situation in life.

_____

_____

5. _____ A single gene determines each personality characteristic.

_____

_____

6. _____ The genetic contribution to personality is complicated.

_____

_____

7. _____ Human beings are able to change their genetics.

_____

_____

Talk It Over

Genes for Crime? It is highly possible that there is a genetic link or contribution to violence or criminality. In other words, our genes may contribute to the possibility that we will become a thief, murderer, or other type of criminal.

Psychologist David Lykken believes that people who want to become parents should be tested and given a license. If both the man and the woman have genes for violence or criminality, they should not be allowed to have a baby. He says that this will reduce crime in society. What do you think?

Beyond the Text

New discoveries in genetics—many due to twin studies—appear very frequently these days. Search the Internet for the most recent discovery. Share the information with the class. Discuss the information and any new vocabulary.

PART 3

Building Vocabulary and Study Skills

---

1 **Words with Similar Meanings.** The words in each of the following groups have similar meanings, but they are not exactly the same. Match the words with their definitions by writing the letters on the lines. If necessary, check your answers in a dictionary.

1. _____ brain   a. a way of thinking or feeling

2. _____ mind   b. the ability to remember

3. _____ memory   c. an organ of the body that controls thought and feeling

4. _____ equipment   a. an instrument

5. _____ machine   b. the things that are needed for an activity

6. _____ device   c. a manufactured instrument that needs power (e.g., electricity) in order to work

7. _____ insight   a. a way of thinking with formal methods

8. _____ knowledge   b. understanding that comes from experience and learning

9. _____ logic   c. the power of using one's mind (especially the right brain) to understand something suddenly

10. _____ colleague   a. a person of equal status or age

11. _____ peer   b. a person who works in the same place as another

12. _____ co-worker   c. a person who works in the same profession as another

2 **Categories (Content Areas).** It often helps to learn words in groups (words with the same stem, words with similar meanings, words with opposite meanings, etc.). One method of grouping words is to put them together in categories, such as people, animals, buildings, and so on. One kind of category is a "content area"—the subject with which all the words are associated.

Example

The following are words associated with the content area of science: *laboratory, neuroscientist, subjects, experiment*

Cross out the word in each line that does not belong, as in the example. Write the category or content area of the words that belong together.

1. genes   ~~nurture~~   nature   biology

   genetics _____

2. infant   baby   newborn   child

   _____

3. doctor   neuroscientist   biologist   musician

   _____

4. creativity   cerebrum   hypothalamus   corpus callosum

   _____

5. drinking   breaking   writing   eating

   _____

6. meditation   disease   insomnia   headache

   _____

7. height   eye color   weight   anxiety

   _____

8. reading   writing   mathematics   dreams

   _____

3 **Word Roots and Affixes.** It is often possible to guess the meanings of new words from word roots (also called "stems") and affixes (prefixes and suffixes). There is a list of many affixes on page 149. Here are some more word roots and affixes and their meanings.

Prefixes	Meanings
a-, an-	no, without
ante-	before
micro-	small
poly-	many

Suffixes	Meanings
-ism	belief in; act or practice
-ist	a person who believes in or performs a certain action

Word Roots	Meanings
anthro, anthropo	man, human
ced	go, move
chrom	color
chron	time
graph	write, writing
hetero	different
homo	same
metr, meter	measure; an instrument for measuring
morph	form
phil	love
psych	mind
somn	sleep
sphere	round; ball-shaped
tele	far
theo, the	god

Without using a dictionary, guess the meaning of each underlined word. Use the list of word roots and affixes. (Not all the underlined words are common.)

1. It is believed that an earthquake <u>anteceded</u> the fire.

    a. caused   d. put out; worked against

    b. happened after   e. was caused by

    c. happened before

2. There were some <u>amorphous</u> clouds in the sky.

    a. without form or shape   d. related to rain

    b. thick and dark   e. bright white

    c. beautiful

3. Many ancient peoples were <u>polytheists</u>.

    a. very well educated

    b. people with many culture centers

    c. people who studied many languages

    d. people who believed in many gods

    e. people who believed in having several wives

4. Movies often <u>anthropomorphize</u> creatures from other planets.

    a. study

    b. give human form or characteristics to

    c. present in a terrible way

    d. depict

    e. try to imagine

5. They wore <u>polychromatic</u> body paint.

    a. beautiful   d. made of natural dyes

    b. symbolic   e. of many colors

    c. complex

6. My teacher didn't appreciate my <u>heterography</u>.

    a. talking a lot in class

    b. different ideas in the speech that I gave in class

    c. logic

    d. spelling that was different from the rule

    e. answers on my geography examination

7. He sometimes has a problem with <u>somnambulism</u>.

   a. sleepwalking   d. breathing

   b. drinking   e. anxiety

   c. lying

8. He used a <u>telemeter</u>.

   a. instrument for seeing something very small

   b. instrument for finding directions

   c. instrument for measuring time

   d. instrument for measuring how far away an object is

   e. instrument for measuring a person's level of anxiety

PART 4   Reading in the Real World

1 **Summarizing a Passage.**   So far in this book you've written summaries of single paragraphs. Here are some suggestions for summarizing a longer piece—in this case, an article.

■ Begin by marking the entire article. Mark the main ideas and important details.

■ Make sure that you truly understand the article. It's not possible to write a good summary of something that you don't understand.

■ In writing a summary, use your own words. Do not simply copy from the article. To use your own words, follow these steps:
   1. Change sentence structure whenever possible. For example, change the active voice to the passive voice or the passive to the active.
   2. Use synonyms whenever possible.
   3. Do not try to find synonyms for technical terms or for words for which there is no synonym.

■ Remember that summarizing is not translation. It's usually easier to write a good summary if you put the original aside and not look at it as you write.

Read this article and mark it as you read. When you finish, compare your markings with those of your classmates.

The Bilingual Brain

When Karl Kim immigrated to the United States from Korea as a teenager ten years ago, he had a hard time learning English. Now he speaks it fluently, and recently he had a unique opportunity to see how our brains adapt to a second language. Kim is a graduate student in the lab of Joy Hirsch, a neuroscientist at Memorial Sloan-Kettering Cancer Center in New York. He and Hirsch have recently found evidence that children and adults don't use the same parts of the brain when learning a second language.

The researchers used an instrument called a functional magnetic resonance imager to study the brains of two groups of bilingual people. One group consisted of those who had learned a second language as children. The other consisted of people who, like Kim, learned their second language later in life. When placed inside the MRI scanner, which allowed Kim and Hirsch to see which parts of the brain were getting more blood and were thus more active, people from both groups were asked to think about what they had done the day before, first in one language and then the other. (They couldn't speak out loud, because any movement would disrupt the scanning.)

Kim and Hirsch looked specifically at two language centers in the brain—Broca's area in the left frontal part, which is believed to manage speech production, and Wernicke's area, in the rear of the brain, thought to process the meaning of language. Both groups of people, Kim and Hirsch found, used the same part of Wernicke's area no matter what language they were speaking. But their use of Broca's area differed.

People who learned a second language as children used the same region in Broca's area for both languages. But those who learned a second language later in life made use of a distinct region in Broca's area for their second language—near the one activated for their native tongue.

How does Hirsch explain this difference? "When language is being hard-wired during development," says Hirsch, "the brain may intertwine sounds and structures from all languages into the same area." But once that wiring is complete, the management of a new language, with new sounds and structures, must be taken over by a different part of the brain.

A second possibility is simply that we may acquire languages differently as children than we do as adults. "If you watch mothers or family members teaching an infant to speak," says Hirsch, "it's very tactile, it's very auditory, it's very visual. There are a lot of different inputs. And that's very different from sitting in a high school class."

Source: "The Bilingual Brain" from *Discover*, October 1997, p. 26. Copyright © 1997 Walt Disney Company.

After You Read

2   **Checking Your Understanding.**   To make sure that you understand the article, answer these questions. Look back at your markings to find the answers. (Note: If you haven't marked information that helps you answer some of these questions, you have missed some of the main ideas or important details.)

1.   Who is Karl Kim? Who is Joy Hirsch?

_____

_____

2.   Where do they do research?

_____

_____

3.   What instrument did they use?

_____

_____

4.   Why did they use this instrument?

_____

_____

5.   Who was in each group that they studied?

_____

_____

6.   Which areas of the brain did they look at?

_____

_____

7.   What was their conclusion about learning a second language?

_____

_____

3   **Summarizing.**   Use your answers to the questions in Exercise 2 to help you write a one-paragraph summary of the article. When you finish, compare your summary with those of other students.

Medical Technology and Bioethics

Before You Read

1 **Getting Started.**   Look at the photos and discuss them in small groups.

1. What are some discoveries in medical technology that have been in the news recently?
2. What are some possible problems of multiple births?
3. What might be a benefit of MRI scans? (What can we learn from them? What is good about this?)
4. New medical technology is extending human life—making it longer. What is good about this? What problems might result from people living longer?

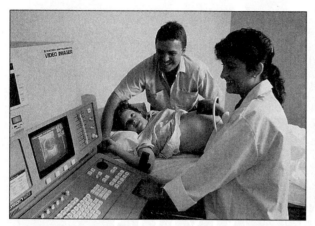

Ultrasound of a fetus

Quintuplets

Mice in a genetic experiment

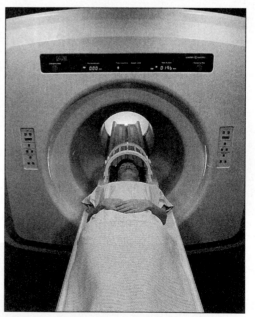

Person having an MRI scan

2   **Preparing to Read.**   Look again at the photos on page 216. Then survey the first reading selection by looking at the subheads. Put a check (✔) by the following topics that you believe will be discussed in the reading.

1. _____ Comparison of Traditional Medicine and Modern Medicine

2. _____ New Discoveries in Medical Technology

3. _____ The Joy of New Life

4. _____ Possible Problems that Result from Multiple Births

5. _____ Questions About Medical Ethics

6. _____ How Science Might Help People Live Longer than Before

7. _____ Answers to Questions About Medical Ethics

Now check the questions that you believe the reading selection will answer.

1. _____ What are some recent discoveries in the field of medical technology?

2. _____ How has the birth control pill changed society?

3. _____ Is it better for a woman to give birth at home or in a hospital?

4. _____ What is one negative consequence of the use of technology to tell parents the gender of their baby before it is born?

5. _____ What are some new ways that a woman can become pregnant?

6. _____ What did people in the past do in order to live to be very old?

7. _____ What are some ways in which technology will help people in the future to extend (lengthen) their lives?

8. _____ What are people doing to find answers to questions of ethics?

3   **Vocabulary Preview.**   Briefly look over this list of words from the reading that follows. Which words do you already know? For the ones that you don't know, *don't* use a dictionary. Try to understand them from the reading.

Nouns	Verbs	Adjectives	Adverb
breakthrough	diagnose	beneficial	rapidly
surgery	treat	ethical	
conception	conceive	fertilized	
fertility	alter	moral	
triplets			
xenotransplants			
concerns			
bio-synthetics			
supply			
physician			

Read

4 As you read the following selection, think about the answer to this question: what ethical questions need to be answered because of recent discoveries in medical technology?

Read the following selection quickly. Do not use a dictionary. Then do the exercises that follow the reading.

Medical Technology and Bioethics

Breakthroughs in Medical Technology

[A]   Every day, when we open a newspaper, turn on TV, or get onto the Internet, it seems there is a new medical breakthrough—a sudden and exciting discovery that, in turn, leads to more changes. Clearly, medical technology is rapidly advancing; some people would even say it is at a *frenetic* pace. The breakthroughs allow doctors to diagnose diseases, treat patients, and extend the length of life in ways that were not imaginable by most people fifty years ago. Many of these discoveries are beneficial, but they are coming so fast that we often don't have a chance to consider the moral questions and ethical problems. As Martin Luther King, Jr. once said, "Our scientific power has outrun our spiritual power."

Consequences of a Medical Discovery—"The Pill"

[B]   There are always consequences to a medical breakthrough. Take the example of the birth control pill, which became available in the 1960s and is now "old news." This gave women more control over their bodies and allowed for population growth control. But it also caused people to question their beliefs about gender roles, sex, freedom, and the family. It contributed to enormous societal change worldwide. Has this been a good thing? The answer reflects each person's religion, culture, and personal values.

Technology and the Beginning of a Human Life

[C]   Some of the most astonishing new medical technology involves the beginning of life. Due to ultrasound and amniocentesis, it is now possible to have a good deal of information about a baby many months before the actual birth. Most people agree that this knowledge is beneficial. Some medical problems, for example, can actually be repaired, through surgery, even before birth. However, there is the question of ethics. In some countries where many parents value daughters less than sons, it is common for a woman to have an ultrasound, discover the gender of her fetus, and then go immediately for an abortion rather than give birth to a girl. The ethical question will become even more difficult in the very near future, when a couple will be able to choose the sex of their child. For many people, a related question is this: when does "human personhood" begin—at the moment of conception, after several months of pregnancy, or at the baby's first breath?

New Methods of Conceiving a Baby

[D]   For couples who have difficulty conceiving a baby, there are now a number of possibilities. One is the use of fertility drugs. These often result in a successful pregnancy, sometimes of twins—but also sometimes of triplets (three babies), quadruplets, quintuplets, and even sextuplets! In such multiple births, the babies are born early, before they are mature enough, and almost always have many painful, expensive physical or mental challenges. Another common method of conception is *in vitro* fertilization. By this method of conceiving a baby outside a woman's body, childless couples may still become parents. This brings joy to many families, but it also raises questions. At a cost of over $75,000 for the delivery of one such baby, should society have to pay for this—or for the very expensive care of premature babies from multiple births—especially when there are many orphaned children who need parents? Expense is not the only ethical question. Another is what to do with the fertilized human eggs that are the result of *in vitro* fertilization. An egg might be frozen for a long time—perhaps decades—before it is implanted in the mother's body. Is this egg a human being? If the parents die, for example, in a car accident, or divorce, to whom do the eggs belong? Can physicians destroy these frozen eggs?

Living Longer?

[E] For centuries, people have hoped to find a "fountain of youth"—some magical water to make them healthy and young for a very long time. Today, the oldest humans are perhaps 105 to 110 years of age. An average person can expect to live to seventy-five or eighty, in some countries. New research into the extension of human life offers the possibility of a medical fountain of youth. Already, the transplant of a healthy organ—a heart, lung, liver, kidney, and so on—for a diseased organ is quite common. The problem is finding enough organs. For this reason, there has recently been research into xenotransplants—the transplanting of an organ from one species (such as a baboon) into another (a human). This has not yet been successful, but now, with increasing knowledge of genetics, scientists are altering pigs with human genes in the hope that these animals can be raised on special farms and soon provide a large supply of organs for transplantation. Of course, there are ethical concerns, including the question of whether it is right or wrong to raise and sacrifice other species to increase human longevity. At the same time, other researchers are working in the area of bio-synthetics. The goal of this is to *create* organs, not transplant existing organs. A good example is skin. Patients with very serious burns can now receive artificial skin, grown in laboratories, instead of real skin. Patients respond well to it, and it allows them to leave the hospital earlier than with older methods. There is a large supply, and there are not the same ethical problems as with other types of transplants. In search of a *genetic* fountain of youth, Italian biologists have been experimenting with mice. By blocking the action of a single gene called [P66.sup.shc],* they have created mice that live 30 percent longer than usual. This may give people great hope, but it is premature to do something similar in humans. Perhaps, with more time, we will have the opportunity to consider the possible ethical questions in extending human life by 30 percent.

The Ending of a Human Life

[F] More than ever before, there are huge moral questions involving the ending of a human life. For example, we have the medical ability to keep a person technically "alive" for years, on machines, after he or she is "brain dead," that is, after the neocortex has stopped functioning. But is it ethical to do this? And what about the alternative? In other words, is it ethical *not* to keep a person alive if we have the technology to do so? And how much care should be given to a dying patient? Forty years ago, it was far easier to give a patient "the best healthcare

* The name of the gene is [P66.sup.shc].

that money could buy" because there *wasn't* as much healthcare as we have now. Today, there seems to be no end to expensive tests and treatments to prevent death. One MRI scan, for instance, costs $2,000 but might not give the physician significant information. Who will pay for this? How can this be available to everyone, not just the rich? How much is too much?

A Need for Answers to Ethical Questions

[G] It goes without saying that we need to find answers to such questions. Some—but not enough—hospitals have begun to hire bioethicists to help both patients and doctors. Some—but not enough—medical schools have responded by including courses in ethics for future physicians. Without far more attention to these questions, our understanding of technology will continue to "outrun" our understanding of what is right and wrong. And we will continue to make the mistakes of the past: upsetting the natural order and suffering the consequences.

After You Read

5 **Getting the Main Ideas.**   Write T on the lines before the statements that are true, according to the reading. Write F on the lines before the statements that are false. Write I on the lines before the statements that are impossible to know from the reading.

1. _____   Recent discoveries in medical technology are happening very quickly.

2. _____   Societal changes that are a consequence of the birth control pill have been good ones.

3. _____   "Human personhood" begins at birth.

4. _____   Fertility drugs and *in vitro* fertilization are two methods that are used by couples who have difficulty conceiving a baby.

5. _____   The transplantation of organs from one species to another is fairly common.

6. _____   Because of advances in the field of medicine, it is easier today for a patient to receive "the best care that money can buy."

7. _____   Most hospitals will soon have bioethicists to help patients and doctors with ethical questions.

6 **Getting Meaning from Context.** On the lines, write words from the reading selection that fit these definitions. The letters in parentheses refer to the paragraphs where the words appear.

1. a sudden and exciting discovery (A): _____

2. look at symptoms to identify a disease (A): _____

3. take care of; try to cure (A): _____

4. make longer (A): _____

5. good, helpful (A): _____

6. medical operation (C): _____

7. place high importance on (C): _____

8. unborn baby (C): _____

9. becoming pregnant with a baby (D): _____

10. causing one to be capable of producing a baby (D): _____

11. changing (E): _____

12. worries, problems, questions (E): _____

13. not natural; made by humans (E): _____

14. amount; available quantity (E): _____

15. give a job to (G): _____

16. medical doctors (G): _____

Use your own logic and the context of the following sentence to answer the questions that follow. Don't use a dictionary.

> Fertility drugs often result in a successful pregnancy, sometimes of twins—but also sometimes of <u>triplets</u> (three babies), <u>quadruplets</u>, <u>quintuplets</u>, and even <u>sextuplets</u>!

1. You know that *bi-* is a prefix that means "two." From the context, you can guess that *tri-* means "three." What do these prefixes mean?

   ■ quad- = _____

   ■ quint- = _____

   ■ sext- = _____

2. What do these words mean?

   ■ triplets = _____

   ■ quadruplets = _____

   ■ quintuplets = _____

   ■ sextuplets = _____

7 **Understanding Reading Structure.**   Here is a list of breakthroughs in medical technology that were mentioned in the reading. Match them to the sections of the reading in which they appeared. Write the letters on the lines. Then look back at the reading to check your answers.

1. _____ ultrasound

2. _____ xenotransplants

3. _____ amniocentesis

4. _____ MRI scans

5. _____ the birth control pill

6. _____ *in vitro* fertilization

7. _____ bio-synthetics

8. _____ fertility drugs

9. _____ organ transplants

10. _____ blocking the action
of a specific gene
in mice

a. Consequences of a Medical Discovery—"The Pill"

b. Technology and the Beginning of a Human Life

c. New Methods of Conceiving a Baby

d. Living Longer?

e. The Ending of a Human Life

8 **Making Inferences.**   On the short lines, put a check mark next to each statement that you can infer from the reading selection. Do not check the other statements, even if you think they are true. On the line after each statement that you check, write the phrases from the selection from which you inferred the information.

1. _____ Medical technology is changing our lives faster than we can determine if the changes are ethical or not.

_____

_____

2. _____ People don't agree on the benefits of the birth control pill.

_____

_____

3. _____ Ultrasound and amniocentesis can "repair" a baby before it is born.

_____

_____

4. _____   In the future, in some countries, people might use medical technology to plan, in advance, to have a son instead of a daughter.

_____

_____

5. _____   Multiple births bring with them financial and medical problems.

_____

_____

6. _____   There are more ethical problems with xenotransplants than with bio-synthetics.

_____

_____

7. _____   Humans, like mice, will very soon be able to live 30 percent longer if the action of a single gene is blocked.

_____

_____

9   **Viewpoint.**   Look back at the last paragraph of "Technology and Bioethics." In your opinion, what does the author believe is a problem today? How does the author suggest solving this problem?

Discussing the Reading

10   In small groups, talk about your answers to these questions.

1. Has the discussion of the birth control pill made changes in the society in your country?
   If so, what are some?

2. Do pregnant women in your country usually have ultrasound or amniocentesis? Do they ever have an abortion based on their knowledge of the baby's sex? Is it legal to do this?

3. Do you sometimes hear (from the news or in conversations) about multiple births? If so, what are some of the problems?

4. Would you like to live to 110 or 120? Why or why not?

Cross-Cultural Note: Life Expectancy

People born in the year 1998 can expect to live, on average, a certain number of years, depending on the country in which they live. Here are some examples.

Country	Life Expectancy at Birth Males	Females	Country	Life Expectancy at Birth Males	Females
Argentina	70.9	78.3	*Kazakhstan*	58.1	69.3
Brazil	59.4	69.6	*Mexico*	68.6	74.8
China	68.3	71.1	*Russia*	58.8	71.7
Egypt	60.1	64.1	*South Korea*	70.4	78.0
France	74.6	82.6	*Thailand*	65.4	72.8
Ghana	54.8	58.9	*Uganda*	41.8	43.4
Hungary	66.5	75.4	*United Kingdom*	74.8	80.1
Japan	76.9	83.3	*United States*	72.9	83.3

11   **Discussing Life Expectancy.**   In small groups, talk about the life expectancy statistics. In your opinion, why do women, on average, live longer than men in all countries? What might be some reasons that life expectancy is so different from country to country?

Talk It Over

Considering Medical Ethics.   There are many controversial issues (questions to argue about) in the field of medicine. Here are some of them. What do you think about each issue—and *why?*

1. Is euthanasia ethical? In other words, is it moral to painlessly kill a person who is incurably sick or brain dead? Why or why not?

2. If a married couple has fertilized eggs frozen in a medical laboratory, and then they decide to get a divorce, what should happen to the eggs?

3. It is now possible for a woman in her fifties or even sixties to give birth to a baby. What do you think about this?

12   **Checking Your Understanding.**   Turn back to Exercise 2 on page 217 and answer the questions you checked. Then answer the question immediately before the reading.

Beyond the Text

Bring to class recent newspaper or magazine articles about the most recent breakthroughs (and their ethics) in one of the following areas and share this news with the class. Alternatively, you can log onto the Internet for this information. One good Website is http://www.bioethics.net.

- *in vitro* fertilization
- determining the gender of a baby at the time of conception
- prenatal (before birth) surgery
- organ transplants
- xenotransplants
- bio-synthetics
- genetics and the extension of life

PART 2	# The Mind-Body Relationship

1 **Main Idea and Summary.**   For each paragraph that follows, practice what you have learned about finding the main idea and summarizing paragraphs. First, read each paragraph quickly, without using a dictionary. Mark the information in any way that helps you to understand it. (For example, you could circle the main topic, underline the important words of the main points, and number the supporting details.) Then write the *main idea* in one sentence. To *summarize* the paragraph, write the main idea and add the important details in as few words as possible. (You might need to write more than one sentence.) The *Main idea* and *Summary* parts for Paragraph A are given as examples.

The Mind-Body Relationship

[A] Western doctors are beginning to understand what traditional healers have always known—that the body and mind are inseparable. The World Health Organization, in fact, recommends that in some countries, urban doctors might have greater success if they take a traditional healer with them as they visit patients. Until recently, modern urban physicians healed the body, psychiatrists the mind, and priests or ministers the soul. However, the medical world is now paying more attention to holistic medicine—an approach based on the belief that people's state of mind can make them sick or speed their recovery from sickness.

Main idea: *Western doctors are paying attention to holistic medicine.*

Summary: *Until recently, Western medicine treated the mind and body separately. Today many doctors believe the mind can influence the health of the body, something that traditional healers have always known.*

[B]   Several studies show that the effectiveness of a certain drug often depends on the patient's expectations of it. For example, in one recent study, psychiatric patients at a major hospital were divided into two groups. One group was given a tranquilizer to make them calm. The other group received a placebo; the members of the second group did not know, of course, that their "tranquilizer" actually had no medication in it at all. Surprisingly, *more* patients were tranquilized by the placebo than by the actual tranquilizer. It seems likely that a person's hope of a cure and belief in the physician influence the effect of medication.

Main idea: _____

_____

Summary: _____

_____

[C]   In study after study, there is a positive reaction in almost exactly one-third of the patients taking placebos. How is this possible? How can a *placebo* have an effect on the body? Evidence from a 1977 study at the University of California shows that several patients who received placebos were able to produce their own natural "drug." That is, as they took the placebos (which they *thought* were actual medication), their brains released enkephalins and endorphins—natural chemicals that act like a drug. Scientists theorize that the amount of these chemicals released by a person's brain quite possibly indicates how much faith the person has in his or her doctor.

Main idea: _____

_____

Summary: _____

_____

_____

[D]   Another study demonstrates the importance of environment on patients' recovery from sickness. A group of doctors and health experts recently changed a Veterans' Administration hospital from a crowded, colorless building into a bright, cheerful one. Although the doctors expected some improvement, they were amazed at the high rate of recovery. After just three months in this pleasant environment, many patients who had been in the hospital for three to ten *years* were healthy enough to be released and to lead normal lives.

Main idea: _____

_____

Summary: _____

_____

_____

[E]   It is even possible that there is a connection between a person's mind and the risk of developing cancer. Doctors are learning that people who express their emotions by occasionally shouting when they're angry or crying when they're sad might be healthier than people who suppress their feelings. Scientists at the National Cancer Institute studied a large group of patients who had had successful operations for cancerous growths. The scientists discovered that those in the group whose cancer later returned were people who suppressed their emotions, felt angry but denied their anger, and refused to admit that their illness was serious.

Main idea: _____

_____

Summary: _____

_____

_____

_____

After You Read

2 **Distinguishing Facts from Theories.** Which of the following statements have been proven, and which are only beliefs that some people hold? On the line, write *fact* or *theory* for each statement, according to the presentation of the information in the reading selection "The Mind-Body Relationship."

1. _____ Urban doctors have greater success if they take a traditional healer with them as they visit patients.

2. _____ A person's state of mind can make a person sick or speed his or her recovery.

3. _____ The effectiveness of a certain drug often depends on the patient's expectations of it.

4. _____ A person's hope of a cure and belief in the physician influence the effect of medication.

5. _____ In a 1977 study, several patients who took placebos were able to produce their own natural "drug."

6. _____ The amount of natural chemicals released by a person's brain indicates how much faith the person has in his or her doctor.

7. _____ There is a connection between a person's mind and the risk of developing cancer.

3 **Applying Information.** Use paragraphs B, C, D, and E of the reading selection to answer this question: If you are very sick, what three things can *you* do to increase your chances of getting well?

1. _____

2. _____

3. _____

Discussing the Reading

4 Each culture has some traditional cures for certain common illnesses or conditions. These are cures that can't be found in a drugstore; instead, people learn them from their parents and grandparents.

1. If there are students from different cultures in your class, move around the room and ask them about traditional cures in their cultures. If all the students in your class are from the same culture, compare your ideas on traditional cures; do these differ from region to region or family to family? Write your answers in the chart on page 228. Then ask your teacher if she or he knows some folk cures from another country. Add any illnesses or conditions to the chart that you want to.

2. After you have filled in the chart, consider the various cures. How are they similar? How are they different? Compare them to the medicine that we find in an urban drugstore. Are there advantages to each, or is one kind better?

Folk Cures			
Student: _____ **Country:** _____	**Student:** _____ **Country:** _____	**Student:** _____ **Country:** _____	**Student:** _____ **Country:** _____
cold			
a cough			
nausea			
itchy skin			
hiccups			
a headache			
a hangover			
other			

PART 3	**Building Vocabulary and Study Skills**

1 Categories.   Circle the words in each item that belong in the underlined category.

1. <u>body parts</u>:
   target   liver   kidney   throat

2. <u>emotions</u>:
   anger   sadness   effect   cure   hatred

3. <u>symptoms of illness</u>:
   insomnia   headache   ulcer   syndrome

4. <u>things that cause disease</u>:
   placebos   infection   bacteria   genetics

5. <u>methods of diagnosis</u>:
   recovery   relaxation   ultrasound   stomachache

6. <u>groups of people</u>:
   organization   tribe   community   society

7. <u>places to live</u>:
   colony   village   mosque   cave

8. <u>types of beliefs</u>:
   tranquilizers   values   ethics   morals

9. <u>expressions of emotions</u>:
   hug   grin   suppress   shout

10. <u>words in geography</u>:
    subsidy   landlocked   harbor   tropical

11. <u>actions of physicians</u>:
    diagnosis   fertility   treatment   surgery

2   **Word Forms.**   Complete the sentences with the appropriate forms of these base words.

heal	treat	spirit	effective	accept
diagnose	combine	be	tradition	participate

1. In most urban and suburban areas of the world, sick people go to a doctor for

   _____.

2. The healer is a _____ of doctor, priest, and psychologist.

3. In _____ village societies, disease is viewed as something

   outside the world—something _____.

4. During the _____ , a doctor asks about symptoms.

5. In village societies, there is _____ of all villagers in the

   healing ceremony, not just the _____ and the patient.

6. Folk medicines are often successful, and scientists are trying to find out the

   reasons for their _____.

7. At communal ceremonies, villagers can express their feelings in a socially

   _____ way.

3   **Word Roots and Affixes.**   Here are some more word roots and prefixes and their meanings.

Prefix	Meaning
hyper-	above; beyond
hypo-	beneath; under

Word Root	Meaning
corp	body
derm	skin
gam	marriage
mort	death
ortho	straight; correct
spir	breathe
xeno	strange; foreign

Without using a dictionary, guess the meaning of each underlined word. Use the list of word roots and affixes. (Look back at the list in Chapter 9, Part 3 on page 209 for additional help.)

1. He went to a <u>dermatologist</u> for help with his problem.

    a. person who studies bones

    b. eye doctor

    c. skin doctor

    d. person who helps people with mental problems

    e. heart specialist

2. The <u>mortality</u> rate is very high in that village.

    a. birth   d. divorce

    b. multiple birth   e. death

    c. marriage

3. The child began to cry when the doctor took out a <u>hypodermic</u> needle.

    a. large   d. for use under the skin

    b. for use in the stomach   e. for use in the muscle

    c. for use on the skin

4. The little girl is <u>hyperactive</u>.

    a. very quiet, shy

    b. more active than is normal

    c. less active than is usual

    d. having difficulty with breathing

    e. good at dancing

5. He's in the hospital on a <u>respirator</u>.

    a. strict diet

    b. special bed to help his back problems

    c. machine to help him breathe

    d. machine that pumps blood (as the heart does)

    e. machine that checks his temperature regularly

6. The physician studied the <u>corpse</u>.

    a. dead body   d. reaction to the placebo

    b. new medical instrument   e. ultrasound

    c. ceremony

7. People in that village believe in <u>polygamy</u>.

    a. many gods

    b. marriage

    c. marriage to more than one person

    d. the necessity of marrying someone from a different village

    e. the economic benefits of gambling

8. They took their child to an <u>orthodontist</u>.

    a. doctor

    b. dentist

    c. doctor who specializes in children

    d. doctor who helps people with breathing problems

    e. dentist who straightens teeth

9. My brother has always been a <u>xenophile</u>.

    a. strange person

    b. person who lives abroad

    c. person who is attracted to foreign cultures

    d. person who doesn't like foreign cultures

    e. person who speaks foreign languages

4 **Improving Reading Skills: Predictions.**   In each of the following sentences, complete the last word. Work as fast as you can and write your time (the number of seconds it takes you to finish) on the line after each group. Try to improve your time with the second group. The first item is done as an example.

1. You should take care of yourself to prevent ill_____*ness*_____.

2. A healer might give medication to his or her pat_____.

3. It's possible to do this, but I'm not sure that it's eth_____.

4. Many patients prefer to be cured by traditional methods rather than by a modern physi_____.

5. In cancer research, it seems that almost weekly there is a new break_____.

Time: _____

6. The woman and her husband were amazed when the ultrasound indicated that they were going to have tri_____.

7. Transplants are now quite common, but the problem is finding a large enough supply of or_____.

8. The patient felt weak; he didn't have any ener_____.

9. Some illnesses are emotional, and some arc phy_____.

10. This is a difficult problem; is there any sol_____?

Time: _____

In these sentences, fill in the last word. (There may be more than one correct answer.) Work as fast as you can and write your time (number of seconds) on the line after each group. Try to improve your time with the second group.

1. Disease is usually caused by _____.

2. New medical breakthroughs bring with them a number of ethical

_____.

3. Healers and physicians treat _____.

4. The patient has been feeling terrible; she has bad _____.

5. Some people believe deeply in _____.

Time: _____

6. Psychiatrists heal _____.

7. The doctor gave him a tranquilizer to make him _____.

8. Environment seems to influence a person's recovery from

_____.

9. It might be beneficial if we shout when we're _____.

10. Doctors are learning that it's not good if their patients suppress their

_____.

Time: _____

Focus on Testing

Understanding Analogies

As you saw in Chapter 8, some standardized tests have a section on analogy. Many of these have multiple-choice answers. You need to (1) understand the two words that are given, (2) understand the relationship between the two words, and (3) choose the pair of words that has the same relationship.

Example

illness:sickness::

   a. well:health   c. sleeplessness:symptom

   b. doctor:physician   d. disease:condition

The best answer is b because *illness* and *sickness* are both nouns and are synonyms. The two words in a are different parts of speech. The two words in c are both nouns but not synonyms; sleeplessness is an example of a symptom. The two words in d are nouns but not synonyms; a disease is an example of a condition.

Take this practice test. Work as quickly as possible (as you would on an actual test) and don't use a dictonary. Your teacher might decide to time you on this test.

1. art:painting::

    a. cosmetics:makeup   c. music:jazz

    b. mosque:building   d. statue:artist

2. physician:treatment::

    a. psychiatrist:tranquilizer   c. archaeologist:the past

    b. biologist:ethics   d. researcher:experiment

3. depict:painting::

    a. write:book   c. watch:movie

    b. see:photograph   d. predict:future

4. express:supress::

    a. diagnose:treat   c. cure:kill

    b. alter:change   d. conceive:extend

5. rank:military::

    a. society:status   c. status:society

    b. power:politics   d. politics:power

6. beautiful:pretty::

    a. ugly:unattractive   c. plump:fat

    b. thin:slim   d. nice:handsome

PART 4   Reading in the Real World

1   **Scanning Magazine Articles.**   Read the following article from *McCall's* magazine and do the exercises that follow. (It's always a good idea to look through the questions *first* and have them in mind as you read.) This article may seem difficult to you, but *don't worry* about the words you don't understand. Instead, concentrate on understanding the main ideas and answering the questions.

Home Remedies Even Doctors Use

[A]   The next time you're sick, you might be able to avoid a trip to the doctor's office by simply pulling something out of the refrigerator. Or the kitchen cabinet. Or even the spice rack. More and more studies are finding that certain foods, spices, and other household staples provide effective relief from common health problems. In fact, many physicians, concerned about the overuse of antibiotics and the trend toward treatment overkill for even minor medical problems, are recommending these simple cures. And patients are more than willing to give them a try, considering today's soaring medical costs and shrinking insurance coverage.

[B]   The treatments here are more than just folklore—all of them come from doctors with decades of experience, and many even boast the kind of scientific credentials usually reserved for prescription medicines. And all are likely to be in your house already. So try one out the next time you or your kids are hit with an everyday illness or injury. But keep in mind that, just like prescription medicines, treatments involving natural substances *can* cause side effects. If you experience any unusual reactions to the therapy, discontinue it immediately.

Baking soda nixes itches.

[C]   Adding about 1/4 to 1/2 cup per quart of cool water, or half a box in the bathtub, will often calm down rashes, chicken pox, or poison ivy. You can soak in it or apply it with compresses, says Lorraine Stern, M.D., an associate clinical professor of pediatrics at the University of California, Los Angeles, and a pediatrician in practice for 21 years, but be aware that it may be drying to the skin. These treatments or a paste made from baking soda and water are also effective for insect bites and bee stings.

Ginger quiets queasy stomachs.

[D]   If your mother gave you ginger ale for an upset stomach, she was onto something. Ginger has a calming effect on the stomach—a fact verified by a study finding that ginger capsules helped counteract the effects of motion sickness. Most of the grocery store varieties of ginger ale and ginger snaps (cookies) are very light on real ginger, but they may have enough to settle slight queasiness. For a more powerful punch, though, you can boil a few slices of ginger root in about 2 cups of water to make yourself a batch of ginger tea. (Ginger tea is also available at some health food stores.)

Garlic fights colds and flu.

[E]   The trade-off here is obvious—the unwelcome scented aftereffects—but studies have confirmed that some of garlic's chemical constituents can kill disease-causing germs. Add two to three cloves per serving to whatever you're making or, for maximum healing power, make this special soup: Toss garlic (again, two to three cloves per serving) and a bit of ginger into a potful of vegetable soup that is heavy on ingredients loaded with vitamins A and C (e.g., carrots, broccoli, spinach, tomatoes, red and green peppers). The latest studies have named vitamins A and C as two of the most effective nutritional infection fighters, and the soup's steam helps clear congestion, covering all approaches on the cold front. To avoid the odor of garlic, try the pill form found in many pharmacies and health food stores.

Acupressure alleviates nausea and pain.

[F] Above your wrist is a point you can press into medical service to relieve nausea, according to Bruce Pomeranz, M.D., a professor of neurobiology at the University of Toronto. Six studies confirm the effect, although *why* it works is still unclear. Find the groove (long, narrow channel) between the two large tendons on the inside of your wrist that run from the base of the palm up to the elbow. About 2 inches above the wrist, press down hard with a thumb or finger for a minute or two until the spot feels slightly achy. Mild queasiness may be relieved immediately; relief of more intense nausea may require about 20 minutes of repeated pressing.

[G]   Another acupressure point—the web of flesh between the thumb and forefinger—seems to moderate pain sensations. Find a spot about an inch into that triangle where you've got muscle, not just skin, and squeeze it until it aches a bit. Repeat two or three times, or hold the pressure for a few minutes. It's especially effective for relieving pain in the head or neck area but can relieve any pain because it triggers the release of endorphins, the body's natural painkiller.

Source: "Home Remedies Even Doctors Use" by Catherine Clifford, from *McCall's*, August 1992, p. 26. Copyright © 1992 by Catherine Clifford.

2 **Application.**   According to the article, what home remedy (cure) might you try for each of these conditions?

Condition	**Cure**
1. You have a sore throat, watery eyes, and are having difficulty breathing.	_____
2. You have a queasy (upset) stomach; that is, you feel seasick.	_____
3. You have a headache.	_____
4. You have a problem with your skin; for example, your skin itches because of an insect bite.	_____

3   **Getting Meaning from Context.**   Find words or phrases that mean the same as the following. The letters in parentheses refer to the paragraphs.

1. something (caused by a medicine) that is in addition to the purpose (B):

    _____

2. put something (or yourself) in water or liquid (C): _____

3. effects (usually unpleasant) that follow another action (E): _____

    _____

4. bacteria (E): _____

5. motion sickness; a stomach problem (two words) (F): _____

    and _____

6. the body's natural painkiller (G): _____

4   In the first paragraph, the writer says that patients are happy to try these home remedies "considering today's *soaring* medical costs and *shrinking* insurance coverage." What do you suppose she's saying about medical costs? In other words, what can you guess that *soaring* means?

_____

_____

What does *shrinking* mean?

_____

_____

Beyond the Text

Bring to class newspaper and/or magazine articles about medical or health-related issues that interest you. Alternatively, you can check health Websites on the Internet. (Two possible sites are www.onhealth.com and www.discoveryhealth.com.) Discuss new vocabulary. Tell the class about the most interesting information.

Video Activities: A New Treatment for Back Pain

Before You Watch.

1. In your culture, is there a difference between "scientific" and "alternative" types of medicines and treatments?

2. What are some ways you know to treat back pain?

3. The following words refer to the human nervous system. Review their meanings: *nerve, spinal cord, brain*. Share what you know about the way information from the body reaches the brain.

Watch.   Read the following statements. Write (T) if they are true and (F) if they are false.

1. _____   The procedure uses electricity to reduce the patients' pain.

2. _____   The treatment takes place in a doctor's office.

3. _____   The treatments are painful.

4. _____   The pain relief from the procedure is immediate.

Watch Again.   Take notes on the two patients before and during/after the needle treatment.

Patient	Before Treatment	During/After Treatment
Doris Dorry	-had back pain for 25 years -pain level was a "10"	
Judy Ellis		

After You Watch.   Put the sentences in the correct order to describe how needles help cure back pain.

_____   This current irritates small nerve fibers in the back.

_____   An electrical current passes through the needles.

_____   The patient feels less pain.

_____   This information is carried to the spinal cord.

_____   Doctors attach needles to the patient's back.

_____   The irritation interrupts the pain message being sent to the brain.

_____   From the spinal cord it travels to the brain.

Chapter 11

The Media

IN THIS CHAPTER

The first reading selection gives you advice on one technique to improve your English—reading a newspaper. The second is a selection of different types of newspaper articles and columns. The last reading discusses what happened when a new kind of newspaper became available in China.

PART 1

How to Read a Newspaper

Before You Read

1   Getting Started.   Look at the photos and discuss them in small groups.

1. What are various ways to learn about the news? Which way do you prefer?

2. Do you read a newspaper in English? If so, how often? Which parts do you read? What is difficult about it for you?

3. What is the major English-language newspaper in your city or country? Do you think this is a good newspaper? Why or why not?

2   **Preparing to Read.**   Survey the first reading selection. In addition to the subheads, look quickly at the first and last sentences of each paragraph. Then check (✔) the following questions that you believe will be discussed in the reading.

1. _____ How can you improve your vocabulary?

2. _____ What's a fun way to spend a weekend with your children?

3. _____ What are some characteristics of a bad newspaper?

4. _____ What are some good English-language newspapers?

5. _____ Who are some of the most famous journalists today?

6. _____ What are the various sections of a newspaper?

7. _____ Why is it important to read the whole newspaper?

8. _____ What are some steps to follow so that you can read the newspaper quickly?

9. _____ How can you use your computer to find the news?

10. _____ How can you find a newspaper that avoids subjects that you're not interested in?

3   **Vocabulary Preview.**   Briefly look over this list of words from the reading that follows. Which words do you already know? For the ones that you don't know, *don't* use a dictionary. Try to understand them from the reading.

Nouns	Verb	Adjectives	Phrases
tricks	register	overstressed	yellow journalism
doorstep		op-ed	"hard news"
pitcher		customized	
tabloid			
gossip			
editorials			
headlines			
password			
mug			

Read

4   **Reading About Newspapers.**   As you read the following selection, think about the answer to this question: what suggestions does the author give for reading a newspaper? Read the selection quickly. Do not use a dictionary. Then do the exercises that follow the reading.

How to Read a Newspaper

[A]   You sometimes ask me for "tricks." You want quick and easy ways to learn this language, to acquire a huge vocabulary, to read fast and understand more, to become good writers. You want magic. You think I have some secret magic tricks that I am holding back—not letting you have. Let me assure you: this is not true. There are no easy tricks. I am not holding back. But there *are* some techniques that work better than others. One of the best techniques I can think of is to read an English-language newspaper regularly. This will allow you to "kill two birds with one stone"—well, actually, *three* "birds": increase your vocabulary, improve your reading skills, and learn something about how to write. One caution, however: newspaper language is very challenging. It *does* become more possible, though, if you read the paper regularly—several times a week—because you will see the same vocabulary over and over and because you will have more background information about continuing stories.

A Perfect Sunday

[B]   When I was young and newly married, my husband and I used to spend most of every Sunday reading *The Times.* It arrived on our doorstep, four inches thick and as heavy as a bomb. We made a big pot of coffee (in summer, a big pitcher of icy lemonade) and lay on the living room floor, surrounded by sections of the paper: national and international news, business, sports, entertainment, book reviews, classified ads. Occasionally, we read something aloud to each other: "Just listen to *this*! You won't believe it." From time to time, we exchanged sections: "Are you almost finished with Entertainment?" It was a lovely way to spend a leisurely Sunday, but it *did* take almost the whole day. That was a time before our children came along, before my husband and I became overworked, overstressed, and underslept, before life started moving at a frenetic pace. Now I can't imagine spending so much time reading the paper. Now I have to be efficient and practical. I have picked up a few suggestions that I can share with you.

Which Paper?

[C]   First, you need to choose a newspaper and know which *not* to choose. In some English-speaking countries, as you wait in the checkout line at the supermarket, you might notice something that looks like a newspaper. You read the headlines: "Woman Gives Birth to Baby with Two Heads!" or "Elvis Presley Seen in Bus Station in Texas" or "UFOs from Mars Land in Soccer Stadium Parking Lot." Trust me. These are not newspapers. They are trash. To be more accurate, they are called "tabloid" newspapers, simply the worst examples of "yellow" journalism—newspaper writing that is full of gossip, half-truths, and too many exclamation marks (!!!). If your goal is just to acquire a little vocabulary and have some fun, go ahead and read them. But don't expect to find actual news or good writing or the truth. For that, you need a real newspaper. For international news, you might try the *Christian Science Monitor* (not at all a religious newspaper, as its name seems to imply) or the *International Herald Tribune.* In the United States, *USA Today* offers national and international news in extremely easy language. For local, national, and international news, find the best paper in the city where you are at the time—*The Bangkok Post, The London Times, The Chicago Tribune.*

What You Will Find

[D]   Next, you need to know about the various parts of a newspaper. This will help you to decide what to read and what to skip. In most English-language papers, the "hard" news is in the first section, beginning on the front page. Hard news includes everything that has happened that day—politics, crime, scientific discoveries, economics, weather, and local events. The "top" (or most important) news story of the day can be found in the upper right-hand corner of the front page. Journalism students soon learn that ethical writing of hard news must be *objective*—in other words, contain only facts, not the journalist's opinion—and *balanced* (contain both sides of a story). In any good newspaper, opinion is clearly separated from hard news. Opinion appears in advice columns ("Dear Abby, My mother-in-law expects us to spend every holiday at her house, and it drives me crazy . . ."), in movie, TV, or book reviews, in editorials, and in letters to the editor. On the "op-ed" (opinion and editorial) page, there are specific columns written by the editor or publisher of the newspaper (editorials) and letters written by members of the public. These are full of opinions on every subject from politics to television to local events. Most of the rest of the newspaper contains advertising. Advertisers *pay* for this space, and it is not news.

How to Get the Most Out of the Paper and Not Spend All Day Doing It

[E]   At this point, you are ready to start reading. When you read a newspaper—especially in a language new to you—it is almost impossible to begin on page one and read through to the last page. Don't even think of trying this. Instead, begin by throwing away the sections that you have no interest in. Unless you're looking for a job or a used car, you can immediately throw away the classified ads, for example. This makes the paper a good deal thinner. Next, *preview* the rest of the paper. That is, briefly look over each section for articles that especially interest you. Then go back to the front page. On this page, read each headline—the title of every article. You might be surprised by how much you can learn from just the headlines. (For more on how to read headlines, see pages 252–255.) After you have read every headline, choose just *five* articles that interest you—no more than five. Then, for each of these articles, read *only* the first paragraph or two. This is where you will find the important information: who, what, when, where, why. If one of these articles absolutely fascinates you, you can read a little more. But in most cases, read no more than one paragraph. Then you can move on to a section that interests you, such as entertainment (often called "Calendar"), business, or sports. (But beware of sports! The language of sports is difficult because it is different from "normal" English.) In these sections, read only the headline and first paragraph of a few articles that look interesting to you—no more. Last, you might look for some small piece of information that you need at the moment—the weather report or where a certain movie is playing; additionally, some students like to read the advice column. The language in this column is conversational, and they can learn about customs, too. Most important—don't worry too much about vocabulary. Guess meaning from the context and use a dictionary for only a few words. If you read the paper several times a week, you will discover many of the same words appearing again and again.

Customized News—Just for You

[F]   Imagine a newspaper that is written just for *you*, with only articles that interest *you*. You are the publisher. You are the editor. You choose the articles. What if you're living in Mexico City, for example, but you'd like the news from London, where you lived for a few years? What if you absolutely hate news about crime and don't want to see it on your front page every day? What if you love some subject—archaeology, for instance— that is often hard to find in your daily paper? Such a specialized newspaper exists—on your computer. There are many customized online news services. They allow you to focus on your priorities and quickly find articles that you'll probably be interested in. With some, you just type a topic under "Search" or choose one of their topics. With others, you register in advance. You choose a name and a password. The computer asks what city you live in and what your interests are: travel? business? movies? global news? local news? and so on. Then, each day, your computer seeks stories that fit your interests. You can usually read a summary of each article. If that summary interests you, you can read the whole article ("full text") and often see pictures and hear audio, too. There are two disadvantages to these computer news services, however. One is that you might miss some fascinating news about a topic that you don't yet *know* interests you. And the other is that you miss the wonderful experience of lying on the living room floor on a rainy Sunday afternoon with a mug of coffee and every section of *The Times* surrounding you.

Here are examples of free online news services. (There is usually a fee, however, for articles from past issues.) If you know of other good ones, share them with the class.

The Los Angeles Times	www.latimes.com
The New York Times	www.nytimes.com
The Times (London)	www.the-times.co.uk
NEWS.COM	www.news.com
MSNBC	www.msnbc.com
The International Herald Tribune	www.iht.com

After You Read

5 **Getting the Main Ideas.** Check (✔) suggestions that the author states or implies. Do not check the others, even if you think they are good ideas.

1. _____ There are some techniques that make it easy to learn this language.

2. _____ It's a good idea to spend a whole day reading the newspaper.

3. _____ Don't read tabloid newspapers if you want to learn about the news.

4. _____ You shouldn't read the whole newspaper.

5. _____ You should read all of the headlines on the front page.

6. _____ You should read only parts of some articles.

7. _____ Don't read the sports section.

8. _____ The advice column is a good place to find conversational language.

9. _____ It's a good idea to look up most of the new words to find the meaning.

10. _____ An online news service is one way to find specific news of interest to you.

6 **Getting Meaning from Context.** On the lines, write words and expressions from the reading selection that fit these definitions. The letters in parentheses refer to the paragraphs where the words appear.

1. succeed in doing two things with one action (A): _____

2. the place where you enter a house (B): _____

3. a container for cold beverages (B): _____

4. a kind of newspaper that does not focus on true news (C):

   _____

5. a kind of journalism that does not focus on true news (C):

   _____

6. the type of news that includes everything that has happened that day (D):

   _____

7. the page of the newspaper that has opinions of the publisher and of readers (D):

   _____

8. the opinion of the editor or publisher, in the form of a column (similar to an article) (D):

   _____

9. the title of a newspaper article (E): _____

10. made specific for a person's needs (F): _____

11. a cup for a hot beverage (F): _____

7   **Making Inferences.**   The selection "How to Read a Newspaper" is written in the first person, "I." What inferences can you make about this person? Write your inferences by answering the questions. Then write the phrases from which you inferred the information; that is, write your *support*.

1.   What is the author's gender? _____

Support: _____

2.   What is the author's profession? _____

Support: _____

3.   For whom has the author written this? _____

Support: _____

4.   What *tone* does the author write in? (In other words, is the tone formal, informal, academic, scientific, conversational, etc.?)

_____

Support: _____

8   **Understanding Chronology.**   Time words show the relationship between events and their order in time. Here are just a few examples.

first	beginning	after that	after	last
second	next	then	at this point	finally

The author suggests reading the newspaper in a certain order. Quickly look for time words in the reading selection; mark them as you find them. Then use them to help you number these suggestions in order.

1.   _____   Preview the newspaper.

2.   _____   Choose a good newspaper.

3.   _____   Throw away the sections that you have no interest in.

4.   _____   Know about the various parts of a newspaper in order to decide what to read and what to skip.

5.   _____   Go to the front page and read each headline.

6.   _____   Look for some small piece of information that interests you (e.g., the weather).

7.   _____   Move to a section that interests you, such as entertainment, business, or sports, and read just the beginning of a few articles.

8.   _____   Choose five articles.

9.   _____   Read only the first paragraph or two of five articles.

9 **Viewpoint.** The author expresses several opinions. Look back at the selection to find the author's opinion on these topics.

Topic	Opinion
1. reading an English-language newspaper	_____
2. spending most of the day on Sunday reading the paper	_____
3. tabloid newspapers	_____
4. ethical writing of hard news	_____
5. the separation of opinion from hard news	_____
6. the language of sports	_____

10 **Checking Your Understanding.** Turn back to Exercise 2 on page 241 and answer the questions that are answered in the reading selection.

Discussing the Reading

11 In small groups, talk about your answers to these questions.

1. Which sections of the newspaper do you prefer? Why?
2. If you sometimes read a newspaper in English, does it help you to improve your English? Which sections help you the most?

Beyond the Text

Find a good English-language newspaper. (If you don't know of one, ask your teacher.) For homework, follow the steps that the author suggests in Paragraph E of "How to Read a Newspaper." Then, in class, discuss your experience. Was this technique helpful to you? Why or why not? What was difficult? What did you enjoy? What did you learn?

Choose *one* of these projects.

1. Register for an English-language customized online news service. (Choose one from the box on page 244 or another.) Then tell the class about this.
2. Find a tabloid newspaper. (Ask your teacher for the name of one.) Read through it and try to discover why the author says it is "trash." Also, try to discover why the author implies that it is not a bad way to "acquire a little vocabulary and have some fun." Do you agree with her?

Focus on Testing

Figurative Language

In Chapter 6, you saw that some words have figurative meanings in addition to their basic, literal meanings. For example, if a writer refers to a tabloid newspaper as "trash," it doesn't literally mean garbage. Instead, it has a figurative meaning of "something of inferior quality or worth very little."

On vocabulary and reading tests, you might be asked for the meaning of words that are used figuratively. *All* the answers for an item might be synonyms or near-synonyms of the underlined word in the sentence. Read the sentence carefully and choose the answer that has the same meaning of the word as it is used in that particular context.

For each underlined word or expression that follows, circle the letter of the appropriate meaning for its context.

1. The Supernovas <u>destroyed</u> the Jaguars 3-2 in last night's playoff game at Space Stadium.

   a. ruined the condition of   d. killed
   b. defeated   e. neutralized
   c. put out of existence

2. The hijacked jet <u>sat</u> on the runway for two days.

   a. rested on a chair   d. took a seated position
   b. remained   e. had a position on a committee
   c. lay, rested

3. They <u>shot</u> that program on a tropical island.

   a. fired a gun   d. went first
   b. filmed   e. took a photograph
   c. saw

4. I hope you can <u>pick up</u> new vocabulary by reading the newspaper regularly.

   a. take hold of and lift up   d. acquire, get
   b. be able to receive (radio signals)   e. arrange to go and get
   c. raise oneself after failure

5. The investigation did not <u>bring to light</u> any unethical actions by the police.

   a. make known   d. cause
   b. put outside, under the sun   e. move
   c. take to a place with electric light

PART 2	# The Daily News

---

1   **Skimming for Main Ideas.**   Readers often glance at material quickly before they read it, to get a general idea of what it is about. As quickly as you can (try to do this in about forty-five seconds), look over the following paragraphs from a newspaper. Then write the appropriate article letter next to the corresponding description.

1. _____ a "hard news" story

2. _____ an editorial

3. _____ a letter from an advice column

4. _____ a review of a TV program

5. _____ a book review

6. _____ a sports article

2   **Summarizing.**   Quickly read each paragraph again, without using a dictionary. Mark the information in any way that helps you understand it. Then use the information that you marked to write a summarizing statement.

A

> ### POLICE ETHICS
> Once again, Chief of Police Ervin Dobbs has proven that his determination to protect the members of his police force outweighs his desire to uncover the truth. After last month's incident in which three police officers may have used unnecessary violence in responding to the actions of a man whom they were arresting, we had hoped for an objective, outside investigation. However, yesterday Chief Dobbs announced his decision to investigate this incident *within* the police department. This is clearly a case of "the fox guarding the hen house." Chief Dobbs' failure to take the initiative in bringing to light possible unethical actions by his officers leads us to question his own ethics. We believe that this decision is part of an undesirable trend in the police department. Perhaps the city council should consider a search

B

> ### CLIFFHANGER
> Making a thrilling last-minute goal, Kevin Brisbane led the Supernovas to destroy the Jaguars 3-2 in last night's playoff game at Space Stadium. Although suffering from a knee injury, Brisbane played brilliantly in the final quarter of the game and was chosen the team's Most Valuable Player. Traded last season from the Thunderbolts, Brisbane has not only been the team's star player but has also worked to bring together a group of loose-

C

SURVIVING "SURVIVOR"

It has been reported that at least half the country tuned in to watch last night's final show of "Survivor"—a ridiculous competition among sixteen greedy, boring people roughing it on a tropical island in an attempt to become the last "survivor" and thereby to win a significant amount of money. I find that I am both relieved that this mindless series has come to an end and horrified that it is only the beginning of a trend. It goes without saying that producers have announced plans to shoot a number of similar programs, as they have in Sweden and the Netherlands, where the concept originated. Already, a related series has put a group of strangers together

D

NEW ZEALAND JET HIJACKED

The Air New Zealand jet hijacked yesterday by three unknown men continues to sit on the runway at Kimpo Airport in Seoul. Ten passengers—one a pregnant woman—were released, but ninety-two others and the seven-member crew remain on board as hostages. The hijackers have not yet made clear their destination but have demanded one million U.S. dollars in cash. Negotiators have not been able to determine the ethnicity of the hijackers or any goals other than the money. In a similar hijack attempt at Kimpo last year, the release of all hostages was successfully negotiated,

E

VIRGINIA WOOLF MEETS MODERN SOUL-MATES

In his third novel, *The Hours,* Michael Cunningham tells the deep and passionate story of one day in the lives of three women in different cities and time periods. One woman, in modern-day New York, spends the day planning a party for a friend. Another, in 1950s Los Angeles, begins to feel a prisoner in her "perfect" family. The third is Virginia Woolf, as Cunningham sees her, in a London suburb, beginning to write her famous novel *Mrs. Dalloway.* With careful and original prose, Cunningham slowly brings their stories together to an exquisite ending. Clearly influenced by the writing of Woolf, Cunningham is perhaps the truest modern inheritor

F

Dear Confused,
It might *seem* impolite to accept a guest's offer to help you in the kitchen at a dinner party, but remember that above all, you want your guests to feel comfortable. Not everyone feels relaxed at a party. It often makes someone feel more "at home" to visit with you while helping out with some small task than to be treated like visiting royalty. It always helps to imagine yourself in the role of guest; what makes you feel comfortable? How do you

After You Read

3 **Distinguishing Facts from Opinions.** It's important for students to be able to recognize the difference between facts and opinions. A fact can be checked and proven, even if you aren't sure if it is true or not. An opinion is an idea that people might disagree about. One way to distinguish the two is to be aware of words that indicate *opinion*. Some of these are modals (*should, shouldn't, ought to*), but most are adjectives or adverbs.

Examples

| good (well) | wonderful (-ly) | horrible | brilliant |
| bad (-ly) | ridiculous | exquisite | interesting |

On the short lines, write F before the statements that are *facts,* according to what is stated or implied in the reading. Write O before the statements that are (or may be) the *opinions* of the writers of the articles. The first two are done as examples.

Police Ethics

1. __F__ Ervin Dobbs is the chief of police.

2. __F__ There was an incident last month in which three police officers may have used unnecessary violence during an arrest.

3. _____ The police chief does not want the truth about the incident to be uncovered.

Cliffhanger

4. _____ The Jaguars and Supernovas played at Space Stadium last night.

5. _____ Kevin Brisbane played brilliantly in the final quarter.

Surviving "Survivor"

6. _____ The people on "Survivor" were greedy and boring.

7. _____ "Survivor" was a competition among sixteen people on a tropical island.

8. _____ There are plans to release other similar programs.

New Zealand Jet Hijacked

9. _____ A jet was hijacked yesterday by three people.

10. _____ Except for a demand for money, the hijackers have not made clear their ethnicity or the reason for the hijacking.

Virginia Woolf Meets Modern Soul-Mates

11. _____ *The Hours* is Michael Cunningham's third novel.

12. _____ It is the story of three women in different cities and times.

13. _____ His prose is careful and original.

14. _____ The ending is exquisite.

Discussing the Reading

4 In small groups, talk about your answers to these questions.

1. Do you sometimes read book reviews, movie reviews, or TV reviews? If so, do they influence your choice of books to read or movies/TV programs to see?

2. In your country, are there advice columns in the newspapers? If so, what kind of advice is given? (Romance? Politeness? Financial?)

3. In your country, are newspapers careful to separate factual hard news from opinion, or is there a mixture?

PART 3 # Building Vocabulary and Study Skills

---

1 **The Grammar of Newspaper Headlines.** Newspaper headlines in English can be difficult to understand. Certain grammar rules are specific to headlines. Here are some of them.

■ Articles (*a, an, the*) are usually omitted (left out). You need to imagine them there. If this is the first (or only) day that a story has been reported, imagine *a* or *an* for a singular count noun. If this is a continuing story, or if this is something or someone well known, imagine *the*.

■ The verb *be* is usually omitted. Imagine it there in the present tense.

Example

President in Madagascar for Meeting =
The president **is** in Madagascar for **a** meeting.

■ A comma is used instead of the word *and*.

■ An infinitive (*to* + verb) usually indicates the future tense. It is an abbreviation of *be going to* + verb.

Example

New Program to Film in Caracas, Quito =
A new program **is going** to film in Caracas **and** Quito.

■ A present participle (*-ing*) without the verb *be* may indicate the present perfect continuous, present continuous, or past continuous tense. You don't know the tense for certain because the verb *be* is not there. To understand the headline, imagine the verb *be* in the present perfect continuous. This most often fits the context; however, if it doesn't, try the present continuous. If that doesn't fit, try the past continuous.

Example

Brisbane Playing at Top Form =
Brisbane **has been** (or perhaps **is**) playing at top form.

- The present tense in a headline usually doesn't mean the present. Instead, it indicates the active voice. You, the reader, will need to decide which tense fits the context. First try the present perfect tense (in the active voice). This works most of the time. However, if this doesn't seem to fit, try (in this order) the present continuous and then the simple past.

   Example

   UFOs from Mars Land on Earth =

   UFOs from Mars **have landed** on Earth.

- A past participle indicates the passive voice. The regular "past tense" (*-ed*) probably doesn't mean the past tense. Instead, it is probably the past participle, and therefore indicates the passive voice. Because the verb *be* is missing, you need to imagine it there in either the present perfect or simple past tense.

   Example

   Jet Hijacked =

   A jet **has been** hijacked.

- The relative pronoun (*that, which, who*) of an adjective clause is omitted.

   Example

   Hostage Released from Jet Dies =

   A hostage **who was** released from **the** jet **has died**.

- A comma (in addition to meaning *and*) might indicate a direct quotation. How do you know? It is followed by the name of a person, organization, or country, and then a verb of speech (e.g., *say, claim*).

   Example

   Media Reports Hurting Police, Dobbs Says =

   "Media reports **are** hurting **the** police," Dobbs **has said.**

Change these headlines into complete sentences, as in the previous examples.

1. Elvis Presley Seen in Bus Station =

   _____

2. Medical Technology Topic of Meeting in Tokyo =

   _____

3. Hikers Find Ancient Paintings in Cave in Spain =

   _____

4. UN Sending Aid to Flood Victims =

   _____

5. New Planet Discovered =

   _____

6. Two Hostages Shot; One Dies =

   _____

7. Thailand, Mexico to Sign Trade Agreement =

_____

8. TV Show Begun in Sweden Now Popular Worldwide =

_____

9. Police Chief Covering Up Errors, Critics Claim =

_____

10. Boy Injured by Truck; Driver Arrested =

_____

2 **Newspaper Language.**   Certain nouns and verbs appear often in newspaper articles, especially in the headlines. Some of these words have a figurative meaning. Here are some examples.

back (v)	support
ban (n, v)	prohibit; not allow
cut (n, v)	decrease (e.g., prices)
declare (v)	say (strongly); express an opinion
eye (v)	consider (something) as a goal or as something that one wants to take
flee (v)	run away; try to escape
hike (n, v)	increase (e.g., taxes)
key (n)	very important factor; something significant
link (n, v)	connect; associate
OK (n, v)	approve
opt for (v)	choose; decide on
probe (n, v)	investigate
seek/sought (v)	try to get; search for
slash (v)	cut (reduce, decrease) deeply (e.g., subsidies, financial aid)
slay/slain (v)	kill
spark (n, v)	begin; initiate
vow (n, v)	promise

Change these headlines into complete sentences. Use both the grammar rules and the list of vocabulary to help you.

1. Study Links Mood to Diet =

_____

2. Smoking Banned in City Restaurants =

_____

3. Tax Hike Necessary, Mayor Declares =

_____

4. City Council OKs Tax Hike =

_____

5. Results of Police Probe Released =

_____

6. President Backs Microlending Program in Rural Areas, Seeks Funds =

_____

7. Mother of Girl Slain in Park Seeking Help =

_____

8. Arrest of Local Man Sparks Anger =

_____

9. High Rate of Diabetes Linked to Diet, Study Finds =

_____

10. Students Opting for Technology Majors =

_____

3   **Hyphenated Words.**   Hyphens (-) have several meanings. For instance, a hyphen can replace the word *to*.

Example

They won the game 3-2.
(3-2 = 3 to 2; i.e., one team had three points, and the other had two)

Hyphens often connect word parts, especially of adjectives but also of nouns.

Example

It was a last-minute decision.
His mother-in-law gave him some good advice.

Complete the sentences with the missing hyphenated words. Choose from these:

old-fashioned	half-truths	op-ed	right-hand
two-day	English language	modern-day	seven-member

1. Hijackers held the _____ crew hostage during

   the _____ negotiations to free them.

2. You can find his letter in the lower _____

   corner of the _____ page of the newspaper.

3. Busy _____ people often prefer a customized online newspaper to an _____ paper one.

4. Several _____ tabloid newspapers are famous for amazing stories that are usually just gossip or contain

_____ .

Beyond the Text

Look through the front section of an English-language newspaper. Bring to class five headlines that contain examples of the grammar rules and vocabulary that you saw on pages 252–256. Share these with the class and try to "translate" them into "normal" English.

PART 4 Reading in the Real World

1 **Vocabulary.**   The following article is from a British journal (magazine), *New States-man & Society*, about newspapers and the changing society in China. It contains many words that are probably new to you and a good deal of figurative language and idioms. This new vocabulary may be divided into three groups:

- words that you can probably guess from the context
- words that you probably cannot guess but aren't necessary in order to understand the main ideas
- words that you probably cannot guess but *do* need in order to understand the main ideas

This article presents the difficulty of guessing meaning from context when there are *too many* new words. For example, here are the first two sentences:

A little more than a year ago, *China Culture Gazette*, official <u>organ</u> of China's Ministry of Culture, was transformed. For years, CCG had been an <u>infamous</u> <u>stronghold</u> of the <u>hard-line</u> <u>apparatchiks</u>, <u>choked</u> with <u>dull</u>, <u>harsh</u> Communist Party <u>propaganda</u>.

In the first sentence, there is one new word, *organ.* You already know at least one meaning of this word, from Chapter 10—part of the body such as the heart or liver. But you see that the word has a very different meaning here. Because there is only one new word in this sentence, you can probably guess its meaning. It refers to *China Culture Gazette,* which sounds like the name of a newspaper or magazine, so you imagine that *organ* means "newspaper."

However, the second sentence is full of new words, so guessing is impossible, and you need a "translation": "For years, CCG had been a famous (in a bad way), safe place for the strict members of the Communist Party and was full of boring, unpleasant ideas (possibly half-truths) from the government.

Here is a glossary of some words from the article. You can look over this list now or look back at it as you read.

Words and Expressions	Meanings
red	symbol of many quite different things (e.g., communism, debt, danger)
nude	without clothes
nudity	the condition of being without clothes
coolest	most popular; most fashionable
like hot cakes	very fast; very many
mushroom	plant that we eat that is famous for growing very fast
mired in debt	owing a huge amount of money
on the brink of	at the edge of; very close to (usually trouble)
bail them out	save them from trouble
ladled out	gave
meagre	not enough
profitable	able to make money
scandal	shocking news about someone's improper behavior
broke	became public (used for news)
pursuit	the act of chasing and trying to catch
newsstands	places where people buy newspapers and magazines

2 **Scanning a Magazine Article.**   Read the following article. Then do the exercises that follow. As you did in Chapter 10, look through the questions *first* and have them in mind as you read. *Don't worry* about the words you don't understand. Instead, concentrate on understanding the main ideas and answering the questions.

Mao Meets Muzak

A little more than a year ago, *China Culture Gazette*, official organ of China's Ministry of Culture, was transformed. For years, CCG had been an infamous stronghold of the hard-line apparatchiks, choked with dull, harsh Communist Party propaganda. With a new issue of its Cultural Weekend edition, the paper changed colour overnight: from red to yellow.

The pictures did the trick. On that day, the four-page Cultural Weekend displayed many nude and half-nude photographs; instantly, it became known as "the coolest paper in Beijing." It also ran a front-page interview on the subject of nudity with Liu Xiaoqing, China's brash movie queen. It sold like hot cakes.

The Ministry of Propaganda was furious. The Ministry of Culture wasn't happy about it, either. Rumour had it that Communist Party general secretary Jiang Zemin, who has a propensity for showing off his "high-culture" taste, happened to pick up a copy of CCG at a subway station. The general secretary couldn't believe what he saw, and afterwards expressed grave concern about the moral health of Chinese society.

With the economic reform and a mushrooming of new papers and journals competing with the old ones, the situation has changed significantly in the past five years or so. CCG had been in the red, politically and financially. In fact, the paper was so deeply mired in debt, it was on the brink of folding. Everyone on the staff knew the party was not going to bail them out: as inflation continued and the price of paper climbed, the government ladled out the same meagre subsidy.

So when Zhang Zuomin, a former Red Guard, took charge of Cultural Weekend, he was given a free hand to make it profitable, and he knew exactly how far he could exercise that freedom. What was remarkable was that CCG's hard-line chief editor stood firmly behind Zhang when the nudity scandal broke. The wily old apparatchik even snapped at his grumbling superiors at the ministries. "Are we no longer 'marching toward the market'?" he demanded, employing a party slogan currently in fashion. "If not, I quit."

In their pursuit of the average reader, many other papers are testing the new boundaries. The average reader is apparently tired of "hard news"—the kind of stories found in the official print media that go on and on about party congresses, production rates and ideological education, while remaining silent about political oppression and abuses of power. How much more inviting is gossip about movie stars and millionaires.

With the new formula, the papers have begun to support themselves, attract advertisements and relieve government of its financial burden, but only at the expense of the official papers. Once-dominant journals are being ignored by readers. Papers like *People's Daily* and *Guangming Daily* still arrive in the offices of all state enterprises, but few look to them for interesting coverage of popular events. They can't compete with what's on the newsstands.

Source: Excerpted from "Mao Meets Muzak" by Jianying Zha and Denis MacShane from *New Statesman & Society*, April 1, 1994, p. 31. Copyright © 1994 Statesman and Nation Publishing Company Ltd. (UK).

After You Read

3 **Checking Your Answers.** Look back at the reading, if necessary, to answer these questions.

1. The first paragraph tells us that the newspaper "changed colour overnight: from red to yellow." These colors are used as symbols. What does this expression probably mean, in the context of this article?

   _____

2. The second paragraph says, "The pictures did the trick." Read the rest of the paragraph to answer this question: if the nude photos "did the trick," what did they do? (In other words, what might this idiom mean?)

   _____

3. In the fourth paragraph, we find that _____.

    a. there were many new newspapers and magazines

    b. there was a lot of competition with the old newspapers and magazines

    c. CCG was nearing failure

    d. the Communist Party was not giving CCG enough money

    e. all of the above

4. In the fifth paragraph, we find that _____.

    a. Zhang Zuomin had the responsibility for a section of CCG, Cultural Weekend

    b. Zhang Zuomin was allowed to do anything to make Cultural Weekend profitable

    c. Zhang Zuomin's boss supported the changes at the newspaper

    d. a and b

    e. a, b, and c

5. In the last sentence of the sixth paragraph, what does *inviting* mean?

    a. boring

    b. asked to go and talk about movie stars

    c. attractive

    d. hard news

    e. not allowed

6. In the last paragraph, we learn that the new newspapers _____.

    a. still arrive in government offices

    b. contain stories about popular events

    c. are more successful than the old style magazines

    d. a and c

    e. b and c

7. What is the main idea of the article? Write this in one sentence.

_____

Talk It Over

Censorship.   In some countries, government censors remove from newspapers and magazines articles that have certain content such as political opinion or sexual references or photographs. Is censorship good or bad? Why do some cultures believe it is necessary? What do you think?

Video Activities: Bye, Bye, Charlie Brown

Before You Watch.   Discuss the following questions in a group.

1. Have you ever seen or read "Peanuts"? (In some countries it is called "Snoopy.") Tell what you know about his comic strip. Do you have a favorite character?

2. What other comic strips do you know?

Watch.   Write answers to the following questions.

1. What did Charles Schultz think of the name "Peanuts"?

   _____

2. Why did Charles Schultz retire?

   _____

3. What unusual event happened on the day this video was made?

   _____

   _____

Watch Again.   Fill in the missing details.

1. For nearly _____ years, the comic strip Peanuts appeared in more than _____ newspapers in _____ different countries. It had approximately _____ readers. It was first published in _____.

2. Charles Schultz never liked the name "Peanuts" because it doesn't have _____. He would have preferred to call the strip _____.

3. The woman at the end of the video will miss the character called _____.

After You Watch.   Read some English language comic strips. Then discuss these questions:

1. Who are the characters in this story? What is the relationship between them?

2. What does each character say? What does each character mean?

3. A comic strip tells a story. Retell the story of this strip in your own words, based on the words and actions of the characters.

4. What could have happened just before the story in this strip? What do you predict will happen in the next strip?

5. What is your reaction to the comic? For example, do you think it is funny, cute, wise, or boring?

Chapter 12

With Liberty and Justice for All

IN THIS CHAPTER

The first reading selection discusses systems of justice in different societies. The second is a selection of stories from the news about legal cases in three countries. Finally, you will read two newspaper articles about an unusual punishment intended to change the ways of two young criminals.

PART 1	# The Concept of Law

Before You Read

1   **Getting Started.**   Look at the photo and discuss it in small groups.

1.   Where does this scene take place? Who are the people and what are they doing?

2.   What might have happened before this scene began? What might happen next?

3.   Would a comparable scene in your culture be similar? Why or why not?

2   **Preparing to Read.**   If you ask questions before and during the reading process and then think about the answers, your reading will be more active; you will probably better understand and remember the material you have read. Look at the photo again and then scan the first reading selection. List questions that you think the reading might answer.

1.   _____

2.   _____

3.   _____

4.   _____

5.   _____

6.   _____

7.   _____

3   **Vocabulary Preview.**   Briefly look over this list of words from the reading that follows. Which words do you already know? For the ones that you don't know, *don't* use a dictionary. Try to understand them from the reading.

Nouns		**Verbs**	**Adjective**
rights	sin	commit	tribal
duties	lawsuit	violate	
punishment	harmony	restore	
justice	sentence	sue	
deterrent	dispute		

Read

4   As you read the following selection, think about possible answers to the preceding questions that you wrote. Read the selection quickly. Do not use a dictionary. Then do the exercises that follow the reading.

The Concept of Law

The Idea of Law

[A]   The idea of "law" exists in every culture. All societies have some kind of law to keep order and to control the interactions of people with those around them. The laws of any culture tell people three things: what they *can* do (their rights), what they *must* do (their duties), and what they may *not* do (illegal actions). In addition, there are usually specific types of punishment for those who break the law.

What Prevents Crime?

[B]   Although all societies have laws, not all have the same idea of justice—what is "right" and "wrong" and how "wrong" should be punished. In most Western cultures, it is thought that punishing criminals will prevent them from committing other crimes. Also, it is hoped that the fear of punishment will act as a deterrent that prevents other people from committing similar crimes; in other words, people who are considering a life of crime will decide against it because of fear of punishment. In most non-Western cultures, by contrast, punishment is not seen as a deterrent. Instead, great importance is placed on restoring balance in the situation. A thief, for example, may be ordered to return the things he has stolen instead of, as in Western societies, spending time in prison.

Kinds of Law

[C]   Another difference in the concept of justice lies in various societies' ideas of what laws are. In the West, people consider "laws" quite different from "customs." There is also a great contrast between "sins" (breaking religious laws) and "crimes" (breaking laws of the government). In many non-Western cultures, however, there is little separation of customs, laws, and religious beliefs; in other cultures, these three may be quite separate from one another, but still very much different from those in the West. For these reasons, an action may be considered a crime in one country but be socially acceptable in others. For instance, although a thief is viewed as a criminal in much of the world, in a small village where there is considerable communal living and sharing of objects, the word *thief* may have little meaning. Someone who has taken something without asking is simply considered an impolite person.

Civil Law and Society

[D]   Most countries have two kinds of law: criminal and civil. People who have been accused of acts such as murder or theft are heard in the criminal justice system, while civil justice deals with people who are believed to have violated others' rights. The use of the civil system reflects the values of the society in which it exists. In the United States, where personal, individual justice is considered very important, civil law has become "big business." There are over 700,000 lawyers in the United States, and many of them keep busy with civil lawsuits; that is, they work for people who want to sue (bring legal action against) others. If a man falls over a torn rug in a hotel and breaks his arm, for instance, he might decide to sue the hotel owners so that they will pay his medical costs. In a country like Japan, by contrast, there is very little use of the civil justice system. Lawsuits are not very popular in Japan, where social harmony (peaceful agreement) is even more important than individual rights, and where people would rather reach agreements outside court.

The Judgment of Disputes

[E]   In most cultures, when people cannot reach agreement on their own, a judge might be called on to make a decision. In North America, a case might be heard in a court of law before a judge chosen by the government and, perhaps, a group of citizens in a jury. In some tribal societies, however, a man or a woman who is thought to have special supernatural power might be chosen by the people to judge disputes. In the 1950s, among the Gisu people of Uganda, the inhabitants of a village had great faith in a man who was believed to have the ability to cause smallpox, a serious disease. On Sundays, they went to his "court," where he charged a fee for his judgments of cases. Although the Ugandan government considered this practice illegal, he was very popular with the people.

Social Justice

[F]   In societies where courts and judges simply don't exist, self-help is necessary and socially acceptable in disputes. If a cow has been stolen, the owner's friends and relatives may get together and help him get the animal back. In small villages, everyone, in a sense, becomes a judge; in such societies, where people's neighbors are also friends, members of their families, or co-workers, the opinions of the villagers are very important. Social disapproval of people's activities can serve both as powerful punishment for and as strong deterrent to crime.

Modern and Traditional Justice

[G]   In some countries, traditional and modern justice exist side by side. A good example of this combination can be found in Tanzania, where people usually take their legal disputes first to family leaders or the representatives of their village "age-set," a group of people of about the same age. If the disagreement cannot be settled by these leaders, then the case is taken to a modern court. The people who are part of the dispute will argue until both sides agree, for the goal is to restore a situation of balance and social harmony. Another example occurred in the United States in the summer of 1994. Two Indian teenagers pleaded guilty to attacking a man in Washington State.* Instead of sentencing the boys to prison, the judge sent them back to their people in Alaska for traditional tribal punishment. It was believed that prison would turn them into hardened criminals but that tribal justice might help them become functioning members of society.

* For more about this, see Part 4 of this chapter.

After You Read

5 **Getting the Main Ideas.**   Write T on the lines before the statements that are true, according to the reading. Write F before the statements that are false. Write I before the statements that are impossible to know from the reading.

1. _____ The concept of law and justice is the same in all cultures.

2. _____ Punishment brings back balance to situations and prevents other crimes.

3. _____ Every country's laws are based on historical customs and religious beliefs.

4. _____ In urban societies, crimes are usually judged in the criminal law system, while personal disagreements are resolved by other methods.

5. _____ In every society, it is illegal and socially unacceptable to commit murder.

6. _____ Traditional justice is more effective than modern justice.

6 **Finding Important Details.**   The reading selection gives examples of concepts of justice in the United States and other Western countries, Japan, and traditional village societies. Choose the important ideas about these systems and write them on the lines, without mentioning the specific society. Then exchange books with a classmate. Write US in the parentheses before the statements about the United States, J before those about Japan, and TS before those about traditional societies. Exchange books again to check the answers. The first one is done as an example.

1. (US) _Punishment is considered a deterrent to crime._

2. (   ) _____

3. (   ) _____

4. (   ) _____

5. (   ) _____

6. (   ) _____

7. (   ) _____

8. (   ) _____

7   **Understanding Vocabulary from Context.**   Here are some vocabulary items that might be new from the reading selection "The Concept of Law." Try to determine the definition of each item from the context and write it on the line. Then check your answers in a dictionary.

1. concept   = _____

2. punishment = _____

3. justice   = _____

4. deterrent   = _____

5. commit   = _____

6. restore   = _____

7. order   = _____

8. sin   = _____

9. violate   = _____

10. lawsuit   = _____

11. sue   = _____

12. harmony   = _____

13. dispute   = _____

14. sentence   = _____

8   **Understanding Outlines.**   Write your own outline for each paragraph of the reading selection. (There may be several correct possibilities.) Then compare your outlines with those of your classmates and explain the reasons for your organization of the information.

I.   The Idea of Law

   A.   What people can do

   B.   What people must do

   C.   What people may not do

II.   What Prevents Crime?

_____

_____

_____

_____

_____

III.   Kinds of Law

_____

_____

_____

_____

_____

IV.   Civil Law and Society

_____

_____

_____

_____

_____

V.   The Judgment of Disputes

_____

_____

_____

_____

_____

VI.   Social Justice

_____

_____

_____

_____

_____

VII.   Modern and Traditional Justice

_____

_____

_____

_____

_____

9 **Checking Your Understanding.**   Turn back to Exercise 2 on page 262 and answer the questions you wrote.

Discussing the Reading

10 In small groups, talk about your answers to these questions.

1. In Exercise 6 on page 265, which follows the reading, you listed statements about various systems of justice. In your opinion, what other cultures or countries do these statements refer to?

2. What else do you know about the system of law and justice in the United States or Canada? Compare it with the system in your culture.

3. What kind of justice system seems most advantageous to you? Why?

4. Are there any famous trials going on now? If so, what are they about?

Beyond the Text

Bring to class newspaper and magazine articles about famous legal trials—past and/or present. Share the articles with the class. Discuss the important information and learn new vocabulary.

PART 2

The Legal System in the News

1 **Skimming for Main Ideas.**   Read the following articles quickly, without using a dictionary. (You'll notice that the headlines have been omitted.) When you finish reading, write the main idea of each article.

A. _____

_____

B. _____

_____

C. _____

_____

The Legal System in the News

A

_____

_____

John Carter, of New Jersey, recently sued McDonald's after he was injured in a traffic accident with a customer of the restaurant chain. The customer, apparently, was drinking a chocolate milkshake and eating French fries at the time his car hit Carter's. Carter sued McDonald's because of the restaurant's failure to warn customers: don't eat while driving.

The result of the lawsuit? The court ruled in McDonald's favor. It was decided that McDonald's had no responsibility to warn customers about something so obvious. However, McDonald's still had to pay $10,000 for its defense. The case was in the court system for three years.

B

_____

_____

A tribal leader in a rural mountain village in Papua New Guinea (South Pacific) had been killed. According to tribal law, in order to restore harmony, the family of the killer had to pay compensation to the victim's family. The exact amount of compensation was $15,000, twenty-five pigs, and a young woman named Miriam Wilngal.

The family began to collect the money and gather the pigs. But there was one serious problem: Miriam Wilngal refused to be part of the compensation. She wanted to finish high school and become a typist.

Her refusal shocked both families and led to a court case. Her lawyer explained that if a tribal law violates the country's democratic constitution, the dispute is heard in National Court. In this case, the judge ruled in favor of Ms. Wilngal and said that the tribal law violated her personal freedom. Her lawyer pointed out, "Women are not animals."

The family members of the man remain angry and continue to believe that a woman is due to them.

C

_____

_____

    In 1970s–1980s India, the news was full of stories about Phoolan Devi, the infamous "Bandit Queen." Born in poverty, Phoolan Devi was a member of the low-caste "untouchables." In her village she had been a child bride and a victim of rape. She became the leader of a gang of *dacoits*—organized robbers and murderers—and a folk hero, a sort of female Robin Hood, almost a goddess to millions of poor, uneducated, rural women.

    In a dramatic public ceremony in 1983, she surrendered to police. Hindi movie music played loudly, and a crowd of 8,000 people watched as Phoolan Devi, a small young woman, walked up the steps of an outdoor stage and held her rifle above her head. She spent the next eleven years in prison.

    In 1994, with her time in prison and a popular movie about her life, *Bandit Queen,* behind her, the former criminal (who cannot read or write) decided on a new career: politics. She ran for a seat in the national parliament—and won.

    However, in January, 1997, the court decided to arrest her again, for murders committed back in 1981. Phoolan Devi claimed that she had not committed these crimes. She then disappeared before authorities could arrest her.

After You Read

2 **Summarizing.**   Go back to the main ideas that you wrote. Use this information to help you write a headline for each article on the lines above the article. When you finish, compare your main ideas and headlines with those of other students.

3 **Making Inferences.**   What can you infer from the reading about the culture or legal system in the United States, Papua New Guinea, and India? List the possibilities.

_____

_____

_____

_____

_____

_____

_____

Discussing the Reading

4 In small groups, talk about your answers to these questions.

1. What do you think about John Carter's lawsuit? Have you ever heard about similar lawsuits? If so, tell your group about them.

2. Do women and men have equal rights in your country? If so, for how long has this been true? If not, in what ways are their rights different?

3. In your country, are there tribal people who have their own tribal laws? If so, do these laws sometimes conflict with national laws?

4. The third article said that Phoolan Devi was "a sort of female Robin Hood." Who was Robin Hood, and what was he famous for? Do you know about other criminals who have become famous folk heroes? If so, tell your group about them.

Cross-Cultural Note: Highlights in International Legal History

System of Laws	*Date*	*What It Was, What It Did*
Ur-Nammu's Code	2050 BC	first known written code of laws; established a system with judges who could order guilty people to pay compensation to the victims of their crimes
Hammurabi's Code	1700 BC	established in ancient Babylon; included the principle of punishment by "an eye for an eye and a tooth for a tooth"
The Ten Commandments	1300 BC	a list of laws received from Moses by God of actions that people should or shouldn't do; later, part of the Bible
The Laws of Manu	1290–880 BC	legal rules that established the caste system in India
The Twelve Tables	450 BC	ancient Roman law; the foundation of modern law; included the principle that the law must be written and that judges must base their decisions on it
The Code of Li K'vei	350 BC	the first Chinese code of laws; dealt with rules concerning arrest and prison for crimes such as robbery
The 17-Article Constitution of Japan	604 AD	foundation of morality and law in Japan; stated that "peace and harmony should be respected"; emphasis on prevention of disputes
First School of Law	1100 AD	established in Bologna, Italy; spread Roman law through Europe
Magna Carta	1215 AD	signed by King John of England; first time that a king agreed that he, too, must obey the law
American Declaration of Independence	1776 AD	declared, for the first time, that certain people did not have—from birth—the right to rule others
Napoleonic Code	1804 AD	included many principles such as individual liberty and equality of all people under the law
The Geneva Convention	1864 AD	agreement that provided some human rights in time of war
The Universal Declaration of Human Rights	1948 AD	established by the United Nations; includes social, cultural, economic, political, and civil rights

Source: The World Wide Legal Information Association (www.wwlia.org/hist.htm)

| PART 3 | **Building Vocabulary and Study Skills** |

1 **Categories (Content Areas).** What categories (content areas) are the following words usually connected with? Write *edu* on the lines before the words about education; *rel* before the words about religion; *med* before words about medicine; *law* before words about law; and *bus* before words about business and money. In a few cases, more than one answer may be correct.

1. _____ classroom
2. _____ jury
3. _____ virus
4. _____ budget
5. _____ justice
6. _____ blackboard
7. _____ courtroom
8. _____ sue

9. _____ priest
10. _____ account
11. _____ symptoms
12. _____ prayer
13. _____ ceremony
14. _____ treatment
15. _____ patient
16. _____ livelihood

17. _____ bargain
18. _____ crime
19. _____ disease
20. _____ advertise
21. _____ worship
22. _____ instructor
23. _____ judge
24. _____ lesson

25. _____ dispute
26. _____ assignment
27. _____ punishment
28. _____ lecture
29. _____ memorize
30. _____ marketing
31. _____ cure
32. _____ illegal

33. _____ credit
34. _____ sin
35. _____ physician
36. _____ prison
37. _____ salesclerk
38. _____ faith
39. _____ compensation
40. _____ exam

41. _____ cash
42. _____ deterrent
43. _____ consumer
44. _____ hospital
45. _____ graduate
46. _____ surgery
47. _____ collateral

2 Divide into groups. The class chooses a content area, such as the law, travel, city life, work, art, journalism, and so on. Within a given time limit, each group writes a list of as many words as possible connected with the content area. Then the class discusses the words. The winner is the group with the most correct words. Then repeat the activity with another content area.

3   **Improving Reading Skills: Prediction.**   Fill in the words missing from the following paragraphs about dealing with lawyers in countries with a legal system like that in the United States. There may be several correct answers. When you are finished, discuss the reasons for your choices.

In disputes in which a reasonable _____ seems impossible, it may be _____ to get the help of a lawyer. _____a good one is not easy. You might want to ask friends for _____, but their suggestions may help only if their cases were _____ to yours. There may also be _____in your area that provide lists of _____ with their specialties. It is important to choose a lawyer who _____ a lot about the particular _____ that you are worried about.

Your first _____is to call the lawyer and _____ an appointment to see him or her. During this first _____ , you may not get answers to specific legal _____, but you can find out about the lawyer's _____ and fees, and you can see if you get a positive _____ from the conversation. If you ask, you may not have to pay _____ for this first meeting. Its purpose is to help you _____ whether or not this lawyer is the best one to take care of your _____.

Lawyers make most of their money by _____ for their time. They usually charge by the hour, and add up _____ for phone calls, writing _____ , filling out legal _____, and so on. To save yourself _____, always be prepared before you call or _____ your lawyer: write a _____ of your questions and _____ before you begin your discussion. Then, during the session, listen _____, take notes, and _____ organized. Always be honest with your _____ and tell him or her all the _____. In addition, provide the lawyer with all the written _____ you have on the case.

4   Find sections from reading selections at the level of the class; that is, they should be neither too easy nor too difficult. Rewrite the material, but leave out every eighth word. Have copies made for everyone in the class. You and the other students try to figure out the missing words from clues in the reading. Then discuss the reasons for your choices.

PART 4

Reading in the Real World

Focus on Testing

Timed Tests

On any test, some questions will seem easier to you than others. If you are taking a timed test, it will help you to answer the easy questions first and then to come back to the harder ones later. In this way, you will be able to finish more—or all—of the test without wasting time.

   The following two articles are about an unusual punishment for a crime. Read the first article and answer the questions about it. Work as quickly as possible, as you would on a test. (Your teacher might decide to give you a time limit.) Remember to answer the easy questions first. If you finish before the time limit, don't begin the second article. Instead, check your answers. Your teacher will tell you when to begin reading the second article.

Tribal court may banish teens to Alaskan islands

- **Admitted robbery:** Indians making restitution to Washington victim.

KLAWOCK, Alaska (AP)—A panel of Tlingit elders began a hearing Thursday to decide whether two Indian teenagers should be banished to uninhabited islands for severely beating and robbing a pizza deliveryman in Washington state last year.

5   Cousins Adrian Guthrie and Simon Roberts, both 17, pleaded guilty to robbery in May for attacking Tim Whittlesey of Everett, Wash., with a baseball bat. Whittlesey's hearing and eyesight were permanently damaged.

   Rather than sending the teens to prison, a Washington state judge agreed to send them north to face the Kuye'di Kuiu Kwaan Tribal Court.
10 The youths could still get prison time later.

   Rudy James, a tribal elder who proposed the alternative at the behest of the youths' parents, says the punishment probably will be banishment for up to two years to separate, isolated islands in Alaska's vast Alexander Archipelago. The hearing in this southeast Alaska fishing village may last
15 through today.

   The tribal elders held court in the Alaska Native Brotherhood-Alaska Native Sisterhood hall, a single-story building used for weddings, funerals, town meetings and bingo games. It was the first time the Klawock court was convened to determine a sentencing referred from a state court.
20 About 75 people attended Thursday's hearing, which lasted two and a half hours and was scheduled to resume this morning. No one was allowed into the hall until it had been ritually cleansed with branches of devil's club, a thorny plant native to the region.

(continued on page 275)

25   Everyone entering the room submitted to purification by being brushed with a cedar bough and wiping their feet at the door.

Guthrie and Roberts entered the room through an "entrance of shame," wearing their tribal regalia turned inside out.

Each boy was allowed to speak and had a tribal advocate at his side. The boys testified that they had gotten drunk on rum at a party the night

30   of the attack. Guthrie said they got the idea from another boy who bragged that he had mugged pizza deliverymen "to make quick cash."

Both were vague when asked about certain details of the crime, including whether it was premeditated.

"It wasn't very planned-out," Guthrie said. "We just went."

35   Both expressed regret.

"I feel sorry what happened to him, the victim, and the shame I've put my family through and having to be here today," Roberts said.

Source: "Tribal Court May Banish Teens to Alaskan Islands" from *Star Free Press*, September 2, 1994, reprinted by permission of Associated Press.

1. A *hearing* (line 1) is probably _____.

   a.   a conversation

   b.   similar to a trial

   c.   the sense by which one perceives sound

   d.   a kind of punishment

   e.   listening

2. *Banished* (line 2) probably means _____.

   a.   sent away (as punishment)   d.   beaten (as punishment)

   b.   punished   e.   not allowed to go to

   c.   put in prison

3. *Mugged* (line 31) means _____.

   a.   borrowed money from   d.   beaten and robbed

   b.   killed   e.   bought (something) from

   c.   hit

4. The tribal elders held court to decide _____.

   a.   if the boys were guilty   d.   if the boys should go to a state court

   b.   how to help the victim   e.   which island to send the boys to

   c.   on a sentence for the teenagers

5. The teenagers committed the crime when they _____.

   a.   were drunk

   b.   had heard another boy brag about a similar crime

   c.   had carefully planned it

   d.   a and b only

   e.   a and c only

Muggers face year in island isolation

• **Teens banished:** No contact with outside world.

KLAWOCK, Alaska (AP)—They'll have sleeping bags, and tools for cutting firewood and gathering food. But they'll have no way to contact the outside world during a year or more of exile to offshore islands whose only inhabitants are wild animals.

5　　Two 17-year-old Tlingit Indian boys, Adrian Guthrie and Simon Roberts, were banished to separate islands by tribal elders for beating and robbing a pizza delivery man.

It is the first case of a state court referring a criminal case to an American tribal panel for a traditional Indian punishment.

10　　Guthrie and Roberts were held aboard a fishing boat Saturday pending their move to the sprawling Alexander Archipelago of hundreds of mountainous islands off the coast of southeastern Alaska. Tribal officials will not disclose their final destinations.

On Saturday, the teenagers were lounging in the sun. One listened to

15　music on a Walkman as two tribal guards stood watch. The boys would not talk to reporters.

They probably would be taken to their islands during the night for security, said elder Byron Skinna Sr.

The teenagers pleaded guilty in May to robbing Tim Whittlesey and

20　beating him with a baseball bat while he was working as a pizza delivery man in Everett, Wash. They stole $47 and a pizza. Whittlesey, 25, suffered permanent damage to his hearing and eyesight.

Twelve tribal elders deliberated for 3 1/2 hours Friday night before banishing the two for a year to 18 months.

25　　Elder Skinna said each boy would be given forks for digging up clams, axes and saws for cutting firewood, and some food to carry them through the first few days. He said they would have sleeping bags and each will build a small shelter, which will be equipped with a wood stove for cooking and heat.

30　　Guthrie and Roberts look much like teenagers anywhere else in the United States, wearing reversed baseball caps and MTV-inspired clothes. But their elders say the boys have been taught how to live off the land since they began to walk.

Source: "Muggers Face Year in Island Isolation" from *Star Free Press*, September 4, 1994, reprinted by permission of Associated Press.

6. *Exile* (line 3) is probably _____.

    a. punishment

    b. banishment

    c. being forced to leave home

    d. all the above

    e. none of the above

7. We can infer that for the next year or more, the teenagers _____.

    a. won't have conversations with other people

    b. will have no electricity for cooking or heating

    c. may have to work hard to survive

    d. all the above

    e. a and b only

8. For the next year or more, the teenagers _____.

    a. will have only each other for company

    b. won't have a radio

    c. will need to gather their own food

    d. all the above

    e. b and c only

9. The victim of the crime _____.

    a. will have problems hearing for the rest of his life

    b. will have problems seeing for the rest of his life

    c. was a baseball player

    d. a and b only

    e. b and c only

10. It is stated or implied that the teenagers who committed the crime _____.

    a. are similar in many ways to other teenagers in the United States

    b. play baseball

    c. know how to survive in the wilderness

    d. all the above

    e. a and c only

Video Activities: Justice and Racism

Before You Watch.   Discuss the meanings of the following words in a group. Check the meanings in a dictionary if necessary.

Justice	Verdict
Jury	Convict (verb)
Defendant	Testimony
Guilty	

Watch.   Discuss the following questions in a group.

1. At the beginning of the video, the announcer says, "Justice is supposed to be blind, including color blind, but is it?" What is the answer to this question, according to the video?
2. Who is more racist, judges or juries? Why?
3. According to Judge Danielson, what is the solution to the problem of racism in the justice system?

Watch Again.   Below are incomplete statements from the video. Try to guess the missing words. Then watch the video again and check your answers.

a. "Because racism still exists in our society, we see it in our court

_____."

b. "_____ may say they're impartial, but sometimes they

make comments to other _____ about the defendant."

c. "Each judge knows that he or she has an ethical _____ to

deal with (racism) when it occurs in the courtroom."

d. "Racism is going to be _____ with us right on into the

millennium, even in our criminal justice system."

After You Watch.   Work in a group. The words below are similar in meaning but not identical. Use a dictionary to learn their exact meanings. Then explain each word and use it in a sentence. You may do this activity in groups.

   bias   racism   prejudice   apartheid

Photo Credits

Page 1 © Michael S. Yamashita/Corbis; Page 2 *(top left)* © Paul Kenward/Stone, *(top right)* © Jim Zuckerman/Corbis, *(bottom left)* © Dave Bartruff/Corbis, *(bottom right)* © AFP/Corbis; Page 3 © Will/Deni McIntyre/Photo Researchers Inc.; Page 10 © Seth Resnick/Stock Boston; Page 21 © Michael Dwyer/Stock Boston; Page 22 *(left)* © Owen Franken/Stock Boston, *(right)* © Vince Streano/ Corbis; Page 25 © J. Maier Jr./The Image Works; Page 43 © David Lee/Corbis; Page 44 *(left)* © Peter Menzel/Stock Boston, *(top right)* © Mercury Press International, *(bottom right)* © Owen Franken/Stock Boston; Page 51 © Tim Thompson/Corbis/ Page 52 © Donald Johnson/Stone; Page 53 © Steven Rubin/ The Image Works; age 63 © Bill Lai/The Image Works; Page 64 *(left)* © Bettman/Corbis, *(right)* © Walter Hodges/Stone; Page 66 © Corbis #cbo29239; Page 83 © Corbis #cbo34577; Page 89 © Ric Ergenbright/Corbis/ Page 90 *(left)* © Ken Fisher/Stone, *(right)* © Brian Bailey/Stone; Page 99 © Cordella Molloy/ SPL/Photo Researchers Inc.; Page 105 © Vanessa Vick/Photo Researchers Inc.; Page 106 *(top left)* © Vince Streano/Stone, *(top right)* © Danny Lehman/Corbis, *(bottom left)* © Steve Raymer/Corbis, *(bottom right)* © David Wells/The Image Works; Page 115 © Dave Bartruff/Corbis; Page 116 © Brian Vikander/Corbis; Page 117 © Mark C. Burnett/Photo Researchers Inc.; Page 118 © Jim Sugar Photography/Corbis; Page 131 © Louise Gubb/The Image Works; Page 132 *(top left)* © Zig Leszczynski/Animals, Animals, *(top right)* © Morris Hubberland/ Photo Researchers Inc., *(bottom left)* © Karl Amman/Corbis, *(bottom right)* © Dolphin Institute/Photo Researchers Inc.; Page 134 *(top)* © James Balog/Stone, *(bottom)* © Raymond Gehman/Corbis; Page 136 © Corbis #cbo08386; Page 161 © Graham Harris/Stone; Page 162 *(top left)* © Rapho/Photo Researchers Inc., *(top right)* © Scala/Art Resource, *(bottom left)* © Scala/Art Resource, *(bottom right)* © National Museum of African Art/Eliot Elisofon, Image No. VIII-58; Page 163 *(left)* © Christie's Images/Superstock, *(right)* © Metropolitan Museum of Art, negative #161066; Page 173 © Peter Menzel/Stock Boston; Page 174 © Bob Krist/Stone; Page 175 © Andrew Lichtenstein/The Image Works; Page 177 *(left)* Paul A. Saunders/Corbis, *(right)* © David Stewart/Stone; Page 180 © Archivo Ioonografico/Corbis; Page 187 © French Ministry of Culture and Communication, Regional Direction for Cultural Affairs-Rhone-Alpes region-Regional Department of Archaeology; Page 188 *(both photographs on this page)* © French Ministry of Culture and Communication, Regional Direction for Cultural Affairs-Rhone-Alpes region-Regional Department of Archaeology; Page 193 © Lester V. Bergman/Corbis; Page 195 *(top left)* © Hulton Getty, *(top right)* © M. Dwyer/Stock Boston, *(bottom left)* © Bob Thomas/Stone, *(bottom right)* © Archive Photos; Page 215 © Adam Hinton/Stone; Page 216 *(top left)* © David Joel/Stone, *(top right)* © Jacksonville Courier/The Image Works, *(bottom left)* Klaus Guldbrandsen/SPL/Photo Researchers Inc., *(bottom right)* © Charles Thatcher/Stone; Page 239 © Bettman/Corbis; Page 240 *(top left)* © Culver Collection/Superstock, *(top right)* © Superstock, *(bottom left)* © Roy Botterell/ Stone, *(bottom right)* © Henry Ditz/Corbis; Page 261 © Hulton Getty; Page 262 © David Young Wolf/Stone.